Expert Advice From The Home Depot®

Moving
1-2-3®

Meredith® BOOKS

Moving 1-2-3®
Editor: Larry Johnston
Copy Chief: Terri Fredrickson
Publishing Operations Manager: Karen Schirm
Senior Editor, Asset and Information Manager: Phillip Morgan
Editorial and Design Coordinator: Mary Lee Gavin
Editorial and Design Assistant: Renee E. McAtee
Book Production Managers: Pam Kvitne, Marjorie J. Schenkelberg,
   Rick von Holdt, Mark Weaver
Contributing Copy Editor: Cheri Madison
Contributing Proofreaders: Kathi DiNicola, Sue Fetters, Courtenay Wolfe
Indexer: Donald Glassman

Additional Editorial and Design contributions from Greenleaf Publishing, Inc.
Project Editor: David Toht
Writers: Steve Cory, Jeff Day, Sarah Hoban
Graphic Designer: Rebecca Anderson
Assistant Graphic Designer: Sandy Peters
Copy Editors: Deborah Dillon, Barbara Webb
Principal Photographer: Dan Stultz, Stultz Photography
Photographers: Rebecca Anderson; Steve Cory; Image Studios;
   Lark Smothermon, Wooly Bugger Studios; Ben Toht; Dave Toht
Principal Illustrator: Ian Worpole
Illustrator: Jim Swanson

Additional Design contributions from Abramowitz Creative Studios
Publishing Director/Designer: Tim Abramowitz
Graphic Designers: Joel Wires, Kelly Bailey

Meredith® Books
Executive Director, Editorial: Gregory H. Kayko
Executive Director, Design: Matt Strelecki
Managing Editor: Amy Tincher-Durik
Executive Editor/Group Manager: Benjamin W. Allen
Senior Associate Design Director: Tom Wegner
Marketing Product Manager: Brent Wiersma
National Marketing Manager—Home Depot: Suzy Johnson

Publisher and Editor in Chief: James D. Blume
Editorial Director: Linda Raglan Cunningham
Executive Director, Marketing: Steve Malone
Executive Director, New Business Development: Todd M. Davis
Director, Sales-Home Depot: Robb Morris
Executive Director, Sales: Ken Zagor
Director, Operations: George A. Susral
Director, Production: Douglas M. Johnston
Director, Marketing: Amy Nichols
Business Director: Jim Leonard

Vice President and General Manager: Douglas J. Guendel

Meredith Publishing Group
President: Jack Griffin
Senior Vice President: Bob Mate

Meredith Corporation
Chairman and Chief Executive Officer: William T. Kerr
President and Chief Operating Officer: Stephen M. Lacy

In Memoriam: E.T. Meredith III (1933-2003)

The Home Depot®
Marketing Manager: Tom Sattler

Note to the Reader: Due to differing conditions, tools, and individual skills, Meredith Corporation and The Home Depot® assume no responsibility for any damages, injuries suffered, or losses incurred as a result of following the information published in this book. Before beginning any project, review the instructions carefully, and if any doubts or questions remain, consult local experts or authorities. Because codes and regulations vary greatly, you always should check with authorities to ensure that your project complies with all applicable local codes and regulations. Always read and observe all of the safety precautions provided by any tool or equipment manufacturer, and follow all accepted safety procedures.

We are dedicated to providing accurate and helpful do-it-yourself information. We welcome your comments about improving this book and ideas for other books we might offer to home improvement enthusiasts.

Contact us by any of these methods:
Leave a voice message at: 800/678-2093
Write to: Meredith Books, Home Depot Books
   1716 Locust St.
   Des Moines, IA 50309-3023
Send e-mail to: hi123@mdp.com.

Thanks to: Bekins Van Lines; Home Sweet Home Inspection Co.; Bill McCarthy, Checkmate Movers; Piano Movers, Inc.; Noel Ramos, H. K. Worldwide Moving; Smartbox; Taylor Moving & Storage; United Van Lines

How to use this book

Moving to a new home is always a complex undertaking. If the move takes you to another city or town, the potential complications increase.

Packing your possessions is only the start. You must then safely transport everything to the new home, unpack it all, make it fit into the new place, and get established in a new neighborhood. Sometimes you must do all this while you are under the additional stress of starting a new job.

Deciding to move

The decision to move involves many factors beyond the scope of this book. Evaluating new neighborhoods, selecting a new home, and selling and buying real estate are just some of the things you may have to do before you move. (One thing you should do when you are buying a home is to hire a home inspector; see pages 102–108.) Once you have made the decision to move and have picked out your new home, *Moving 1-2-3* begins.

Planning your move

The first chapter of *Moving 1-2-3* is **Planning your move**. This chapter will help you decide whether to hire professional movers or do the job yourself. Many choices are available. Some of them involve little labor on your part, some require a lot of physical work. This chapter will help you assess those options. It also includes valuable advice that can help you reduce the amount of goods and furniture you have to move, which can save time, money, and effort.

The pro move

The second chapter, **Using a professional mover,** explains how to find and evaluate a moving

▲ Measure the rooms in your current home, then measure the rooms in your new house to get an idea how your furniture and other possessions will fit. If you have a good idea where everything will go before you arrive at the new house, the move will go more smoothly (see page 112).

company. It includes discussions of various kinds of professional moving services, from the full-service professional van lines to methods that allow you to save money by doing some of the work yourself. Advice on costs, liability for damage, and tips for moving nonfurniture household goods such as boats and motorcycles is also included.

The DIY move

In chapter 3, **Making the move yourself**, you'll find all the facts about do-it-yourself moving. This chapter covers all aspects of moving your own household, from packing boxes and wrapping furniture to loading and driving the truck. It also shows ways you can do some of the work, such as packing boxes, while leaving other work to the pros. Throughout this chapter and the rest of the book, you'll find tips and tricks such as **Safety Alerts**, **Closer Looks**, **Work Smarters**, and **Good Ideas** that will help you make the move go more smoothly.

Readying the new place

Chapter 4 is called **Preparing your new home.** The chapter starts with information about professional home inspections. You should consider hiring a home inspector if you are buying a house or other dwelling. The chapter also shows how to make some common repairs and upgrades at your new house. The best time to paint rooms and replace flooring is before you move all your furniture into the house, for instance. The chapter will also help you become familiar with your new home.

Moving day

The final two chapters, **Preparing for moving day** and **Settling in,** bring the big event into perspective. These chapters show you exactly how to organize the time before the move, what to do with the kids, how to move the pets, how to cope with the myriad details that go with moving, and how to establish yourself in your new home and community.

Packing and tracking your possessions

PACK CAREFULLY AND KEEP TRACK OF THINGS
Packing your goods is a critical part of the move. It's important to pack everything carefully in sturdy, well-sealed boxes to prevent damage. Even if you hire professional movers, you may pack some items yourself. Chapter 3 shows what kind of packing materials to use (pages 59–63), how to pack boxes correctly (pages 68–81), and how to prepare furniture and appliances for the move (pages 82–89). You should also set up an inventory system as you pack so you'll know what's in what box and where the box should go in the new house (pages 36–37).

Moving 1-2-3®
Table of contents

Planning your move

When you move you pack up the things that make up your everyday life and say goodbye to them for days, weeks, or even months. Then if everything goes well, the boxes arrive in good shape and on time. You unpack all those little things you've done without and begin putting your life back together. Never before and perhaps never again will your toaster look like a long-lost friend.

Whether the move is across town or across the country, getting things to arrive on time and in one piece takes planning, patience, and energy.

Planning is the most important of the three. A well-planned move will always go better than a last-minute panic. Even more so than with most projects, the job of moving a household is easy to underestimate. Reestablishing your routine in a new home will always be smoother if you know what is in each box and where each piece of furniture will go. But when do you start planning?

Start as soon as you can. Professional movers and real estate agents say you should start planning at least two months before the move. Anyone who has moved recently will tell you it's never too early to pack

Chapter 1 highlights

ON YOUR MARK, GET SET...
Take a quick look at everything you'll need to do to get ready.

8

SHOULD YOU DO THE MOVE YOURSELF?
Find out if renting a truck and gathering your friends is the right way for you to move.

10

FULL-SERVICE MOVERS
Hiring the pros is the easiest but most expensive way to move.

12

PORTABLE CONTAINERS
Midway between professional and do-it-yourself moving, this is the latest wrinkle in moving.

14

SELF-SERVICE MOVERS
Have a trailer delivered to your house, load it, and let the pros do the driving.

15

SCALING DOWN
Pare down to the essentials so you don't have to pay to move things you don't want or need.

16

HAVING A SALE
Organize a sale and earn some extra money—while getting rid of stuff you won't have to move.

18

SELLING YOUR TREASURES ON THE INTERNET
Your collectibles and junk can bring big bucks in online auctions.

20

STOW IT, DON'T SHOW IT
Get rid of the clutter before you show the house by renting space in a self-storage yard.

22

FROM RENTER TO HOMEOWNER
Moving isn't all about getting rid of stuff. New homeowners have to budget for new tools and services.

23

CLEANING HOUSE
Take a look at what can go in the trash, what you can recycle, and what's hazardous waste.

24

---

away the things you don't need daily, like holiday decorations, books, or the good china.

Decisions, decisions

When you get ready to move, you have lots of decisions to make. You not only have to choose a mover, you have to decide on the type of mover. You have the traditional choice between the professional or do-it-yourself move, but you also have a new middle ground. Some companies will deliver portable storage containers to your house; others drop off a trailer. In either case you load it, and when you're ready, the company moves it to your new home, where you unload it.

Once you've settled on a mover, the job begins. What do you take and what do you leave behind? You will have to clean your closets, garage, attic, and basement, and then decide what to do with everything. A yard sale is the traditional way to raise a bit of money while getting rid of excess baggage. With specialty items (and they don't have to be all that special), you might make more money in an online auction.

If the house is still cluttered despite a thorough cleaning, rent a self-storage shed so that the house shows better. You will probably end up with things you don't want and can't sell. Options include donating to charity, recycling, and throwing it away, but make sure you know what properly goes in the trash and what is hazardous waste.

On your mark, get set...

Moving is a huge job, and while you'll probably never enjoy it, you can make it more bearable if you do it over a period of months. If you wait until the last minute, you'll end up moving everything—clothes that don't fit, books you don't want, broken furniture that you can't fix—and it will cost you in labor and money. Waiting until the last minute won't allow time to transfer your children's school records or get copies of their vaccination history. Given everything that you have to do, you probably won't have time to wind your watch.

So plan ahead. Here are some of the things you'll need to think about, in the approximate order you'll need to think about them. You'll find a more complete, week-by-week list on pages 164–165.

Do it yourself or hire a pro? This is probably the most important decision you'll have to make—and the easiest. Hiring a pro means that someone else does most—or all—of the work. Doing it yourself means that the burden falls on you and any friends you can round up. Hiring a pro means paying for all those services; doing it yourself means saving a lot of money. And of course there is that middle ground, the pod or "self move," in which somebody delivers (and moves) a shipping container or truck trailer that you load yourself.

Look into all three options as soon as you decide to move and get estimates from several companies for each option. Make your decision and your reservations early.

Get boxes, tape, and packing material. If you like your boxes of uniform sizes and strong, talk to a truck rental company or moving-supply dealer. If you like your boxes cheap, talk to a moving company about used boxes. If you like your boxes free, check with grocery stores, liquor stores, and florists. You'll also want to buy packing material and 2- or 3-inch-wide packing tape that comes on a dispenser (a tape gun), so that you can apply the tape then cut it off along a serrated edge. (See pages 62–64.)

Start packing. If you hire pros to handle the move, you can leave some or all of the packing to them. You can also do the packing yourself, though you should ask the mover whether or not items that you pack are covered by insurance. (Your homeowner's insurance won't cover damage incurred during a move—see pages 49–50.)

Your initial packing should include the things you can do without until you move into your new home. You won't need Christmas decorations in June and in most parts of the country, you won't need your fishing pole in December. But go beyond the obvious. Scrapbooks, collections, and pictures on the wall in the office, den, or spare bedroom can be packed early just as well as later, and early is a better time. Pack up blankets if it's summer and the air-conditioner if it's winter. Almost anything in the attic is ripe for packing. Pack a box a day until you're down to the things that you use every day.

Start scaling down. After a few years in a house, you end up with extra stuff—an old shovel, some beat-up folding chairs, an old winter coat, a bunch of CDs that you can't stand, and all the things you picked up at yard sales. It's going to cost you to move it all—van lines charge by the pound; if you're doing it yourself, a larger rental truck costs more than a smaller one. It's time to have your own yard sale. The easiest place to start might be with clothes. Every time you change clothes, put what you've worn in the left-hand side of the closet. (Clean it first if necessary.) After several weeks get rid of everything on the right-hand side of the closet—those items obviously aren't a key part of your wardrobe. Tackle the garage next, then books. (For more on scaling down, see pages 16–17.)

Do your paperwork. Fill out a change-of-address card at the post office. Give the bank and credit card companies your new address. Open a checking account in your new town. Get doctor's records, dentist's records, and immunization records. Talk with the new school about your kids and find out what's needed for enrollment and when it's needed. Ask your insurance agent about insuring the new home, at least until you can get a local agent. Arrange to have the utilities turned off in your old house (schedule it for a couple of days after your move) and open accounts for the new house. Cancel the newspaper.

Keep packing. Start doing with less at home. As the move approaches work room by room, packing everything you can do without, whether it's clothes, china, or paperclips and pencils. Pack things that you don't need on a daily basis.

Make plans for the kids. All but the youngest kids will want to feel involved in the move. Find ways to get them involved: Older kids can move or pack boxes. Younger ones can label boxes; the youngest can draw pictures on them. If necessary line up a babysitter for the day of the move. (See pages 168–169.)

Make plans for pets. Movers aren't allowed to transport pets. Get a pet carrier for dogs and cats; hamsters, gerbils, and rabbits can be transported in their cages. Plan well ahead for fish—they'll need a spill-proof container and perhaps a battery-operated aerator. Visit your pet store to see what you need to move your fish and give the staff time to order items they may not have. (See pages 170–171.)

Make plans for plants. If using a mover see if they'll handle plants. (Most won't.) Regardless of who's doing the moving, transfer all plants into nonbreakable containers. Prune them a couple of weeks before the move. Spray for insects and water them normally. The day before the move pack them in boxes with air holes. For more on moving plants, see pages 78–79.

Pack the kitchen last. As moving day approaches, start living out of the pantry, refrigerator, and freezer. Don't restock unless you have to—there's no point in paying to move something you can get for the same price in your new town. When the fridge and shelves are empty, eat microwavable meals or eat out.

 CLOSER LOOK

FIFTY WAYS TO LEAVE YOUR HOMESTEAD

There is more than one way to get your household from here to there. Some ways involve more work than others; some involve more money than others. All of them do the trick, however, and settling on a method is a question of how much money you're willing to trade off for a given amount of work. The options are listed briefly below. You'll find more thorough explanations in the pages that follow.

You can rent a truck and do it yourself. This is the most labor-intensive choice, but the least costly one. You do all the packing, all the lifting, and all the driving. Depending on distance involved and the size of the truck, driving could well be the hardest part. (See pages 97–99 for more information.)

You can hire the pros and let them do all the packing. Packers arrive at your house a couple of days before the move and pack everything for you. On the day of the move, the movers load the van. When they arrive at your new home, they'll unpack it and you can even have them put everything where you want it. Needless to say, this is the the most expensive option. (For more information, see pages 12–13.)

You can hire the pros and do some or all of the packing yourself. (See pages 33–34 for more information.) This saves money, but you need to find out whether the movers will be responsible if any of the items you pack (PBO or packed by owner) are damaged.

You can have a shipping container delivered to your home and pack it over the course of several days. The moving company will then haul it to your new home, where you have several days to unpack it. (For more information, see page 14.)

You can hire a self-service mover who will leave a 28-foot trailer at your home, give you two days to pack it, then deliver it to your new home. You can unpack it yourself or hire the unpackers provided by some self-service movers. (See pages 33–34.)

 REAL WORLD

HANDLE WITH CARE

A divorce or a pending divorce can make planning a move even harder. If there are children involved, you will have to get the court's permission to leave the state and may even need it to move across the state. Check with your attorney to see what's required and how long it takes.

If you are moving out of the house that you and your spouse shared, you will need a property settlement before you take anything. You and your spouse can usually enter into a legally binding agreement before the divorce, but make sure your attorney is involved. If you can't agree, the court will decide. Even with an agreement, sorting through things can be emotionally draining. It's often a good idea to have a close friend there to help you through.

Should you do the move yourself?

CLOSER LOOK

ADVANTAGES:

Cost, cost, cost

Complete control over schedule

Flexibility on the details

DISADVANTAGES:

Driving a large truck, especially
   over a long distance

Lifting

Finding helpers

Packing and unpacking

Sometimes moving everything yourself is a necessity—your budget won't permit hiring someone else to do it. Sometimes it's a practicality—your new home is so close to the old one that you can just wheel your stuff down the street on a cart.

The shorter the move, the smaller the load, and the healthier the workers, the more sense do-it-yourself moving makes. Smaller loads are easier to pack, easier to manage, and will fit into smaller trucks that you're likely to be more comfortable driving. Short distances mean that you won't need to take a lot of time off work and that you won't have to drive cross-country in a truck that is unfamiliar and perhaps rough-riding.

But there are other costs beside the truck and what it does to your bones. As you're figuring out the costs, make sure you add in boxes and packing material. Add in the time

and stress involved. And don't forget that once you're on the road, you'll need to pay for gas, tolls, and food. If it's a long move, you'll need to pay for motel rooms.

Talk to two or three companies about the truck you plan to rent. A truck too small, one designed for something else, or one that isn't there when you go to pick it up can turn a move into a disaster.

Begin by knowing how big a truck it will take. You'll need roughly 150 cubic feet of truck space per furnished room. To translate from cubic feet to truck length takes some math (length in feet = volume in cubic feet divided by height × width of the truck box in feet). A 10-foot truck usually has about 400 cubic feet of space, enough to move an efficiency or studio apartment. If you have six rooms to move, you'll need about 900 cubic feet, about the capacity of a 24-foot truck. The chart on page 58 gives you an idea of the truck sizes that various rental companies recommend. Ask the companies you have in mind and if in doubt, err on the side of a bigger truck.

Once you know the size truck you need, make sure that you're getting a moving truck. A truck built for moving will have a ramp so you can walk in and out of the truck. It may have a side door as well as a back door, in case you have to unload from the street. The floor should be hardwood and be clean of stones and debris. There should be fixtures on the walls for straps that will secure the load.

Equally important, make sure you can drive the truck. Does it have an automatic or a manual transmission? Do you need a special license to drive it? Are you comfortable backing it up? And don't forget the amenities: Is it air-conditioned? Does it have a radio? A CD player?

Compare both prices and service. Some companies charge for mileage (or mileage beyond a certain threshold), others don't. If you're planning on stopping to visit friends and relatives during a one-way move, be aware that most companies will allow you a certain number of days for the move and charge extra if it takes longer.

Make sure the rental agreement is for a truck that's guaranteed to be there when you go to pick it up. Some companies and some of their independent dealers have policies that encourage them to rent the truck for the most

money possible. If so, someone making an expensive cross-country move can end up with the truck that you thought was reserved for your less expensive local move.

Take care of other essentials while you're at the rental lot. Rent a hand truck (see page 65) and lots of packing blankets. The hand truck will help you move dressers and stacks of boxes; if you're moving a refrigerator, ask for an appliance hand truck. Dollies, which are small frames on wheels, slip under bookcases and the like, allowing you to roll them out the door with very little lifting. As you load wrap furniture that's easily damaged in blankets to protect it. You'll also need straps to tie furniture and boxes to the wall and to prevent loads from shifting.

Make sure you have reliable helpers lined up for the day of the move. Check to make sure that your helpers have a clear path to the truck and that nothing is likely to trip them as they work. Make sure they know what they are doing: Lift with the knees. Stop if it hurts. Lift, don't drag things across the floor and be careful with the furniture.

Load heavy things first and put them on the floor of the truck. Put lighter items on top of the heavier things. Remember that it will take longer to stop a truck when braking than it does in your car, and that once the truck is full, it will take even longer.

(For more on moving yourself, see pages 46–51.)

BUYER'S GUIDE
BUY USED BOXES
You can get free boxes from grocery and liquor stores, but they'll all be different sizes and hard to pack. Call a local moving company instead and ask whether they have any used boxes. Their boxes will be two or three uniform sizes, and since the moving company isn't allowed to reuse them, they're usually half-price. Don't underestimate the power of uniform boxes to make loading easier.

CLOSER LOOK
WHAT DOES IT REALLY COST?
When you figure out the cost of a do-it-yourself move, make sure you figure in the cost of taking time off work. Figure out the cost of fuel and tolls. (A 15-foot truck gets only 6 to 10 miles to the gallon.) Add in the cost of packing blankets, a hand truck and dolly, and food for the helpers. Figure in the cost of motels, if any, and meals on the road.

BUYER'S GUIDE
WEIGH FLAT RATES CAREFULLY
Moving companies charge a flat rate for a load up to 3,000 pounds. But you may have less furniture and miscellany than the flat-rate allowance. If you pay to have pros move a ton of your possessions—2,000 pounds—they're going to charge you for an extra 1,000 pounds, or 50 percent more than you are actually moving.

Should you really do it yourself?

Rental companies claim that you can save up to 50 percent of the cost of a full-service move by doing it yourself, and in many cases you can. But doing it yourself isn't for everybody. If you answer no to any of the following questions, consider hiring a pro instead of doing it yourself.

- Am I in shape? Can I lift without hurting my back? Am I strong enough to lift heavy boxes?
- Do I have friends willing to help me load?
- Do I have anybody to help me unload?
- When I add in the cost of everything involved, am I really saving money?
- Can I drive a truck?
- Can I back up without hitting everything in the vicinity?
- Do I have the time to do this? Can I spend the week on the road that may be required for a long move? Do I need to start a job immediately after I arrive?
- Can my friends and I move a piano (or other large furniture) by ourselves?

Full-service movers

The larger the move and the greater the distance, the more sense it makes to hire a professional mover. Even if your move is a small one, things will likely go smoother if you hire a pro. Time limitations, a bad back, a piano, lots of stairs, or many pieces of heavy furniture may be reasons to hire a pro.

Choosing a mover
If you're considering hiring a pro, start by contacting three movers. Recommendations from friends and neighbors are helpful; so is the website www.moving.org. It's run by the professional trade organization American Moving and Storage Association (AMSA). Working from your zip code and the answers to a few simple questions, AMSA contacts movers in your area, and the movers contact you.

Once you have the names of three movers, double-check the Better Business Bureau or go to the BBB website to see whether there have been complaints. Do a separate search of the Internet for the name of each company, looking for complaints or praise. For information on safety records, go to www.safersys.org, a site run by the Federal Motor Carrier Safety Administration (FMCSA).

Once you've chosen three carrier candidates, discuss packing options with each. Generally you have three choices. The easiest but most expensive option is to let the mover

pack everything. Your second option is to do part of the packing yourself—all the nonbreakable items, for example—and let the mover pack the rest. The third option is to do all the packing yourself. While it's the cheapest option, it's not risk-free: Movers will generally not be responsible for damage to things you packed yourself.

Discuss insurance too. The options are typically a minimal policy offered by the moving company, a slightly upgraded policy, and a full replacement value policy. (For more on insurance, see page 32.)

Getting an accurate estimate
Don't accept an estimate based only on a phone conversation—in fact, rule out any mover who tries to give you one. Walk the movers through the house, showing them everything you want to move, and get a written estimate of the cost of the move. If a mover won't give you a written estimate, hire a different one.

Unfortunately comparing estimates can be tricky. All estimates are based on the expected weight that the truck will carry. A binding estimate says that the mover will do the job for a certain fee, regardless of the weight of the load. A nonbinding estimate says the mover will move you for a stated amount, plus no more than 10 percent. A not-to-exceed estimate provides you with a binding bid, but you will be billed at that rate or actual cost, whichever is lower.

Try to get prices for all three kinds of service so that you can compare prices directly for the same levels of service. If one company's price is dramatically lower than the others, be wary. A company quoting an unusually low price may charge for other services at the time of delivery.

Making an international move

If you're moving abroad, what you need to do and how you need to do it depend on where you're going. While one country may allow you to import certain items, another may not. The best place to start your international move is to find a company with experience in moving to your destination. Most van lines have an international division. Find out where the company is most experienced. You should also contact your future home's nearest consulate or their embassy in Washington, D. C. to review regulations with them. (See page 35 for more about finding an international mover.)

You'll need a visa to move wherever you're going: Work on it in advance. Arriving as a tourist and then changing your status to that of a resident can be difficult, if not impossible, in many countries.

Your host country will generally let you import your household goods, including clothing, duty-free. Rules are likely to require that you haven't been a resident of the country for the last year and that you will be a full-time resident rather than a seasonal resident.

You generally can import your car duty-free too, as long as you will be living in the country a given period of time (often 12 months). The vehicle usually has to be private, rather than commercial, and generally has to be at least a few months old. You may have to convert it to meet safety, antipollution, or other standards in the country you're moving to.

You can often import food duty-free, but only as much as you would normally have on the shelves at home. Alcohol and tobacco are not duty-free.

Firearms regulations are complicated and vary widely. Check with the consulate well in advance. Transportation of ammunition by private parties is generally not allowed because of the danger of explosion.

Find out in advance what you'll need to open bank accounts; have all the necessary papers ready when you arrive.

Advantages/disadvantages of a full-service mover

ADVANTAGES:

All work is done for you.

Price includes packing and all packing materials.

Movers drive truck; you drive in peace.

Movers unload and unpack everything. Everything is in place the day you move in.

Trucks have heavy-duty suspension that provides better protection for your valuables.

DISADVANTAGES:

Cost

Time involved in getting estimates

Understanding the variables

CLOSER LOOK

MOVING VALUABLES

At some point in getting ready for the move, you're going to look at a crystal vase, an heirloom teapot, or an antique muzzle loader and wonder: What's the best way to move this?

The first part of the question is really "How do I move this without breaking it?" The other part of the question is sometimes more difficult to voice: "How do I move this without it getting stolen?"

Small valuables such as jewelry, coins, or stamps are easy to pack and take with you. Pack with tissue paper, rather than newspaper, so the ink won't smudge whatever it comes in contact with. Repair anything that's broken or loose before the move.

Beyond whatever you can pack and carry yourself, your valuables are in the hands of the movers. Most movers won't insure items they

haven't packed, so it's best to let them do the packing. Small pictures and paintings should be wrapped, placed on edge, and put in heavy cardboard containers. Large paintings may require a custom-built wooden case. Large valuable antiques should be shipped in a custom-built wooden crate.

When the moving company representative comes to the house to give you an estimate, point out the pieces you think need special care. Ask the mover to separately quote the price of having the items carefully crated. If you decide in favor of crating, let the movers know well in advance. Ask what kind of insurance the company can provide and ask the company that insures your home about additional insurance you can buy to cover art and valuables in transit. If your items are rare or extremely valuable, contact a company that specializes in moving art and antiques to move them.

Avoid Internet scams

The Internet is a great way to compare prices, but provides no guarantee of good service. You will get what you pay for, and if somebody is going to charge you considerably less than the going rate, expect them to provide considerably less service too. Many Internet movers are really brokers who turn your shipment over to any available carrier. If you're pricing over the web, ask to know exactly who is handling your move.

A legitimate mover will come to your home, examine what you're moving, and give you an estimate. Scam movers may try to give you an estimate over the phone or over the Internet without seeing your household furnishings.

If legitimate movers ask for a deposit, it will be a small one. If someone asks for a large deposit, it's probably a scam.

Legitimate movers charge by weight, as verified on a state-inspected scale. Scam movers will charge by the square foot or cubic foot, which you cannot easily verify.

Portable containers

Midway between do-it-yourself moving and hiring a pro are portable storage containers, often known as pods, which stands for "portable on-demand storage."

Here's how they work. The mover delivers the container to your home. You then have several days before the move to fill it with your household goods. The filled container is then delivered to your new home by a professional trucker. You are allowed several days to unload it. In short, you do the lifting and save some money, but still have the security of a professional driver. For an additional fee you can usually store your container in the company's facilities for as long as necessary.

How it works

The container is delivered to your house on a moving truck and lowered to the ground. Since it sits roughly 4 inches off the ground, there's no need for a ramp. But perhaps the biggest advantage is the several days you have to load the container. The panic of trying to get everything packed—and packed safely—is eased. You can schedule your helpers over a few days and evenings and finish up on a Saturday or Sunday.

Unlike a rental truck, which has to be back to the yard within a certain number of days, a container gives you the option of storing what you move for an unlimited amount of time for a fee. You have access to the containers and their contents, which are usually stored in a large warehouse. Because they are in a warehouse, however, you won't have the same access you would at a self-storage warehouse. You'll have to call a day or more in advance so that your container can be pulled out of storage.

Once the container is delivered to your new house, you usually have another five days (depending on the company) to unload it. If necessary you can get more time, but there is an extra charge.

Figuring the cost

The cost will depend on the distance you're moving and the size of the container you're using. You can usually get an estimate at a container mover's website; but remember, it's only an estimate. Where you are moving, how many bedrooms you have, and whether you need storage are all variables that affect the cost. Some companies simply tell you how much a standard container can hold and let you figure out what size you need. One company projects that their 12-foot-long, 8-foot-high, 8-foot-wide container can hold the contents of a 1,200-square-foot house. Their 16-foot version can hold the contents of a 1,500-square-foot house.

Check to see what the containers are made of before you strike any deals with container movers. Containers may be aluminum, aluminum and plastic, or plywood. Choose a company with durable, weather-resistant containers.

Get three estimates. Compare the cost with that of moving it yourself, not forgetting gas, tolls, meals, and motels. You'll have to add in the cost of packing materials for both pods and moving it yourself. Also check against the cost of a full-service mover (see pages 12–13, 31) and a self-service mover (opposite page).

Ask the company about insurance and understand exactly what you're getting. One container mover provides around $1,000 of free insurance and charges for coverage beyond that. Include added insurance in the cost of the move.

Ask about a guaranteed arrival date. While containers are often picked up by company trucks, the over-the-road transportation is usually done by independent truckers and trucklines over which the container company has no control. If your furniture's arrival date is going to be fluid, you'll want to know that in advance so that you can decide whether or not the money you'll be saving is worth the risk.

Self-service movers

S elf-service movers, like portable containers, are a middle ground between moving it yourself and hiring a pro. A self-service mover delivers a trailer to your home instead of a container. You save money by loading it yourself, but still have the security of a professional driver to haul your goods.

A trailer is at least 28 feet long, enough to handle a four-bedroom residence. However self-service movers charge you by the percentage of the truck's floor space that you actually use. If your four-bedroom home only fills up three-quarters of the truck, you'll only pay three-quarters of what you would if the trailer were full.

Estimating the load space you need

Some self-service movers set a minimum load below which they won't take the job. Others will accept loads of any size, but charge you for a minimum amount of space even if you use less. Usually an efficiency apartment is below the threshold; condominium units and apartments are usually above the minimum.

An average room will fill about 3 linear feet of truck space, or (since the truck is 8 feet wide) 24 square feet. You're better off letting the mover do the estimate however. Some base estimates on the square footage of your house. Others have an online list on which you check off the items you're moving.

Once the truck arrives at your house, you typically have 48 hours to load it. Some companies count only business days, so you could get an extra two days without paying an extra charge if you have the trailer over the weekend. Once the truck is on the road, it can travel about 500 miles in a day, and you can often

track where it is, either online or by calling the company. Once the truck arrives at your new home, you'll have 48 hours to unload it.

For a fee, some movers will provide workers who will help you load and unload the truck. One firm charges $300 for two men for three hours and about $60 an hour for the pair thereafter. Given the problems you may have lining up helpers at the new location that might be money well spent.

Details of the move vary from company to company. All require a temporary wall, called a bulkhead, to keep your load from shifting. All trucks have metal fasteners for bulkheads on the sides of the truck, and the bulkhead comes in pieces that are already on the truck. Some companies, however, have you supply plywood to put between the bulkhead and your cargo. Some have you install the bulkhead; others have their driver install it. Once the bulkhead is in place, most companies load cargo in the rest of the truck and deliver it before they deliver your things. This saves you money, but ask whether any additional cargo is tightly sealed.

Some companies provide a loading ramp. Others charge you for using one. In any event, you will need to rent a hand truck and a dolly. You will also have to provide your own packing materials (see pages 62–64).

Insurance varies too. One company offers $5,000 of free insurance. Another offers $1,000. Additional insurance costs about $10 per $1,000, with the cost declining as you buy more. Yet a third mover offers coverage at $2 a pound, up to a maximum of $20,000. Often a company that offers lower insurance also charges less for the move.

CLOSER LOOK

PACK TO SAVE

Self-service moves differ from full-service moves in two respects. The obvious one is that with a self-service move, you load and unload the truck yourself. The other difference could wipe out your expected savings on the move. Full-service movers charge you by the actual weight of the cargo. The cost of the move is the same regardless of floor space used. Self-service movers charge you by the square foot, so the price may vary: Depending on how carefully you pack, two different people loading exactly the same cargo could use significantly different amounts of floor space.

Load high and wide. Heavy things go on the bottom, fragile things on top. Stand couches on end. Fill dresser drawers with lighter items. Fill voids with linens stuffed in pillowcases, and stack things as high as possible. Be fastidious. What it costs you in effort, you'll save in dollars. (See pages 94–96 for more on loading.)

Scaling down

Do not, under any circumstances, move everything you own: Movers charge for every pound they move, so every pound they move is a pound you pay for. The farther you move, the more you pay.

Scale down. Pare back. Simplify, simplify, simplify. You don't need all that stuff.

You do need to draw up some ground rules. What goes and what stays? High school yearbook? High school textbook? Fifteen pairs of dress shoes? Snowshoes? Everybody has to make up their own mind, but there are a few guidelines you can follow.

Work room by room, tackling one room at a time. Divide everything into three piles, at least mentally. Things you use go into the first pile. Things you don't use go into the second pile. Things you sometimes use go into the third pile. Pack up the first pile to move and get rid of the other two.

Almost every attic or basement in America holds at least a couple of boxes that were never unpacked after the last move. If you haven't needed them in this house, you probably won't need them in the next house. Check them for beloved, if forgotten, heirlooms and toss the rest of the stuff.

Emptying the closets

Studies show that people wear 20 percent of their clothes 80 percent of the time. This means that up to 80 percent of your wardrobe is expendable. To separate trash from treasure, first try on all your clothes. Put those that fit well and look good back in the closet. Put those that don't fit or are outdated or shabby in a pile. If you're saving a favorite suit until you lose 10 pounds, maybe you can get rid of it.

Every morning choose that day's wardrobe from the closet. At the end of the day, put everything you wore either into the left-hand side of your closet or the wash. After a few weeks, the best of your wardrobe will end up on the left-hand side of your closet. The candidates for sale or donation are on the right.

Any clothes that have spent more than a year stored in the attic or basement are clothes you can get rid of.

Measure the closets in your new home and take along only as many clothes as they will comfortably hold. Allow 2½ inches for men's or women's suits, 2 inches for dresses, 1½ inches for slacks and skirts folded over a hanger, and 1¼ inches for shirts or blouses.

Books, books, books

Books are extremely heavy, but they are often also old friends. Get rid of old thrillers, diet books, outdated fix-it books, old travel guides, textbooks, and others you're unlikely to ever open again. Check the hardcovers to see whether any are first editions or otherwise desirable and try selling them on eBay (see pages 20–21) or to an antiquarian book dealer. When you're down to the core of your library, go through it carefully. Ask yourself which of those books you're likely to read or refer to again. Get rid of anything you can bear to part with.

Precious collectibles

These can be a tough call. Are they heavy? Do you display them, read them, or play with them? Is your collection of vintage sporting goods really collectible or is it just a hodgepodge of old stuff you don't use? Could you sell your items and make enough money to rebuild the collection at your new home?

All that food

Stop buying food a month before you move and start cooking with what's in the cupboards. There is probably nothing there that you can't get at your new home. If you buy it fresh at the new home, you won't have to pay to move it. And now is the time to quit loading up at sales and start using frozen food from the freezer compartment and deep freeze. Unless you make a very short move, you can't take frozen food with you.

Tackling the garage

Dedicate a day to cleaning it. Back out the cars and work section by section. Pick up everything piece by piece and sort it into one of three categories:

1. This is something I use.
2. This works but I don't need it.
3. This is broken, useless, will cost more to move than it's worth, or is obvious rubbish.

Pack category 1 as you work your way across the garage. Set category 2 aside for a yard sale. Put everything in category 3 in the trash.

 GOOD IDEA

DONATING GOODS TO CHARITY

Several charitable organizations can use the items you no longer need. If you have usable items that you'd like to donate, look into giving them to organizations such as the ones below. Most are nationwide, though not all may operate near you.

Vietnam Veterans of America and Military Order of the Purple Heart accept donations to resell to help veterans.

Goodwill Industries accepts donations of household goods that they resell to pay for training people who face barriers to the job market. Some stores recycle and resell computers.

HopeLine, operated by Verizon Wireless, accepts donations of any carrier's used cell phones to benefit the victims of domestic violence.

Dress for Success accepts donations of interview- and work-appropriate clothing to give to low-income women who are entering the workforce.

Salvation Army accepts clothes that they sell through Salvation Army Thrift Shops. Proceeds from sales benefit the needy and homeless, disaster relief, and job-training programs.

City missions and rescue missions provide housing for the homeless. They usually accept clothing and small household items, which go directly to their clients. Some operate thrift shops that raise money by selling donated items.

Food banks operate in many towns and cities. You can donate canned goods to local food banks, which distribute the food to people with low incomes.

Local church and local charity resale shops accept donated items. Many churches operate thrift shops and use the money to support their programs, as do many local charities. Some collect usable household goods to distribute to families in need. Check in the phone book under thrift shops for the ones in your area.

Having a sale

Paring down your possessions can be a lot of work. But once you pare down, getting rid of what you don't want can actually be profitable: Think yard sale. There's nothing complicated about having a garage or yard sale, but a well-organized one always makes more money than one you just throw together.

Get organized

Start by making sure there are no local regulations against garage or yard sales. Then start organizing what you want to sell as if you were stocking a department store: Put china in one box, tools in another, books in yet another. Put clothes on hangers and sort and label them by size. When the time comes, display each in its own area. Department stores categorize because it makes it easy on their customers, and a customer who can find what he or she wants is more likely to spend money. Your customers are no different.

Look at things closely as you divide them into categories. If something is broken, throw it out or fix it. First impressions are lasting, and a customer who comes across a broken lamp is likely to decide that everything else is junk too. Clean everything. Run dishes and glasses through the dishwasher

and hose down garden tools to get off the dirt. Polish the bowling ball. Vacuum the sofa. A customer who comes across a yard sale where everything is clean and well organized will linger and more importantly, buy things.

Pricing

As you're organizing and paring down, put a price tag on each item before it goes in its box. As a rule stickers from an office supply store make good price tags, but larger items, like sofas or lawnmowers, should have larger string tags that are easy to see. Set the asking price of an item in good condition at one-fifth to one-third of the original price, but temper your pricing with some common sense. A $15 hammer might sell for $3 to $5. On the other hand, you'll be lucky to get $1 for a rusted hammer with a cracked handle. Don't expect to get $600 for a 5-year-old computer or $25 for a $75 piece of outdated software. Visit a few yard sales before you have yours to get a feel for local asking prices. Set prices in dollar amounts—$1, $2, $3—or in 25-cent increments. Setting odd prices results in a change-making nightmare. Price items such as glasses, plates, and silverware together—five for $1, instead of 25 cents each.

Promoting the big event

Saturdays are usually best for yard sales. Some people schedule their sales for Saturday and Sunday, and reduce the prices on Sunday. Avoid holiday weekends with the possible exception of Memorial Day, which in some areas is the unofficial start of yard sale season. A couple of days before the sale, mow the lawn and remove any hazards. If the sale, or part of it will be in the garage, clean it up.

Advertise your sale. Put up notices on bulletin boards at the grocery store and laundromat. Run an ad in the paper. Several sites on the Internet list yard sales; search on "yard sale" and take advantage of them. Whether your ad is on the laundromat wall or the web, list popular items that you have for sale—children's clothing and toys, antiques, tools, and costume jewelry, among others. (Check local sales in advance to see what's hot.) Yard sale afficionados often try to hit promising sales an hour or two early to beat others to the punch. Unless you want your breakfast interrupted, add "No early birds" to your ads. (They'll come over anyhow.)

On the day before the sale, put signs along the road announcing the sale. Use big dark lettering that's easy to see from the street. Put arrows on the signs or use arrow-shaped signs directing people to your sale.

Display the clothes on their hangers on a clothesline where people can browse through them. Put large items on the ground and small items on tables rather than on blankets on the ground. Dress up the tables a bit by covering them with tablecloths. Put items that are sure to lure buyers, like antiques, unusual items, or children's furniture, near the street. Put tools or sporting goods there too, so men will see them as they drive by.

Be prepared, be flexible

Remember that the price on the sticker is the asking price. Be flexible, but not too early in the day. If someone makes a low bid on an expensive item early in the morning, take the person's name and number and call if it doesn't sell.

Yard sales may not be the best place to sell big ticket items such as refrigerators. Expensive items usually sell better and bring in more money through classified ads. If you are selling something that's on the expensive side, let buyers bid on it. Have prospective buyers fill out a 3 × 5 card with their name, phone number, and what they're willing to pay for it. Call the high bidder at the end of the day.

Set up a table and chair for yourself, so people know where to come with questions or to make purchases. Start the day with $75 to $100 worth of change on hand in quarters, ones, fives, and tens. Keep half the money inside where you can get to it easily and the other half in a fanny pack or pocket instead of in a box at your table. This lets you walk over to help someone without having to leave the cash unattended. Make change without flashing all the bills around. Have a calculator handy and always leave the customers' money out until you've made change to avoid disputes about how much you were given. Put it under a paperweight, jar, or the calculator while you make change.

Selling your treasures on the Internet

A pair of snowshoes, $77.
1974 black rotary telephone, $30.
The Turkish edition of the Sherlock Holmes adventure *The Hound of the Baskervilles,* $10.

This is the stuff that online auctions are made of. If 135 million people came to your yard sale, you could probably sell your snowshoes, phone, and foreign language Sherlock Holmes collection at prices like those too. The best way to show your goods to that many people is to have at least part of your yard sale online.

Online auctions are the perfect place to sell the vintage items you find in your closet. And vintage doesn't have to be all that old or all that good. A battle-worn 1964 GI Joe recently brought in $12 online. A pair of Levis from 1966 sold for $300. A 40-inch Santa Claus lawn ornament from the '50s or '60s went for $51.

Not everything you have is a candidate, so once you've collected things for a yard sale, make a list of items that are unusual, collectible, or remotely interesting. Go to an online auction site and search for similar items to see what they're selling for. You might find a camera like your old Brownie Starflash is worth $20—not a lot, but probably more than you could get at a yard sale. In addition to the general merchandise auction sites, search for special interest websites that have for-sale ads or auctions.

Once you've decided what to sell, register with the auction site so that you can list your items. Making the actual listing is a matter of walking through a basic online form. Toward the end of the process, you'll have the chance to attach a digital photo to your posting, as well as to specify the postage and handling charges for each item. List each item on only one auction site at a time.

Making the listing

The secret to getting the best price is preparing a good listing. Start with the title or headline. "Old clock " is descriptive, but not a very good title. People find items at online auctions by typing in key words and having the auction house search for them. "Old" is seldom one of the words they type in. "Vintage Coca-Cola Clock" is likely to bring a lot more people to your item.

Once you've written a headline, write a description of the item. Be specific: List the maker, the model number, the year made, the size, the color—everything you can think of that will help someone who wants to bid. Point out the good points, but mention any imperfections too.

Setting the price

You probably got a good idea of the item's value when you were deciding whether or not to sell online. It doesn't hurt to take another look to see what similar items are selling for. Then decide how you want to sell the item.

You can auction it, which allows the bidding to start where it will. You can also set a minimum bid, which is posted with your listing as the starting price for the auction.

You could opt for a listing with a reserve price. A reserve price is much the same as a minimum price, except that bidders don't know what the reserve price is. Before bids exceed the reserve price, the listing simply says "reserve not met" and bidding continues. An optional "Buy It Now" price gives bidders the chance to preempt the auction by paying your set price before bidding begins.

Another option is simply to post a price and sell the item to the first person who is willing to pay it.

All the pricing strategies have their advantages, but if you're cleaning house, it's best to set a low minimum bid and sell without a reserve. Bids might seem low at first, but much of the bidding occurs in the final hour of the auction.

In order to make a profit, auction houses charge the seller for listing with them. Online auction fees are generally low. At eBay expect to pay 5.25 percent on the first $25, plus 2.75 percent on the balance up to $1,000. Expect to pay 1.5 percent on the balance above $1,000. That means you'd pay $1.31 on a $25 item. On a $100 item, you'd pay $1.31 on the first $25, plus $2.06 on the next $75, for a total of $3.37.

There is also a small fee for posting a listing; if the article doesn't sell, there is no cost beyond that.

Once you make the sale, you can have the purchaser send you a check. (Wait for the check to clear before shipping the item.) You can also arrange to have the auction house forward the winner's payment to you for a small fee. This is convenient for the buyer because the auction house will accept credit card payments. It's also convenient for you because payment is guaranteed. Then you should pack the item securely and ship it to the buyer promptly. Packing and shipping can take some effort for large or fragile items.

 CLOSER LOOK

ADDING PHOTOS TO YOUR ONLINE LISTING

Most online auction listings include a photo of the item. Generally you can add one photo per listing at no charge. A second photo or a series of photos costs extra.

If you want to add a photo to your listing, you'll need to either take a photo with a digital camera or have a print of the photo transferred to a CD. If you're using a digital camera, follow the instructions with the camera software to connect the camera to your computer and download the picture. If you're using film, have the photo developed by a lab that will create a CD in addition to the photos. (Most chain stores that develop photos offer this service.) When you're ready to post the picture, put the disk in your computer.

The online auction house makes transferring the photo simple, though you may need to download some free software first. In the course of making your listing, you'll come across a button that says "add picture." When you click on it, it prompts you to click on the file that contains your picture. Clicking on a second button adds the photo to your listing.

Selling through classified ads

Newspaper classified ads are a good way to sell items such as cars, refrigerators, lawn tractors, or tablesaws that are a bit expensive for yard sales and too bulky or heavy to ship to an online buyer. The price of an ad depends on the circulation of the newspaper and the size of the ad.

- A 2-line, 10-day ad in one metropolitan newspaper with a circulation of 365,000 costs about $20, for example.
- A suburban paper with a circulation of 50,000 in the same area charges $25 for a 4-line ad that runs until the item sells.
- The weekly shopping news in that area is delivered free to 40,000 homes. It charges $10 for a 15-word ad and 20 cents per word beyond that.

Start your ad with a word that describes whatever you're selling, using capital letters to call attention to it. Ads are listed alphabetically, so starting with a description like "Almost New" will get it placed higher in the column than "Used" or "Refrigerator." In the space you have left, describe the item in detail, listing its strong points. Close the ad with your phone number. (When comparing rates between competitive papers, remember that your phone number will take up at least one line, so a 2-line ad might not be such a good deal.)

You can usually place an ad over the phone, on the web, or by mail. When you do you'll have the chance to dress up the ad. You can usually add a headline in bold type, a footer that runs across the bottom in bold, borders, and other eye-catchers. All come at a cost, but it usually pays to use at least one of the choices to make your ad stand out. If displaying your ad more prominently sells your wares more quickly, you'll save the money you would otherwise spend on future ads.

Stow it, don't show it

Once you begin packing you'll be overwhelmed by boxes. You may be able to live with the confusion, but if your house is still on the market, sending potential buyers through a maze of boxes isn't the best way to land a sale. Uncluttered houses show best. If your house is being shown while you're packing, look into renting a self-storage unit on a month-to-month basis.

Start by looking for a place with good security. The facility should have a high fence, and there should be some way to keep an eye on the units—closed-circuit cameras, alarms, night watchmen, or all three. The entrance should be controlled so that only those renting storage units can get in. Doors on individual units should lock with a cylinder lock like you have on the exterior doors of your house. Cheap garage-door handles or padlocks are too easy to break off.

Your homeowner's insurance may not cover loss or damages outside the home, so ask whether the rental fee includes insurance or whether it's extra. If insurance isn't available from either the storage yard or your homeowner's insurance, rent elsewhere.

A storage unit that has a floor raised above the ground will give you some protection against water damage caused by rain. Insulation will moderate extreme changes in temperature. Look for both, but remember that some things store better than others: Books, paper, and clothes will tolerate changes in temperatures; paintings, Christmas candles, and antique furniture may not. Jewelry is too valuable to keep in a storage unit. If you can't keep it in the house, rent a safe deposit box at a bank.

Preparing items for storage

Pack storage items for the move so that you don't have to repack them when moving day arrives.

Keep your boxes off the floor by placing them on pallets or 2×4s laid flat. Keep them away from the walls and pack them tight against each other to avoid moisture damage caused by condensation.

Make an inventory and keep it in a safe place; you may need it for insurance. You'll probably also want to check the list from time to time to determine whether an item has been packed or is somewhere in the house.

Label all boxes. Pack dishes in boxes designed to hold them (see page 60). Pack with packing paper and use paper to fill up any empty spaces.

Pack books flat in the box. Clothing, curtains, and drapes should be cleaned and then hung in wardrobe boxes (see page 59) available from movers. Dirty fabrics may attract mice or other pests.

Place plastic tarps or other protective covers over sofas and upholstered furniture.

Humidity will cause metal items to rust. Wipe down bicycles, lawnmowers, filing cabinets, and other metal items with WD-40 or light oil.

Leave the refrigerator door open to prevent mold and mildew. Drain gas tanks on equipment and store flammable items elsewhere.

You can't take it with you

Although it may be tempting to pack up your favorite chandelier when you move, there are some things that by common agreement stay with the house. Anything attached to the house usually stays with the house.

This covers a pretty broad range, and some real estate agents have created checklists to make sure everybody understands what goes and what stays.

Chandeliers and lighting fixtures top the list of things that stay with the house. Desk lamps and freestanding lamps are an exception. Fluorescent lights installed above a suspended ceiling stay. Plug-in fluorescent lights in the basement or garage usually aren't considered to be attached, but it's usually not worth the cost of moving them.

Unless otherwise noted in the listing, all major appliances stay—the dishwasher, stove, refrigerator, washer, and dryer.

In some cases the seller has tried to take a home's antique hardware, but hinges, doorknobs, and other hardware are part of the house. Shutters, built-in cabinetry, and doors all stay. All plumbing fixtures stay.

The sale of a house is a negotiation, however. Sellers and buyers ask for, and sometimes get, exceptions to the general rules. It isn't uncommon for a seller to specify in advance that the refrigerator or washer and dryer, for instance, will not stay with the house. It isn't unheard of to do the same with a chandelier. If you want to take any of these with you, however, discuss it with your real estate agent in advance and make sure the excluded items are noted in the sales literature for the house. If you intend to take something that would normally stay, the safest bet is to remove and replace it before you show the house.

REAL WORLD

DITCHING YOUR WHEELS

Households often end up with a second (or third) car that won't be going to the new home. It may be a low-end car that isn't worth trading in. It may even be so low-end that no one wants to buy it. Having a clunker out in front isn't the best way to show a house, but what do you do with the car?

One of the first places to check is with local vo-tech schools. They're often looking for cars that students can work on. Check with them about selling or donating the car.

Or contact your favorite charity. Nearly all charities can make arrangements to send donated cars to auto auctions in order to raise funds. They'll arrange to have someone haul the car to the auction and will send you a receipt so you can deduct the sale price of the car from your income taxes as a charitable donation.

From renter to homeowner

Owning your own home is a part of the American dream, but as you move from renter to homeowner, you might not be worrying so much about what to get rid of as all the stuff you'll have to buy.

You won't have a landlord to mow the lawn anymore for instance. If finances are tight check the newspaper's want ads or yard sales for a used lawnmower in good shape. Have the blade professionally sharpened.

You'll need a hose and sprinkler and if you have a garden, a trowel and hand fork, and perhaps a shovel too. Buy them as you need them. Raking leaves is a yearly ritual from which there is no escape. Buy a leaf rake when the time comes and find out how you can dispose of the leaves.

Plan ahead for snow. Have a snow shovel and some salt or sand on hand well before the first snow. If you have a long driveway or sidewalk, buy a snowblower before the first snow falls. If you plan to have a contractor remove snow, arrange the contract before snow flies. You might still need a shovel if the contract only covers snowfall over a set amount.

While windows will get dirty on their own, they will not wash themselves. Clean inside with window cleaner and newspapers. Clean outside with one of the spray-on window cleaners that attaches to the hose.

The law of averages

It is not all hardware you'll be paying for. Banks and mortgage companies require homeowner's insurance. When you're paying for your first home, the yearly charge for insurance can come as a shock. However lenders will often total the cost of insurance and let you add the monthly average to your mortgage payment. The insurance company bills them directly, and they make the payments.

Taxes are the second big shock of the financial year. You can wrap them into your monthly payment as well and let the bank or mortgage company make the actual payment.

Come winter, homeowners in the north will start paying for heat. If you have oil heat, you can usually buy a season's worth in the fall at a discount. It's a big expenditure all at one time, but it amounts to considerable savings. If you have gas heat, electric heat, or central air-conditioning, you can ask to go on a budget plan in which the utility totals the yearly costs and lets you pay the monthly average.

Cleaning house

GOOD IDEA

A s you get ready for your move, you'll find a lot of things that you want to get rid of. Some you can throw in the trash. Others can be recycled. In the garage especially, you'll find things like old motor oil that must be recycled. (It's illegal to dump oil on the ground or down the drain.) Still other things contain solvents or mercury or other heavy metals and have to be taken to a hazardous waste site.

It's hard to know what's hazardous, recyclable, or just ordinary trash; check with local waste authorities. Here's what to do with some things you're likely to find as you clean house:

Aerosol paint cans. Empty cans can go in the regular trash. Those with paint in them must go to a hazardous waste site.

Art and photographic supplies. Take them to a hazardous waste site.

Batteries. Alkaline batteries can be thrown in the trash. Rechargeable batteries—Nickel Cadmium (NiCd or NiCad), Nickel Metal Hydride (NiMH), Lithium Ion (Li-ion), and Small Sealed Lead (Pb) batteries—can all be recycled and should not go to

landfills, where the heavy metals in them can leach into the water supply. Several national chains, including The Home Depot, and several cell phone providers participate in recycling programs. Contact the Rechargeable Battery Recycling Corporation at www.rbrc.org or by calling (800) 8-BATTERY to find local recycling sites.

Brake fluid, transmission fluid, power steering fluid. Treat these as hazardous waste.

Car batteries. Car batteries contain lead and sulfuric acid. Most states require that anyone selling car batteries also collect batteries for recycling, and 90 percent of automobile batteries are recycled. If you have an old battery, take it to your service station or to any store that sells car batteries.

Cell phones. Old cell phones often end up in the drawer as you upgrade to new models. To recycle them and the rechargeable batteries in them, call the Rechargeable Battery Recycling Corporation (RBRC) at (877) 2-RECYCLE or go to www.call2recycle.org. RBRC can also give you information about recycling rechargeable batteries from portable phones.

Computers. Computers contain lead, cadmium, mercury, and toxic flame-retardants. It is illegal for businesses to throw old computers in the trash; home computers should also be kept out of the trash stream. Some areas have programs that redirect old computers to schools or other institutions. Other areas accept computers, fax machines, and televisions at their hazardous waste collection site. Search "computer recycling" or "computer disposal" on the Internet.

Detergents and cleaners. Flush liquids down the toilet one at a time. Throw solids in the trash.

Fertilizer. The best solution is to put fertilizer on the lawn or garden. If you can't spread it for some reason, give it to a neighbor. You can put it with curbside trash as long as it doesn't contain herbicides. Fertilizers containing herbicides must be disposed of at a hazardous waste site.

Fluorescent lightbulbs, high-intensity discharge bulbs. Both contain small amounts of mercury and are considered hazardous waste. Check to see whether there are local recyclers or dispose of them as hazardous waste.

Fluorescent light fixtures. If the ballast is electronic or has "No PCBs" written on it, dispose of it at curbside. If the ballast is oil-filled or does not say "No PCBs," dispose of it as a hazardous waste.

Herbicides. Take to a hazardous waste site.

Mattresses. The few mattress-recycling plants in the country deal only with commercial customers. Check to see whether your municipality has one of them. Or you may be able to give your mattress to a charity, as long as it's clean, dry, has no tears, and is in excellent condition. If not and you don't want to take the mattress to your new home, your only choice is to throw it out. Every municipality handles mattress disposal differently; check to see what the proper procedures are in your town.

Motor oil. Once used, motor oil contains heavy metals. Do not pour it down the drain or into the ground. Take it to your mechanic to add it to the oil the garage recycles. Many auto-parts stores collect oil for recycling too. Don't contaminate the oil by mixing it with bleach, ammonia, antifreeze, or other household chemicals, and don't store it in containers that once held household chemicals.

Paint, latex. Remove the lid and let the paint dry out. Once the paint is dry, you can put the can in the trash. Get rid of small amounts of latex paint by using it to paint cardboard, which you can throw out once it's dry. To dry larger amounts quickly, mix the paint with kitty litter and pour it in 1-inch layers into a box lined with a plastic bag. Let each layer dry before pouring in a new one. Disposing of wet paint releases pollutants and the paint is likely to drip from the garbage truck onto the roadway.

Paint, oil-base (alkyd). Amounts less than 1 cup can be treated like latex paint. Take larger amounts to a site that handles hazardous waste.

Paint removers. Paint removers and strippers contain both volatile organic compounds and potential carcinogens. Dispose of them at a hazardous waste site.

Propane tanks. Some dealers will take back old tanks. You may also be able to sell the tank. If you are disposing of the tank, it is considered hazardous waste. Even empty tanks have residual propane in them and may explode if crushed or shredded.

Refrigerators, dehumidifiers, air-conditioners. Because of the damage that escaped refrigerants can do to the earth's ozone layer, the refrigerants in appliances must be recycled before the item can be disposed of. Municipalities generally do not do this and won't accept such appliances. Contact a local appliance dealer. There is usually a charge for picking up, recycling, and disposing of the appliance.

Roof tar, driveway sealer. If hardened, most municipalities let you dispose of it at curbside as long as the lid is off the can. If the tar or sealer is solvent-based and still liquid, take it to a hazardous waste disposal site. If latex-based, dispose of it as you would latex paint.

Shellac. Treat as hazardous waste.

Tires. Old tires can be recycled or retreaded. Take them to your mechanic or to a tire dealer for recycling. There may be a disposal charge.

Turpentine, paint thinner. While these are toxic and must be disposed of at a hazardous waste site, you can also give them to a friend who can use them. If you have either of these liquids that have been used for cleaning brushes, pour it into a glass jar and wait a few days until the paint settles to the bottom of the jar. Pour the clear liquid back into its original can and it's as good as new. Let the paint dry and throw it out in your regular trash.

Varnish, oil-base. Like oil-base paint, oil-base varnish is considered a hazardous material.

Varnish, water-base. Even though it's water-base, the varnish contains enough solvents to be considered hazardous waste. Pouring it down the drain is illegal, and when it hardens it could also clog the pipes. Treat as hazardous waste.

🚫 **SAFETY ALERT**

HAZARDOUS WASTE

Many common household products contain poisons or volatile organic compounds and are therefore classified as hazardous waste. Hazardous waste cannot be collected at curbside, but most communities stage hazardous waste collection days periodically or have permanent collection sites. Usually you take the waste to a centrally located site where it is sorted and sent to be disposed of safely. Among the things classified as hazardous waste are these:

Antifreeze	Gasoline	Paint thinners and solvents
Brake fluid	Glues, epoxies	Photographic chemicals
Car batteries	Insecticides, herbicides	Propane tanks
Computer monitors	Kerosene	Rechargeable batteries
Computers	Lighter fluid	Refrigerators
Driveway sealer	Motor oil	Shellac
Fertilizers with herbicides	Oil-base paints (latex paints are	Swimming pool chemicals
Fluorescent light tubes and ballasts	not hazardous waste)	Television sets

Using a professional mover

The advantage of using professional movers is that they do the heavy lifting for you. Your heavy lifting comes in advance: evaluating, hiring, and managing them. It's a process that can be immensely stressful. After all, you're entrusting total strangers to pack up all of your possessions, load them on their truck, and drive away, while you hope they'll all reach the same place you're headed, safe and sound. Add to that chilling stories you've heard about movers holding entire truckloads ransom over billing disputes, or priceless heirlooms lost or ruined by careless handling, or families living out of their suitcases for weeks because all of their household goods are somewhere in transit—but no one's sure where.

There's never a guarantee that any move will go perfectly, but knowing what to expect and what to watch for ahead of time means that you'll be better prepared to manage your move when things start to get hectic. Rest assured: There are lots of honest and careful movers. In addition federal laws and state regulations offer you protection throughout

Chapter 2 highlights

FINDING A REPUTABLE MOVER
Knowing what to ask—and who to ask—will help you in your search.
 28

COSTS TO EXPECT
A good estimate should cover what you'll need.
 31

CHOOSING MOVING SERVICES
Choose your mover based on what you have to move and how much you want to do yourself.
 33

FINDING AN INTERNATIONAL MOVER
If you can't take delivery of your things right away, know where they're going to go.
 35

UNDERSTANDING INVENTORY SYSTEMS
Good documentation means everyone's on the same page.
36

MOVING SPECIAL ITEMS
Unusual items—like boats and cars—require special movers.
 38

AN OUNCE OF PREVENTION
Know the warning signals of dishonest and careless movers.
 41

THE EXTRAS
Additional charges don't have to be a shock if you know what to expect.
 42

CLAIMS AND COMPLAINTS
You can get satisfaction; you just need to know how to ask.
44

the moving process. The next few pages will offer resources to help you make an informed decision about who it is you'll eventually decide to entrust with those possessions.

This chapter will guide you in selecting the right mover, preparing for the move, and successfully orchestrating the many factors that have to come together to make a successful move.

Finding a reputable mover

Checking out your mover

A number of resources are available for checking the credentials, licensing, or history of complaints against a mover.

The Federal Motor Carrier Safety Administration (FMCSA) website, www.protectyourmove.gov, provides a list of registered and insured movers. The site also provides links to state moving associations, attorneys general offices, Better Business Bureaus, and consumer protection agencies.

www.moving.org is sponsored by the American Moving and Storage Association, a nonprofit trade group of about 3,200 professional movers. AMSA has a certified mover program; participants voluntarily abide by a code of conduct that covers service, charges, and disputes. These movers have also agreed to arbitrate disputes of up to $5,000 arising from loss or damages to your shipment. You can also reach the group at 1611 Duke Street, Alexandria, VA 22314; (703) 683-7410.

The Better Business Bureau can provide information on complaints filed against a moving company. You can find local information through the group's website, www.bbb.org.

Hiring the right mover takes some homework, but it's work that pays off. The more research you do on the front end, the fewer headaches you'll suffer on moving day and in the months after. The best approach is to ask a lot of questions. And get everything you and the mover agree to in writing.

Get at least three written estimates from licensed movers. The best place to start gathering names is on a personal level. Do you have friends or relatives who have moved recently and were pleased with their movers? You might also ask your real estate agent for a recommendation.

If you decide to look for a moving company in the telephone directory, you can check out its record with the Better Business Bureau or with local consumer groups (see box, left). Many states have trade associations for movers; you can often verify licensing and complaint information about particular movers through them as well as through your state's attorney general. The American Moving and Storage Association (AMSA) has a certified mover program as well as a mover referral service.

Be more cautious about movers found on the Internet. Make sure they list a local address (not just a phone number) and information about licensing and insurance.

Getting an estimate

Once you've narrowed your search, you'll need an on-site visit from a moving company representative who can give you a written estimate on the goods you're going to move.

Be as thorough as you can when showing the mover what's going; include items in the basement, attic, or storage unit and discuss any particular packing or handling needs for larger or fragile items. If you've omitted anything from the estimate—but then include it when you actually move—your moving costs will be higher than expected.

A number of websites have sprung up that offer you estimates when you fill out an online form. Sophisticated as they may seem, such sites are little better than companies that pretend to give you accurate estimates over the phone. Both are bad ideas. The only way for a mover to have a truly accurate assessment of what you'll be moving is to actually visit your home.

Moreover the mover needs to know the particulars of your move. Do you have furniture or items that will require special crating or packing? Does your new home have any logistical features that the movers need to know about? If you're moving to a narrow city street, for example, a mover may need to move your shipment off a large truck and shuttle it to your home in a smaller one. If you're moving to a third-floor walkup or if your building has a small freight elevator or a spiral staircase, the mover needs to know that as well.

More importantly the in-home estimate gives you a chance to meet the mover or representative and ask questions about the company. Sketchy or contradictory answers from the estimator may well be a warning that you should look elsewhere.

Twenty questions

A cross-country move can cost as much as a new car; even a local move can be a major investment. Approach hiring a mover as you would any significant purchase. Gather all the information you can from the moving company representative, including answers to these important questions:

1 Can you give me references of satisfied customers?
This doesn't always provide the most telling information: What mover is going to give you the name of a dissatisfied customer? But it can be helpful to ask past clients specific questions about how the company handled the move. In other words, don't just call and ask, "Did you like them?" Find out exactly what the mover did well— and maybe not so well.

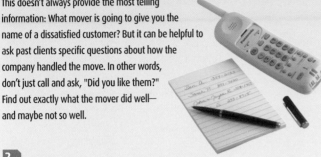

2 How long has your company been in business?
Longevity isn't always the only indicator of reliability, but a company that's been in business 50 years may have a more solid reputation than one that's been around only 2 years. Check also to see how long it's been owned by the current owner.

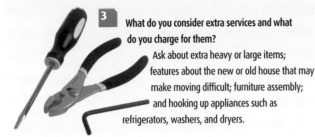

3 What do you consider extra services and what do you charge for them?
Ask about extra heavy or large items; features about the new or old house that may make moving difficult; furniture assembly; and hooking up appliances such as refrigerators, washers, and dryers.

4 Is your company licensed in state and for interstate transport?
The US DOT number as well as the state license number can be checked with the licensing agencies. Moving companies are required to display these numbers in any advertising.

5 If it's a local move, how does your company charge—by the hour, by number of movers, by weight?
Make sure this information is specified on the written estimate.

6 What kind of liability coverage does your company provide?
Many companies will give you printed material explaining their coverage. If they don't, be sure that you have written and signed proof of the coverage that you want for your load.

7 Who does the packing and loading?
If you want your items to be treated professionally, you want professional movers. Find out if the crew is employed by your mover or if they're temporary or day workers.

8 Are workers covered by workers' comp and public liability insurance?
Are you liable if a mover falls down your stairs or drops your entertainment center on his foot? What if your house is damaged or your mover damages someone else's property? Most states require movers to have workers' comp in order to be licensed. You also need to be sure the mover is covered for property damage claims. Ask to see proof of business insurance.

9 Was I given the required printed information?
By law any mover giving you an interstate estimate must give you a copy of the Federal Motor Carrier Safety Administration's (FMCSA) *Your Rights and Responsibilities When You Move.* You should also get an easy-to-read summary of the mover's arbitration program, a notice of availability of the mover's tariff (price list) for the estimate of charges, and an accurate understandable statement on the company's complaint and inquiry procedures. In-state movers aren't legally bound to give you this information, but good ones do anyway.

10 How do you determine the weight of my shipment?
The mover can do this at either the point of origin or the destination. Your mover should be able to explain which method it uses.

(Continued on page 30)

11 **Do you charge extra for travel time to and from my house?**

It's not an unreasonable thing to charge for, but you do want to know about it ahead of time and you do want to know what it costs.

12 **What kind of cancellation policy do you have?**

Find out how much notice you need to give to cancel a move and whether there's a fee involved. A reputable mover should allow you to cancel up until a few days before the scheduled move.

13 **How do I pay for the move?**

Many movers require cash, cashier's check, or money order upon delivery. More are beginning to take credit cards, but you need to ask about this ahead of time. Do not pay a deposit until you sign a contract. Beware of companies that ask you for an unusually large amount of money up front.

14 **How do you pack items with special requirements, such as electronics, glass-fronted furniture, antiques, and musical instruments?**

Wrapping delicate furniture with pads often isn't enough; it may require special crating. Other items may need special packing, labeling, and handling.

15 **Do you guarantee pickup and delivery dates? What happens if you miss one or both dates?**

You should specify exactly what dates you'd like to move. For interstate and longer moves, your mover may not be able to guarantee an exact day; instead you may be given a specific—and reasonable—time period. (You may be able to contract for a guaranteed day, for which you may pay more.) While the FMCSA mandates that movers notify you if there's a delay, they don't go into detail about compensation. That's what you need to ascertain before you sign a contract with the mover.

16 **What kind of inventory system do you use?**

A variety of inventory systems are used to track your household items. The mover should be able to explain its method clearly. Make sure you understand it; you'll need to check it at the end of the move.

17 **How much of the work can I do myself?**

A mover should be able to quote you prices for different levels of service, depending on how much of the packing you do.

18 **If I pack myself, are there restrictions on the types of boxes or containers I can use?**

Some movers want you to use only their boxes and packing material; others allow you to choose and pack your own. Ask about nonmoving-box alternatives, such as plastic storage bins.

19 **What supplies do you provide? What's included? What do I pay for?**

Movers generally sell you boxes, packing wrap, and tape, but you can often get such materials elsewhere for less. Some unscrupulous movers charge for extra tape and wrap used on the day of the move.

20 **How do you handle disputes and complaints?**

Interstate movers are required by law to offer neutral arbitration to resolve disputes on loss or damage. They are also required to have a complaint and inquiry procedure in place for customers and they must give you a clear written description of this procedure. The procedure must include: a telephone number for the mover; the ability for you to contact the mover's principal place of business by telephone; a clear statement about who must pay for complaint or inquiry phone calls; and a written or electronic recording system that records all complaints and inquiries it receives from you. Local movers may not be covered by these regulations, but ask—or contact your state's moving organization.

Costs to expect

If you're moving locally, you'll often pay an hourly rate; this rate should include a truck and the services of two or three movers. You may sometimes need to pay a minimum number of hours for moving time as well as a minimum charge for travel time. Make sure your estimate includes all of this information.

Fees for interstate and long-distance moves are based on the moving company's cost per pound, the weight of your load, and the distance it travels, as well as any additional packing or unpacking services. The mover cannot charge you by the room or by volume, unless it can be converted into a weight-based rate. In such a case the mover must give you a written explanation of the formula used to calculate the conversion to weight.

Binding and nonbinding estimates

Movers generally offer two types of estimates: binding and nonbinding.

Nonbinding estimates give you a general idea of how much it will cost to move your goods, but the final cost will be based on the actual weight of your load, so it could exceed the estimate. By law, however, at the time of delivery you need only pay 10 percent over the estimate; the balance—as well as any additional services that you requested but that were not on the estimate—will be billed 30 days after delivery.

Binding estimates are just that: They bind both mover and customer to the estimated price, no matter what the weight of the load. You must pay on delivery. If you're unable to do so, the mover can place your shipment in storage—at your expense—until you do pay. If you request more services than those described on the estimate, the mover can charge you for them, but not on delivery; it must bill you later.

Some movers offer not-to-exceed estimates. Consumers using these will either pay the maximum estimated amount listed on the estimate or the amount based on the actual weight of the shipment—whichever is lower.

GOOD IDEA

GOING BY THE BOOK

The Federal Motor Carrier Safety Administration's pamphlet *Your Rights and Responsibilities When You Move* is a handy booklet to have on hand throughout the move. If you're planning an interstate move, any mover that gives you an estimate must, by law, give you a copy of the publication. But why wait? You can get up to speed before the estimator comes by downloading a copy from the FMCSA's website, www. protectyourmove.gov.

If there's ever a time to read the fine print, it's when you're dealing with moving documents, so don't be intimidated by the many pages of consumer protection regulations. They're well organized and written clearly and concisely, and outline every step of the process. Using a question-and-answer format, the book explains your rights from the estimate through dispute resolution. It even lists, up front, the 13 most important points you need to remember from the booklet. And it includes a helpful glossary.

Level of liability

Movers have to assume liability for the value of the goods being moved, but there are different levels of liability. The moving company representative must be able to explain the differences and provide written information on what kinds of coverage the company provides.

Released-value or *limited liability* is the minimum coverage required by law and costs nothing extra. However, it doesn't provide a lot of coverage either. For interstate moves loss or damage settlements are based on the weight of the article multiplied by 60 cents per pound (often 30 cents for local moves, although this varies by location). So if the mover drops and breaks an antique china teapot that weighs 3 pounds, the company is liable only for $1.80. Likewise, a 10-pound DVD player will only be worth $6.

You have to pay extra for *full-value* protection. This level of coverage holds the mover liable for the full replacement value of lost or damaged goods, as long as that value doesn't exceed the total declared value of the shipment. Rates and deductibles for this type of coverage vary from company to company, so it's especially important to get a written explanation of this coverage. Many companies can limit their liability on items of extraordinary value under this type of coverage, unless the items are specifically listed in the shipping documents. So if you're moving valuable items such as antiques, artwork, silver, furs, or coin or stamp collections, list all of these items on a separate inventory list.

A mover may also offer to sell you separate liability insurance from a third-party insurance company. If you buy this insurance through your mover, the mover must issue a policy or written record of the policy purchase.

You should also determine whether you have any coverage under your homeowner's insurance. And don't forget: Movers' liability does not extend to boxes that you've packed yourself.

How do I decide?

Once you have a number of estimates in hand, you'll need to choose. Don't decide on price alone, particularly if one price is dramatically lower than other estimates you've gotten. As with any other consumer transaction, if it seems too good to be true, it probably is. Instead take into account these factors:

■ How well did the estimator answer your questions? Did the estimator ask questions about your particular needs?

■ Do the mover's licensing and insurance check out? Do the company's references give them good marks?

■ Does it seem to be a professionally run operation? Some consumer groups even recommend visiting the mover's offices or warehouse.

Timing is money

If you have any say in the matter, think carefully about when you'll move. When you move can affect how easily you can get a mover. Summer is the most popular time to move because the weather is good and school is out. The beginning and end of the month are also in demand, as that's usually when leases run out and real estate closings are scheduled. If you live in a large city, you may also encounter several days a year when rental leases turn over (in Chicago, for example, May 1 and October 1 are big moving days). The best advice is to book as

far in advance as you can—six weeks is good—to avoid settling for lower-quality movers at the last minute.

If you're planning a smaller, local move, try to schedule your move early in the day. Local movers often book multiple moves in a single day, so it's to your advantage to schedule your move in the morning when the crew is fresh. You don't want to be the crew's third move of the day—particularly if you're on the top floor of a walk-up building.

Choosing moving services

S ome companies are best suited for long distance, big household moves; others can be ideal for moving from one apartment to another in the same city. You can also choose a company depending on how much work you want to put into the move. Here are the types of moving services you can choose from.

National moving companies

National movers with well-known names—United, Mayflower, Bekins, Viking, and others—offer advantages such as full-service packing and shipping, as well as long distance and large load capabilities. Some offer technically sophisticated extras such as online tracking and computerized inventory systems; others offer helpful relocation and packing information.

While a nationally known name provides affiliation with a nationwide network, most local agents for van lines are independently owned businesses, much like a franchise. They'll have a local company name as well as their nationwide affiliation. The local agent's name is the one you should use to check insurance, licensing, and complaint history when evaluating a mover.

Local moving companies

Local moving companies may offer some, but not all, of the services that a national mover does. Their trucks may be smaller, and they may not offer as many services. They may also be exactly what you're looking for, in terms of the size of your move, price, or availability. They may offer complete packing services or they may only load and transport boxes and furniture on the day of your move. If they're only doing in-state moves, they are bound by the rules of your state licensing agency or moving association but not by interstate moving regulations.

Self-service movers

Self-service moving is a hybrid method that has become popular over the last decade. It falls between hiring paid movers and renting a truck and moving yourself. Among the better-known names in the field are ABF U-Pack Moving, MoveAmerica U-Load, City to City Moving, and PODS.

Here's how it works. The company delivers an empty moving container to your door. This can be a trailer (see page 15) or smaller portable storage containers that are shipped together. You're given a set period of time for loading. Some

Containers let you load at your own pace, store your goods if needed, and leave the driving to the pros.

companies allow 48 hours; others give up to five days. You're responsible for packing and loading the container. The company then picks up the full container and delivers it to your destination, where you become responsible for unpacking and unloading it.

Self-service movers cost less than full-service movers and save you the hassle and costs of driving your own rental truck—something to consider if you're planning on moving a long distance. You maintain control over how your items are packed and loaded, and you can pack and load at a somewhat slower pace than if you were using full-service movers. Many self-service companies provide additional services such as storage, moving boxes, and packing supplies; packing and moving advice; and links to companies who can provide movers to help with the heavy lifting.

You have to exercise the same caution in checking out self-service movers as you would with any other mover. Check the mover's licensing and insurance; verify that the company's drivers are licensed, professional drivers; and check—using the company's DOT number—that it has current active authority for common carriers.

Service options

You may decide to use all of a moving company's services or you may opt for only some of them—or even hire out parts of the moving process to other vendors altogether.

Loading and transport only. You're responsible for packing, labeling, and organizing all of your boxes. As mentioned before, most companies do not accept liability for boxes that they haven't packed. You're also responsible for disassembling furniture and unhooking any appliances and then assembling and hooking up everything in your new home.

Partial packing. Because movers don't accept liability for boxes they haven't packed, you should consider packing unbreakable items like clothing and books yourself and paying the mover to handle items that could be damaged in the move.

Specialty items. You may decide to hire a separate specialized packer or mover to prepare and move musical instruments, artwork, or valuable antiques.

Total package. The moving company is responsible for packing your entire household, transporting it, and unpacking and setting it up in your new home. It's an expensive option if you're paying for it yourself, but it's often included in corporate relocation packages. Be aware that "packing everything" means just that, so if you're planning on leaving things behind or transporting some items yourself, you'll need to keep these separate and make it clear to the movers that you're doing so.

Pros can pack your entire household or simply the furniture. The cost of this service should be weighed against the fact that when the company packs, it is liable for the safety of your goods.

Finding an international mover

If finding a mover in this country seems complicated, searching out a reputable international mover can appear downright daunting.

Fortunately there are several international mover credentialing programs and networks to help you find and evaluate an international mover:

- Fédération Internationale des Déménageurs Internationaux (FIDI) Accredited International Mover (FAIM) certification means the mover participates in a regular independent audit that measures a range of company standards. You can find a list of accredited movers at http://www.fidi-faim.com/faimsite/finding.html.
- The American Moving and Storage Association's RIM (Registered International Mover) certification ranks companies on professionalism and performance as well as their participation in continuing education. You can find its list at http://www.promover.org/education/rim.htm.

- The Overseas Moving Network International (OMNI), a United Kingdom–based network, also certifies international movers. Its website is http://www.omnimoving.com.

What to look for

Look for a mover that can deliver your goods directly to your new home, rather than simply to a port in that country. Many large U.S. companies do have international departments that can handle this.

You'll also have fewer packing options; because of the shipping cartons used in international moves, the company wraps and packs your items.

As with domestic moves, you should get at least three in-home estimates. However, be aware that international movers charge based on both weight and cubic measurement. Ask for a detailed explanation of what services are covered and what you'll pay extra for.

Your mover should also be able to explain the following:

- What paperwork you'll need, including passports, work permits, export forms, and proof of ownership or insurance
- What you can't ship due to customs regulations in your destination country
- Liability and insurance on your load

(For more about making an international move, see page 13.)

USING A PROFESSIONAL MOVER 2

BUYER'S GUIDE

PROFESSIONAL STORAGE

Especially with international moves (but with domestic moves as well), your new house may not be ready when you move, or you may not be able to arrive at your new home at the time the movers do. In this case your mover may temporarily store your load.

If a mover is going to store your belongings, it must do so in a licensed warehouse in its name. Do not allow a mover to put your load in a self-storage or public storage facility. In addition to being against the law, these facilities may offer less-than-ideal conditions to store your load.

You should know where the warehouse is and pay it a visit if possible. Is it clean and well-tended? Does it look secure? Is the temperature regulated?

You should also find out whether you can gain access to the warehouse if you need to retrieve something from your belongings. If so will you be charged for the privilege? Ask about insurance protection too.

The mover should give you a storage warehouse receipt that includes the address where the load will be stored, a detailed inventory of the load, the storage charge, and any kind of loss- or damage-protection information.

You'll also need to know what you'll pay if you must leave the load in storage longer than you'd anticipated, and whether there will be additional charges to move the load again.

Understanding inventory systems

Once you've accepted an estimate, the mover must prepare an *order for service.* This is not a contract; you can cancel the order within three days, though you may have to pay a cancellation fee if you agreed to a cancellation charge in your nonbinding estimate. The FMCSA requires an order for service to have 15 elements, which include your mover's name, address, and USDOT number; pickup and delivery dates; contact information; terms and conditions of charges; and estimated charges. The pamphlet *Your Rights and Responsibilities When You Move* (see page 31) lists all 15. Both you and the mover should sign and date the order.

The *bill of lading* is the actual contract and it must be presented to you before or on the day of your move. It is required to have the same information as the order for service. By law it must include the mover's name and address, contact information, the form of payment the mover will accept at delivery, the identification number of the vehicle into which your shipment was loaded, evidence of any independent insurance coverage for the shipment, and dates for pickup and delivery. Attached to the bill of lading should be the estimate, the order for service, and the inventory of your items.

You are responsible for reading and understanding the bill of lading. If you don't understand or agree with something on it, don't sign it until you are given a satisfactory explanation.

A copy of the bill of lading must accompany your shipment anytime it's in the mover's possession, including during storage. You should keep a copy with you at all times.

Inventory

Movers use inventory sheets so that they—and you—can keep track of everything that's being moved. This is mandatory on interstate moves, but a conscientious local mover will use some form of an inventory system as well.

As your furniture and boxes are being loaded on moving day, the mover will tag each item with a color-coded numbered sticker and note on the inventory sheet every item that goes into the truck. He'll also describe the condition of each item, as well as any scratches, dents, and dirt on it. Try to accompany the mover as he does this to ensure that the physical description on the form is accurate.

After the inventory is done, double-check it to make sure it's complete and accurate and that the description of each item's condition is correct. (Movers often use a shorthand notation to indicate damage or wear, so make sure you understand exactly what's been noted.) Be sure to check things like scratches on tabletops and other furniture; if there are preexisting scratches, be sure to note their location and size.

You have the right to note any disagreement and you should do so, since you'll need accurate documentation should a dispute arise. Finally both you and the driver should sign each page of the inventory. You'll receive a copy and the mover will keep one. If carbons are used make sure you have a clear, legible copy. The mover must then attach the inventory to the bill of lading.

When the load arrives at your new home, you'll use the inventory list to check off the items as they're unloaded and placed inside the new house. Once again make sure that each item is accounted for and that it's in the condition noted on the form. You and the driver will sign each inventory sheet as the items are moved in. Do not sign any sheet if it contains language that claims to release the mover or its agents from liability—that's against the law.

Some larger national moving companies use bar-code scanning systems for inventory. While this may expedite the inventory process, you still should be certain that the documentation is correct and accurate.

If you've packed your own boxes, you can prepare your own inventory sheet for boxes and their contents, particularly if you're moving items of value. When you're marking the outside of such boxes, don't use overly descriptive labels; boxes with notations like "camera equipment," "silverware," or "DVDs" may tempt thievery and disappear before they're inventoried. Instead simply indicate in which room the box should be placed and add a reference number; you can then cross-check it on your own inventory.

Moving special items

Some of your stuff won't fit in boxes. Oversized items such as cars, boats, and motorcycles pose special problems and can add to the cost of the move. In addition delicate items like pianos and antique furnishings require careful packing and loading. Here's how to handle the unusual items in your move.

Transporting cars

Perhaps you don't have time to make a coast-to-coast drive when you move. Or perhaps your family owns two or more cars, but wants to make the trip together in only one.

It may be possible for your household mover to move your car. But this can be expensive—remember, you're being charged by weight. You may want to seek out a separate auto transporter to do the job.

In some ways finding a mover for your car—an auto transporter—is like finding a mover for the rest of your household goods. You need to do some investigation.

As when finding a regular mover, ask around for referrals (you can even ask your mover for a recommendation). Get several in-person, written estimates. Check out the transporter's address, licensing, and insurance information; also check to see whether any complaints have been lodged with the Better Business Bureau or with state or local consumer groups.

You'll be charged on the distance you're moving the car; the make, model, weight, and size; the insurance coverage provided by the transporter; the service that the transporter provides; and whether or not the car is operable. (Inoperable cars usually cost more to move.)

You may choose door-to-door service, where the car is picked up at one residence and delivered to another. You should also consider terminal-to-terminal service, which could save you money. With this option you drive the car to a dropoff point where other cars are being transported and pick it up at a similar place at your destination.

Be especially clear on the transporter's insurance, what it covers, and whether there is a deductible. Ask to see a certificate of insurance. You should also check with your own auto insurance company to see what your policy covers. Also ask the transporter what sort of vehicle will transport your car: an open carrier or a closed truck.

When you're getting an estimate, ask the transporter what you'll need to do to prepare the car for moving. Among the things that will be recommended are the following:
- Have the car in good working condition and free from fluid leaks.
- Remove any external items such as bike carriers or ski racks; retract or remove antennas.
- Deactivate any alarm system.

- Do not load personal belongings into the car. Transporters aren't liable for any damage or theft for such items.
- Do not move the car with a full gas tank; half to a quarter full is fine.

You and the transporter will inspect your vehicle before you hand over the keys (be prepared to turn over a complete set). The inspection report should detail the condition of the car and include any scratches, dents, or other flaws. Read the report carefully and question anything you don't agree with. Make sure you have a legible copy.

As you take delivery of the car, inspect it carefully and note any damage or changes. Both you and the driver will have to sign the final report, so it's up to you to make sure it's accurate.

Moving motorcycles

Motorcycle transport is another specialized area; call on a motorcycle dealer for some guidance. Some movers will ship motorcycles with your household goods, although they're generally subject to an extra handling fee. If your mover does so, ask whether the bike will be crated or just wrapped in moving pads. Also you should review your liability coverage for the bike, although you can check your vehicle insurance to see if you're covered.

The procedure for checking out a motorcycle mover is similar to other movers—review their licensing and insurance information and be sure to get several quotes. Ask whether the bike will be crated or shipped on a pallet—either is generally acceptable—and whether it will be shipped in an enclosed truck or an open trailer. An enclosed truck is preferred for protecting your bike from both the elements and thieves. Like auto shipping you can pay door-to-door or terminal-to-terminal, but many companies will warn you that the transport trailers are large and sometimes unable to navigate narrow city streets. In that case you may have to make arrangements to pick up the bike elsewhere.

Check to see what liability your shipper covers. It should insure your bike for its book value. Also check your own policy to see what's covered.

Unlike cars you don't have to do a lot of special prep work to ship a motorcycle, but it is usually recommended that you disconnect any safety alarm and make sure the bike is free from leaks. When dropping off the bike, get a written inspection report of its condition. You'll need this to check when you take delivery of the vehicle.

Make sure you're clear about payment too. Some companies do ask for a deposit, and many request cash or a cashier's check, rather than credit cards or a personal check.

Transporting boats

Good research is essential when scoping out boat transporters too. You can start with your own boat dealer—who does it recommend? Get written estimates and make sure the company has experience moving the type of boat that you want to move and can move the distance you want to move. As with all other movers, the lowest price isn't necessarily what you're looking for.

Be as specific as possible when asking about what kind of equipment your boat will be moved on. Find out whether you need particular permits for moving, such as a wide-load permit, and where the boat will be picked up and delivered. If you're moving the boat across state lines, the transporter must be a licensed interstate carrier.

Proper insurance is a must as well. Find out what the transporter's liability is and ask to see a good, legible certificate of insurance.

When the driver shows up, you'll both survey the exterior of the boat and he'll fill out a cargo condition report. You'll need to check this when the boat is delivered and note whether any damage occurred in transit.

Before moving the boat, drain the fuel and water tanks, disconnect and secure the batteries, and stow all gear securely in the cabin.

Canoes, rowboats, and kayaks can often be shipped in the moving van atop the load. Extra charges can vary widely. One homeowner got bids from two well-known moving companies to move a fiberglass canoe as an extra. One company wanted an extra $700. The other company charged only an extra $70. If you transport a boat inside the truck trailer, be sure to clean the boat thoroughly.

GOOD IDEA

SHIPPING YOUR SHIP

Boat owners can get help online from the Boat Transport Guide at www.boat-transporter.org. The site calls itself "a nonprofit resource for boat transport," and includes lots of nitty-gritty information on moving boats, including a detailed tutorial on how to research a company's safety and insurance history through the FMCSA's Safety and Fitness Electronic Records (SAFER) System. It also includes a list of recommended boat carriers—with the caveat to research any company you're thinking of using.

Ask local music stores, theaters, or college music departments for mover recommendations. When you get estimates ask specifically what kind of experience the company has and how they pack and load a piano for moving. What kinds of protection do they use for the exterior—and the interior—of the piano? What kind of vehicle will the piano be moved in, and how will it be secured in the vehicle? What kind of provision does the mover make for tightly angled stairways, narrow doorways, and other obstacles? Is the mover prepared, for example, to use a crane or pulley system to move a piano off a balcony if necessary? Make sure the mover sees the piano, where it's moving from and, if possible, where it's moving into. And insure the instrument for its full replacement value.

When moving day arrives, you and the mover should review a written statement of the condition of the piano, inside and out; do the same when the piano is delivered to its new home.

Handling clocks and antiques

Grandfather clocks should be disassembled, packed, and reassembled during the move. You should have a specialist do this. Ask local clock dealers for names of shippers. Antiques also require delicate handling. Your mover may be capable of handling such items, but you'll need to decide, based on the value, the age, and the fragility of your antiques, whether you want to call in a specialist, perhaps f or preparation of the items or crating. Local antique dealers can guide you if you decide to do so.

Moving pianos

If you're moving yourself consider hiring professionals to move your piano. Piano moving is strenuous specialized work, and if you value your piano—as well as your back, walls, floors, and overall sanity—let the pros handle it.

Even if you're hiring movers for the rest of your household goods, think about hiring a separate piano mover. They will have specialized equipment for the job, along with more expertise in disassembling, packing, and reassembling it. Just as valuable are experience and know-how about moving large, heavy delicate objects in and out of tight places.

An ounce of prevention

Everyone knows a moving horror story; they've either lived through it themselves or know someone who has. Some are the result of carelessness or outright incompetence; others are clear-cut cases of fraud.

Probably the most common and dreaded moving scam goes like this: The mover gives you a great quote, a really great quote, on your move. Your goods are loaded and they arrive at your destination. The bill is presented and it's much higher than the quote. If you don't pay what the mover is asking, your goods don't get unloaded. You are over a barrel.

Many people, desperate to get settled in their new home and with no recourse at hand (and probably some fairly burly guys looming over them), pay up. They don't have to: By law the customer is required to pay only 10 percent more than the estimate at the time of delivery and the balance must be billed no sooner than 30 days later. But they've chosen a disreputable mover and are stuck in a nasty situation.

It is worth knowing who to avoid. The most popular tool of choice for moving scammers is the Internet. Type "moving companies" into your favorite search engine and up pop pages full of movers who promise instant online estimates, great deals, and fast service. Many of these companies are trucking load brokers and not movers themselves. The people who show up to move you aren't employees of the company you dealt with—or maybe aren't employees of any moving company.

The best defense against these scams is to do your research before asking for quotes (see pages 28–30). Get an in-person, written estimate, and research a company's background before you agree to hire the firm.

The proliferation of rogue movers is one reason behind the FMCSA's protectyourmove.gov website (see page 31). While the agency provides helpful hints for avoiding scam artists, it also includes details of recent prosecutions of rogue movers. Among the "techniques and ruses" one company used to overcharge customers was putting only a few items in each box in order to overcharge for unnecessary packing materials. This also allowed them to misrepresent the volume of goods. In addition they packed moving trucks in a way that deceived customers about the volume of their goods, made false statements to customers regarding the capacity of the moving trucks, pressured customers to sign blank bill of lading forms, and falsified information about the weight of the moving trucks.

There are also a number of websites devoted to moving complaints; the best known and most helpful is movingscam.com, started by a victim of a scam mover.

CLOSER LOOK

WARNING SIGNS OF A MOVING SCAM

The old saying "If it seems too good to be true, it probably is" applies to quotes from moving companies. To avoid entrapment check for these warning signs:

- The mover doesn't offer—or refuses—to come to your home for an in-person estimate.
- The estimate you're given is astonishingly low.
- The mover's website doesn't list a local address or required licensing information.
- You're given an estimate based on volume rather than weight. This is against the law for interstate moves. If the mover claims inflated charges are the result of excess weight, remember that the truck must be weighed on a certified scale. You have the right to be present at the truck's weighing.
- The mover arrives on moving day with a truck with someone else's name on it or even with a rental truck. In this case some advocates say you should fire the movers.

The extras

While your moving charges will be based primarily on the weight of the load and the distance it travels, there are plenty of opportunities for additional charges on your final bill. Some are reasonable, others less so. To avoid any unpleasant surprises when the driver presents you with the bill on moving day, you need to talk with your mover—at the time of the estimate—about possible add-on charges.

Acceptable add-ons

Many homes have circumstances that complicate the mover's job. They require extra time and labor and are a legitimate extra expense. These could include the following:

■ Excessive distance from the truck. Moving companies will often add a charge if the truck can't get close to the entrance to your house or building. This is often any distance over 75 feet, but you'll want to check. If it's particularly far the movers may have to unload the larger truck into a smaller "shuttle" to get to your building.

■ Stair carries. If your apartment building doesn't have an elevator and your new home is on the fourth floor, your mover may charge you extra.

■ Handling charges for bulky or big items—nothing quite so large as a car or boat, but oversized items like hot tubs, playhouses, riding mowers, and snowmobiles.

■ Extra services such as assembling or taking apart some types of furniture or household items. For instance movers may take apart and reassemble a bed frame without charge, but an extra item like a swing set or pool table could require more time on their part and more money on your part.

■ Any extra stops to pick up or deliver additional items.

■ Hiring any kind of third-party service for specialized assembly or packing, such as electrical fixtures or appliances. Movers aren't electricians, plumbers, or utility technicians and shouldn't be expected to do that type of work (nor does their insurance cover that type of work). A good mover can give you recommendations of third-party providers it works with and will probably urge you to get this work done before moving day.

■ Delays due to the customer's being unprepared. If you haven't contracted with the mover to pack your items, you need to be ready to go when the movers arrive. This means all boxes packed and sealed properly, beds stripped, and items dismantled that need to be taken apart ahead of time. If the mover needs additional packing supplies because the customer hasn't packed properly, they may charge you not only for the materials, but for the time it takes to deliver the materials.

Tipping the workers

One item you should also budget for: tipping your movers at the end of the job. Like any service business, tipping is never required for movers, but always appreciated—and always appropriate if the movers have done a good job. Recommendations as to how much to tip vary; some suggest a straight 15 percent; others range from $25 to $50 per worker, depending on the degree of difficulty of the move, the conscientiousness and cooperation of the movers, and other extenuating factors. It's one set of charges on which you have to use your own judgment. You should never be charged a tip on your bill of lading however.

GOOD IDEA

THE CARE AND FEEDING OF YOUR MOVERS

You'll earn some good will by keeping plenty of liquids—water, soft drinks, sports drinks—on hand for the movers. It's hot hard work, and they can use the refreshment. Some customers even offer food, particularly if there's not a quick lunch place nearby or if the workers don't take a break.

What movers can't—or shouldn't—move

It's against the law to ship hazardous materials with your household goods without telling your mover. And if you do tell your mover, the mover likely won't allow you to take them because it would then have to comply with requirements for hazardous materials carriers.

The FMCSA's *Your Rights and Responsibilities When You Move* (see page 31) is clear about what sorts of items you can't ship with your household goods: explosives, flammable liquids and solids, oxidizers, poisons, corrosives, and radioactive materials. Some examples of these are paints, paint thinner, gasoline, fireworks, lighter fluid, oxygen bottles, propane cylinders, and automotive chemicals. There are some exceptions for small quantities of medicinal or toilet articles, but you should discuss these with your mover ahead of time.

Other items aren't covered by law, but by common sense. Don't include any kind of perishable food or substance; not only can it disintegrate, but it could also attract insects or rodents. You also shouldn't ship large amounts of cash, securities, important papers, or valuable jewelry. Either carry them with you or ship and insure them separately.

Most movers don't want to move houseplants, either, and will not accept liability for them. They may be willing to take them if the move takes place within one day and within a short distance—say, under 150 miles. If you're moving across state lines, you may encounter state and federal laws governing the movement of plants across state borders. Talk to your mover—and think about whether you really need to move that 8-foot ficus or just buy a new one later.

Claims and complaints

1 f you believe that your mover didn't treat you—or your belongings—right, you have options available to try to set matters straight.

Your first avenue for claims should always be with the moving company itself, and the sooner the better. The most common complaints fall into three categories:

■ If anything is lost or damaged, note it on the mover's copy of the inventory sheet before you sign it. If you don't discover the loss or damage until after you've unpacked, you must file a loss and damage claim within nine months after delivery.

■ You may feel that you've been overcharged, particularly if you've used a nonbinding estimate or if you feel you've been charged for services that weren't provided. You'll need to file an overcharge claim with the company.

■ If you have unforeseen expenses because of a delay in pickup and delivery, you may be eligible for some reimbursement. Your belongings must be shipped with what's called "reasonable dispatch," which means that your mover needs to pick up and deliver on the dates you have requested—unless the mover encounters delays that are beyond its control, such as weather, road construction, or equipment breakdown. If the delay occurred because of such circumstances, you may still want to file a delay claim, although under "reasonable dispatch," the mover isn't contractually obliged to pay you. On the other hand, if your mover missed a guaranteed pickup or delivery date and no such mitigating circumstances were in play, you are entitled to an agreed-upon reimbursement rate. But you'll still have to file a claim.

Arbitration

If the moving company doesn't settle your claim to your satisfaction, you can request arbitration. The company is required by law to have an arbitration program, and you should have received information about it when you first received an estimate. Be aware that under federal regulations, only loss or damage claims on interstate shipments are subject to mandatory arbitration.

Filing a complaint

If you want to go on record with a complaint against your mover or if you believe your mover has broken the law, you can file a complaint with FMCSA's Household Goods Consumer Complaint Hotline at 1-888-DOT-SAFT (1-888-368-7238) or online at www.1-888-dot-saft.com/CC_main.asp. You should include your name, address, and telephone number, as well as those of the mover; the origin and destination of your shipment; the mover's DOT and MC numbers (if available); and a short narrative of specific violations that you allege. The complaint will be maintained in the carrier's file as part of its permanent record, and if FMCSA decides to take enforcement action against the mover, you may be contacted to provide additional information. You should also contact your own state's attorney general, the Better Business Bureau, and your state's moving association.

Making the move yourself

A good move is well organized, with all the boxes clearly marked and placed in the correct rooms at the new home. Items that you may need while moving are kept in easy reach, rather than being stuffed into hard-to-find boxes. Floors and doorways are protected from harm. Moving boxes are the right size and weight either for carrying on a hand truck or lifting by hand. The contents of the boxes are wrapped securely, so they will not get damaged.

Whether you decide to do all the work yourself—or enlist aid for heavy lifting, packing delicate items, or even driving—this chapter will help you. Start by measuring the rooms in your new home, if possible, (see page 112) so you can precisely map the arrangement of furniture in the rooms. Create a system to keep yourself organized and take steps to ensure against theft and damage. Decide which boxes and packing materials you will use and gather them well ahead of time.

Chapter 3 highlights

Do-it-yourself options

For many homeowners a do-it-yourself move is a necessity—hiring pros is just not in the budget. Others do so by choice, consciously carving out enough time in their schedule to save major money that can go into new furnishings or home improvements. Either way a little self-assessment will save you unpleasant surprises once your move is underway.

Counting the human costs

First decide whether you have the time, energy, and patience to make a do-it-yourself move. Expect a workout comparable to a week-long backpack through a national park. Keep in mind that it's easy to underestimate everything that is involved in a move, especially if you haven't done one for a decade or so.

Organizing. This chapter will help you simplify the organizing process. Moving is a major organizational challenge, but it's also a great opportunity to reassess your possessions and declutter your life.

Lifting. The contents of an average three-bedroom house (two adults and two children) weigh 10,000 pounds. Even if you're using a hand truck (or dolly) to move boxes and furniture onto the truck, you may still need to hoist some of them. And taking the hand truck up and down stairs can be difficult. In some situations you will need to hand-carry many boxes. Many furniture items must be carried by hand. Do you have the physical endurance and can you round up enough able-bodied helpers to get the job done at both ends of the move? Think about the friends or family who may be helping you. Are they really up to the challenge? Find out whether your homeowner's or renter's insurance would provide coverage if someone is injured in the process.

Driving. Taking a 26-foot truck on a crowded freeway can be a harrowing experience, especially if you're exhausted after a long day of loading; you may not be up to the challenge. See the "Driving tips" section (page 97) to get a better idea of the factors to consider in choosing whether to drive yourself.

Saving money

The primary motivation for moving yourself is the money you'll save over hiring professional movers. Typically if you pack your possessions and drive them to your new home in a rented truck, you'll cut your moving bill in half. But each move is unique, with its own set of considerations that affect not just the monetary cost, but also your investment in time and energy. Before you commit to doing it all yourself, add up the real costs. Compare the cost to two or three estimates from moving companies (see pages 31–32) so you can accurately assess the advantage of a do-it-yourself move.

Time and loss of income. Packing all your stuff, renting a truck, moving furnishings, driving the truck to a new location, unloading, and unpacking takes up a big chunk of time. Can you do all this without significant loss of income?

Truck or trailer rental. To rent a truck or trailer, you'll sign a rental agreement for a specified number of days. The charge will include a deposit to be refunded upon return of the vehicle (provided it is left in good shape) and a certain number of free miles. Check the contract to see if there are extra-mile charges or fees for one-way rentals. The rental fee will probably be higher during the peak moving season in the summer, as well as on a weekend rather than a weekday, or around the first or last days of the month. To calculate how big a truck you need, see page 58. For additional questions to ask before signing a rental truck contract, see page 93.

Fuel cost, vehicle wear and tear. Calculate the cost of fuel used while driving the rental vehicle—a 26-foot truck fully loaded will average about 10 miles per gallon. If you are driving your own vehicle, factor the cost of wear and tear.

Towing your car. How many cars do you have? Are you going to drive or tow them? A trailer package from a rental company can cost an additional $150, plus another $45 to install a trailer hitch. And another deposit will also be added. See page 93.

Insurance. When you move yourself, the basic insurance offered by the rental company will generally cover only damage due to a major catastrophe like fire or accident. Damage to fragile items because you had to slam on the brakes will be considered a packing problem and will not be covered. It's generally a good idea to pay extra for cargo insurance, available from the rental company on a per-day basis, to cover accidental loss or damage to possessions while in the truck. Be sure to read the fine print. For additional information on insurance, see page 32.

MAKING THE MOVE YOURSELF **3**

GOOD IDEA

SAVE YOUR RECEIPTS
If you are moving in conjunction with a job and will itemize on your tax return, you can deduct most moving expenses at tax time. Save all receipts in a clearly marked small box or envelope.

3

MAKING THE MOVE YOURSELF

GOOD IDEA

SENDING OUT ITEMS FOR PROFESSIONAL CLEANING
If you're not moving far, send area rugs to be cleaned, then have them delivered to your new home. You can do the same for furniture that needs to be cleaned, reupholstered, or refinished.

Your homeowner's insurance will probably not provide much coverage for a move. Most policies don't cover possessions in transit. If they do there may be limitations concerning mileage or interstate travel. If you have just sold your house, the policy may expire during your move. Even if the policy does cover the move, your deductible may be so high that it will not offer reimbursement for the usual moderate amount of damage. Your automobile insurance policy will probably not provide coverage either; most policies exclude coverage for drivers operating a moving van.

Packing materials. The cost of boxes, if you're buying rather than scavenging them, will be roughly the same whether you do it yourself or use a moving company. However you will probably need to rent a hand truck and a supply of moving blankets.

Travel expenses. In addition to the cost of gas, you will also pay for tolls, meals, and lodging if you're driving a long distance. When calculating how long it will take, factor in the need to drive slower than you would in your car and the possible need to modify your route based on clearance or construction issues.

Helpers. Be sure to factor in the cost of hired hands, plus food and beverages for any friends and relatives who are helping with loading and unloading at both ends of the move. If your children are small, you may need to pay for a babysitter while you load and unload the truck.

Possible damage to your past or future home. If your old home is damaged while you are moving out, you may need to compensate the incoming family. If the damage occurs to rental property, the landlord may pocket your security deposit to cover the cost of repairs. Check your homeowner's or renter's insurance policy.

Crating special items

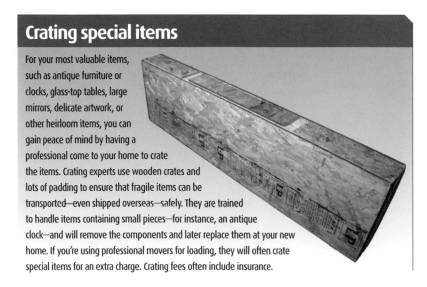

For your most valuable items, such as antique furniture or clocks, glass-top tables, large mirrors, delicate artwork, or other heirloom items, you can gain peace of mind by having a professional come to your home to crate the items. Crating experts use wooden crates and lots of padding to ensure that fragile items can be transported—even shipped overseas—safely. They are trained to handle items containing small pieces—for instance, an antique clock—and will remove the components and later replace them at your new home. If you're using professional movers for loading, they will often crate special items for an extra charge. Crating fees often include insurance.

Hiring pros for part of the work

You pack, they drive. Self-service moving companies will deliver a truck or trailer to your home for you to pack and load, then a moving company driver will pick it up and deliver it to your new home. In some cases another family (or two) may share the truck with you. Charges are usually assessed based on the percentage of the truck that your possessions take up. The truck may take several days longer to reach your new home if other families are involved. For more about this option, see page 15.

Hire help for loading and unloading. Both self-service and full-service moving companies provide workers on an hourly basis. Check the fine print for extra charges. You can also round up college or high school kids, but if you do, be sure your homeowner's insurance will cover damage to your possessions and possible injury to a helper.

Piano movers. Pianos—even small uprights and spinets— are amazingly heavy. They can cause serious injury and damage if anything goes wrong when moving one, especially up or down stairs. Unless you have already moved one yourself or know someone who has, it is almost always best to hire a pro. See page 40 for more on moving pianos.

Hire a handyman to help disassemble and reassemble. Some aspects of moving require carpentry, plumbing, or wiring expertise. If you prefer to have someone else take care of this work for you, hire a general handyman or someone with more specialized skills. A few national moving or crating companies will send pros to your old home to do the work needed to get you ready to move and then send workers to your new home to help you get set up. Items that call for special skills include:

- Appliances such as the washer, dryer, refrigerator with icemaker, or dishwasher
- Heirlooms such as grandfather clocks and china cabinets with curved glass fronts
- Recreational equipment, including pool tables, exercise equipment, and swing sets
- Some furniture items such as waterbeds and wall units
- Light fixtures, ceiling fans, and other electrical items

The container storage option

New players in the self-move category—and an increasingly common sight on streets and driveways—are containers that can accommodate the contents of one room or a room and a half. The rental company drops off the containers; you load and padlock them. Then the rental company picks them up and delivers them to the new home or a storage facility. It generally takes several days longer to reach the destination than the traditional moving truck because the move is coordinated with other boxes in the area. It's also a convenient option for families who are downsizing and want to move a roomful of stuff into a storage facility.

 REAL WORLD

LIVING WITH BOXES

Moving may mean that you will live among an ever-growing pile of boxes at the old home and an ever-decreasing pile at the new home. Kids often find this fun, while grownups get tired of it quickly. Plan activities and meals that make living among boxes at least bearable, and perhaps even fun. Board games, card games, and rented movies will likely fill the bill.

 **WORK SMARTER**

USING A STORAGE FACILITY

Make a meticulous list of the contents of each box that will go into storage. Keep in mind that items sent to storage tend to stay there longer than originally intended. If you will be storing rugs or draperies, have them cleaned first to protect from mildew. You'll need to call a few weeks ahead of time to retrieve items from storage. Corporate relocation agreements usually don't pay for storage of motor vehicles or boats.

Getting and staying organized

Before you start transferring dishes and books into boxes, devote a few hours to planning how you will pack and label. The order in which you pack your stuff, how you pack, and the way you label your boxes are all important to a smooth move. Pages 62–64 show the packing materials you will need; pages 68–87 describe various packing techniques.

Getting started

If you have the opportunity, measure the rooms in your new home and plan where furniture and other large items will go. Also measure doorways to make sure furniture pieces can fit through them. You will find a detailed guide to doing this on page 112.

Keep these goals in mind :

■ All boxes should be packed with things that go together and should be clearly labeled so you can move them into the correct room in the new home.

■ Any items that you may need while packing, driving, or unpacking should be put in separate boxes or other containers and kept where you can easily access them.

■ All unsafe items should be left behind. The list of such items is surprisingly long (see page 55).

■ Boxes should be the right size so you can move them easily—either with a hand truck or carrying by hand.

■ Allow plenty of time for packing; it always takes longer than you think. Make an estimate and add a cushion of 50 percent to be safe.

■ Gather more supplies than you think you'll need and keep them in a centralized location. Don't run the risk of reaching your peak packing momentum only to find you've run out of tape.

 GOOD IDEA

CONTROL BOX WEIGHT
Set a maximum weight for boxes you will lift and carry by hand. Most people can repeatedly lift 30 pounds without straining. Moving boxes are usually rated to hold 65 pounds (the limit is printed on the bottom and assumes proper taping). Pack heavy items in smaller boxes, saving larger boxes for lighter, bulkier items. Weigh boxes on a bathroom scale occasionally to prevent overloading.

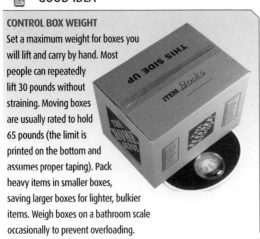

 WORK SMARTER

START WITH WHAT YOU WON'T NEED
Start by packing items you seldom use and tackle big projects first. Bring down the contents of the attic. Tackle cluttered closets and the junk room. When you're done with these, it may look like you've made no progress at all—your most noticeable everyday stuff is still in place—but you'll soon see rapid improvement. Pack everyday kitchen items last so you can use them as long as possible.

Making an inventory

Keeping an inventory of the contents of your boxes may seem like an unnecessary extra task at a time when you are overloaded with work. But it really takes but a minute or less for each box. If you hire a company to drive the truck and a box ends up missing, an inventory sheet will help you deal with the insurance company. In any case the sheet will help you find those inevitable essential items you (or your child) need when you reach your new home.

Keep a notebook handy (a wireless "neatbook" or a spiral notebook will do) on the supply table along with several pens and markers. You may prefer to keep your inventory on a laptop computer. (But back it up on removable media.) Before sealing each box assign it a number. Note the contents of the box on a list in your notebook and include its destination room. Then mark or apply labels to several sides of the box showing the number and the destination room. Keep the list with you in the car (or truck) as you travel to your new home.

Labeling

Clearly label each box with the room where it should end up in the new home. Many people like to use color-coded labels to speed the unloading process. You can also include a brief description of the contents on the outside of the box, but be careful how you label your most valuable possessions (see page 54). If you are sharing a moving truck with another family (often the case when you hire a moving company to do the driving), be sure to put your last name and new address on all the boxes too.

Because boxes get rotated during loading and unloading, mark each box on at least two sides.

Use "fragile" labels so movers or helpers will know to handle with care. With a thick black marker, indicate "this side up" and "top" for all fragiles and electronics.

A "not sure" pile

While you're packing, if you find that you frequently stop and ponder whether you should keep something and pack it or throw it away, try adding a third category: "Things I'm not sure what to do with." Put everything that causes you to pause for a few seconds in the "not sure" pile and leave it for a day or two. It will be much easier to decide after that.

WORK SMARTER

PACKING SMALL ITEMS
To prevent small items—like teapot lids or glass miniatures—from being lost, broken, or mistakenly thrown out with the packing paper, wrap them in brightly colored tissue paper before placing them in the box. Or wrap them in the usual packing paper or bubble wrap, then place them in a gallon-size resealable bag with a FRAGILE sticker affixed.

REAL WORLD

GET APPRAISALS

Have your most valuable items appraised before you move, especially if the appraisal you have is very old. That way you have paperwork to justify a claim for the current value of the item in case anything goes wrong. It's also a good idea to keep a photo of the item with the appraisal document. Keep this paperwork with other important papers that you will carry with you.

Protecting your stuff

While making an inventory identify and document your most valuable items, like antiques, china and crystal, silver service, furs, imported rugs, museum-quality collections, rare books, and precious artwork. Provide a description and an appraised value for each item. If you're hiring someone to load and drive, they will ask you to provide the company with a list of items with a value in excess of $100 per pound per article on a "high-value inventory checklist."

A moving truck or trailer is sometimes a magnet for thieves. While both loading and unloading, make sure that all boxes and possessions are either in view or under padlock at all times. This can be tricky if the path from your home to the moving truck involves turning a corner or climbing several flights of stairs. Neighbors may be able to help you keep an eye on things.

A travel box

There are a number of items you should keep with you while you travel—in the car or in the cab of the truck. Pack a box of travel gear and label it with a sign: **DO NOT PUT ON TRUCK.**

Papers to have handy for the trip. Maps and driving directions, moving inventory, moving rental paperwork, appraisal documents, medical and automobile insurance cards, phone list.

GOOD IDEA

AVOID LABELS THAT INVITE THEFT
One family labeled the outside of their boxes with detailed information about the contents. While they were gone for a short time, thieves broke in and stole the boxes labeled "fine china" and "computer." For your most precious stuff, consider using a less obvious label name or a code name—something like "Maggie's stuff"—or use a separate label color.

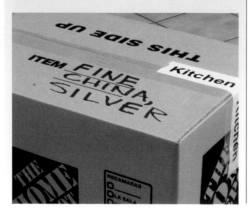

Other valuable papers to carry in a valise or briefcase for safekeeping. Items with credit card numbers, bank checks, stock certificates and bonds, tax records, IRAs, real estate papers, list of user names and passwords, legal documents (wills, passports, etc.), insurance policies, medical and family history records, school records, birth certificates.

Travel items. Keys to your new home, extra cash including change for tolls, prescriptions (refill before you leave), a first aid kit, camera and film, sunglasses (and reading glasses, if needed), bottled water, snacks, tissues, hand cream, etc., an extra layer of clothes, especially if you're driving a long distance, children's items such as toys or DVDs (if your car has a DVD player).

Valuables to hand-carry

For peace of mind, hand-carry smaller valuable items—irreplaceable photos and negatives, computer software, jewelry, coin and stamp collections, or sports memorabilia—to your new home. Or have them shipped via certified mail and keep the receipt with you.

Leave behind hazardous materials

Moving companies have developed a long list of potentially hazardous items that includes several common household cleaning products. Changes in temperature and pressure can cause items on this list to leak or even explode. Try to use up what you can and pass along useful items to a neighbor. For the rest contact a municipal official for disposal information. (Local appliance dealers can help you determine what to do with unwanted appliances. See page 25.) If you are moving locally, you can box up some hazardous items and transport them in your car.

Batteries are not permitted inside moving vans for long distance moves. As you pack remove batteries from clocks, radios, flashlights, etc. Put them in a resealable plastic bag and keep them in a bag to carry with you in your travel box.

If you do load hazardous items into the moving truck and they cause damage to your possessions or those of another family sharing the truck, you may be held liable. Here are some items that should not be packed in a moving van:

- Alcoholic beverages, including wine and beer; bottles or cans of soda
- Matches and lighters
- Kitchen and cleaning liquids such as vinegar, ammonia, disinfectants, bleach, detergent, dishwasher soap, cleaning fluids, polishes, and acids
- Aerosol cans of any sort
- Scuba-diving tanks (unless empty)
- Gases used in welding; wood filler; and etching acid
- Any paint, primer, enamel, shellac, stains, varnish, lacquer, and paint or varnish remover
- Auto windshield washing fluid, engine-starting fluids, rust-preventing compounds, and flares
- Propane or any gas used for cooking or heating (including propane tanks), charcoal briquettes, brick matches, pool chemicals, cleaning fluids, lighter fluids of any kind, and weed killers
- Chemicals and petroleum products, such as kerosene, gasoline, oil, and any rags soaked in a flammable or corrosive product, turpentine, and chemistry sets
- Explosives such as small arms ammunition, loaded weapons, cigarette loads, and fireworks

3

MAKING THE MOVE YOURSELF

Open-me-first boxes

Keep items you'll need soon after you arrive in separate boxes; make sure they are loaded last. These boxes should contain the things you need to help you get your life back to normal as soon as possible after the move. You'll probably have several boxes. Label them "open me first" and assign each a destination room in the new home. Start collecting items for these boxes ahead of time so they are partially packed before the final week of your move, but allow plenty of space for adding final items on moving day.

If you will arrive a day or two before the moving van, shift some of these items into your travel box (page 54) and consider taking sleeping bags rather than bedding for the first night or two. Consider these other priority items:

- After a long day of loading or driving, a few kitchen comforts can make a big difference in morale. You may even want to prepare a simple meal that you can heat and serve on your first night. Bring disposable cups, plates, utensils, can opener, wine opener (and maybe a couple of wineglasses), dishcloths and towels, paper towels, trash bags, plastic bags, aluminum foil, and dishsoap. (Remember dishwasher soap is on the Hazardous Items list.) You may also want cooking utensils, such as a saucepan, frypan, ladle, teapot or coffeepot, a toaster or toaster oven. Other suggestions: a bag of apples, your favorite item to warm up in the toaster or toaster oven, a few canned or boxed food items, and breakfast bars.
- Beverages can include coffee (and filters) or tea and bottled water or juice. Don't pack anything carbonated for loading in the truck such as beer, champagne, or soda pop (cans or bottles) because these are considered hazardous. (However you can take them in the car.)

A suitcase (or box) for each family member

Have everyone place an open suitcase in a convenient location so they can toss in things they will want to have with them during the move and before the boxes get unpacked. Each person should have a change of clothes, books or magazines, a towel, prescription drugs, a toothbrush, and other personal items. For the kids include a few favorite toys, videos, and books for bedtime. And pack paper and pencils.

⊘ SAFETY ALERT

SEAL 'EM TIGHT
To pack expensive medicines seal caps with masking tape. Wrap jars individually and pack them upright in small boxes. If a prescription will be needed during the trip, carry it with you.

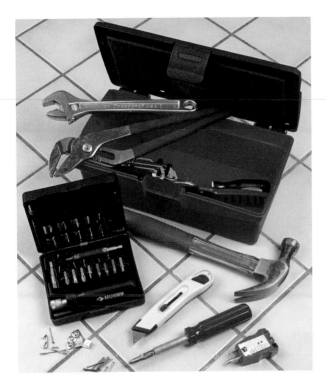

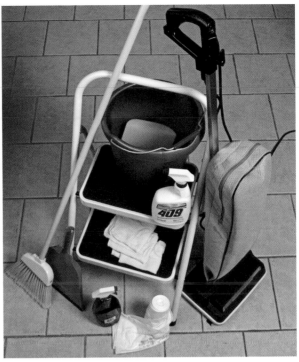

A traveling tool kit

In a toolbox or just a sturdy box, assemble tools that you may need for disassembly, repairs during the move, and reassembly and mounting to walls at the new home. The kit should include a utility knife or two, several screwdrivers (or a four-in-one screwdriver), an extension cord, a flashlight, an adjustable wrench, hammer, pliers, tape measure, scissors, and an assortment of nails, screws, and wall hangers.

Cleaning supplies to set aside

After all is loaded onto the truck, some cleaning is usually needed. If you don't hire someone to clean your home after it is empty, keep some cleaning products to do it yourself. Gather these items during a few days before the move. Many cleaning products cannot be loaded onto a moving truck. (See the hazardous materials section on page 55.) When you're done cleaning, you will have to dispose of many of the cleaning products, perhaps donating them to a neighbor.

Nonhazardous supplies should be loaded last onto the truck so they'll be handy for cleaning your new home. These can include rags, scouring pads, sponge, dishsoap, trash bags, broom, dustpan, bucket, and vacuum cleaner. A step stool or ladder is helpful for cleaning high areas, hanging curtains, or putting in lightbulbs. Here are other things to remember:

- If the windows in your new home will be bare, plan for provisional coverings—perhaps some sheets that can be tacked up for the first few nights until you are able to make more permanent arrangements.

- Pack a land-line telephone and answering machine, as well as a phone list.
- Pack remote controls, keeping the batteries separate.

Sealing spillables

You shouldn't pack anything perishable, but if you have some open nonperishable jars or bags and boxes of dry goods that you'd like to move in your car, put them in plastic bags to prevent spillage. Don't pack any open liquor bottles.

TIME SAVER

SHOE BOX
Pack a box of family shoes and clearly label it. When you get to your new home, you'll be able to quickly find your favorite slippers or the footwear you need for work, dinner out, or jogging.

GOOD IDEA

AVOID HEAT DAMAGE
Some items are vulnerable to damage if the temperature inside the moving van gets very hot, as it will do in the summer: candles, CDs and DVDs, computer software, records, audio and video tapes, undeveloped film, and floppy disks. To prevent damage carry these with you or ship them separately.

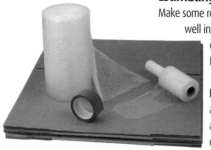

REAL WORLD

TIMELY RENTALS

For rental trucks, rates are determined by the availability of equipment in the area you are coming from and the need for equipment in the area you are going to. Typically weekends, holidays, and the end of the month may cost more because they are busier times, but there are no specific times that are always cheaper. Reserve the truck at least 8 weeks ahead of time. (See pages 92–93 for more information on truck rentals.)

GOOD IDEA

ENLISTING AND REWARDING FRIENDLY HELP

If friends drop by to help you load or pack, a generous supply of food and beverages will make the occasion as pleasant as possible. A pizza with soda pop is standard fare, but today all kinds of food is available for carryout or home delivery.

Estimating packing needs

Make some rough calculations as to schedule and packing well in advance of your move, so you won't be overwhelmed when it comes to crunch time. Here's what to bear in mind.

How much time? Packing time varies greatly according to the situation. But as a general rule, a typical family of four should allow one full day to pack each room of the house, except the kitchen, office, basement, and garage, which may take two or three days each. Bathrooms, hall closets, and wall hangings will take another day or two. It's best to start with an estimate and then add a cushion of as much as 50 percent more time. If you have a lot of fragile items or if your family includes small children or elderly members, it will probably take longer.

How many boxes? Use the chart (below right) for a ballpark estimate. If you purchase boxes from a truck rental company, expect to pay about $200 for a 4-bedroom home, plus another $100 or so for the kitchen and an equal amount for the home office. If you need wardrobe boxes for hanging garments, expect to pay $15 to $20 for each.

What size truck?

The goal should be to have enough space to accommodate your stuff, to make loading and unloading easy, and to complete the move in one trip. Even if you're making just a local move, larger is better. More floor space lets you stack lower and spread things out. So even if you don't need every inch of space, you'll find having extra room takes some of the work out of loading and unloading.

Get the right size truck

You'll need about 150 cubic feet of cargo space on the truck for each room you're moving. Trucks vary from dealer to dealer, so discuss what you're moving with the rental agent. One company makes the following recommendations when renting their trucks:

14- to 15-foot truck:
2 to 3 furnished rooms

18- to 20-foot truck:
4 to 5 furnished rooms

22- to 24-foot truck:
6 to 8 furnished rooms

26-foot truck:
8-plus furnished rooms

Box calculations

Moving companies and Internet companies that sell moving supplies provide use of a "box calculator"—a software program that lets you plug in the number and type of rooms you are packing to arrive at an average number of boxes needed for moving. To be safe add a cushion to the calculator's total; it's a good idea to have more than you need.

TYPE OF DWELLING	APPROXIMATE NUMBER OF BOXES
Studio apartment	10–20
1-bedroom apartment	20–35
2-bedroom apartment	25–40
2-bedroom house	25–45
3-bedroom house	30–55
4-bedroom house	40–65
Larger house	70 plus

The right box

Boxes for moving should be clean and sturdy. Those that are ripped or starting to come apart will only get worse during the course of the move. For ease of loading try to gather boxes that are similar in width and length (the height can vary); this will make them easy to stack.

Though scavenging boxes (page 61) will save money, many people find the convenience of new boxes worth the price. Orderly stacks of new boxes are easy to keep organized, so you can quickly pull out the right-size box. If you purchase boxes from a moving company, they will usually buy back what you don't use. Also check online companies that specialize in moving materials. They may charge less and can deliver boxes and other supplies in just a couple of days.

Some companies sell box kits that include a variety of box sizes typically needed for specific rooms. Whether you buy a kit or just order boxes, have a variety of boxes on hand for packing.

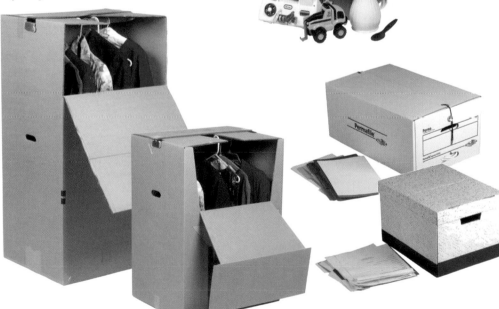

🔍 **CLOSER LOOK**

WILL YOU NEED TO LIFT THEM?
Before you order boxes think through your routes at both ends and figure whether you will need to hand-lift some or all of the boxes, or whether you will be able to use a hand truck to move all of them into the new rooms. If you can always use a hand truck, then obtain mostly extra-large and large boxes; they will make packing easier. If you need to carry by hand, go for more medium and small boxes.

💡 **GOOD IDEA**

BUY THEM USED
To save money (and trees), check with moving companies and Internet sources about the possibility of purchasing used moving boxes, usually at half price. Or ask around about buying boxes from someone who recently moved. You can also check with your local recycling center or with a classified source. When done with your boxes, consider taking them to a recycling center or passing them along to someone else by means of an ad in a local newspaper.

Wardrobe boxes
Wardrobe boxes have double-strength cardboard and a metal hanger bar, so you can simply transfer hanging items from your closet to the moving box. These generally come in two sizes, a shorter one for shirts and folded-over pants and a taller one for dresses, coats, and other long clothing. Wardrobe boxes can also be used for large items such as hanging plants and large lamps. Many people keep them after the move to use for off-season storage.

Boxes for paperwork
If you have a sturdy filing cabinet and will be able to transport it with a hand truck, it's usually best to just wrap the cabinet and move it with the files inside. Otherwise, buy boxes made for paperwork. These sturdy boxes come in a variety of sizes to hold legal- or letter-size files. They are also ideal for manuals, receipts, and other important documents. Most have an easy-open top or removable lid, so no taping is needed—and you can easily get at the papers.

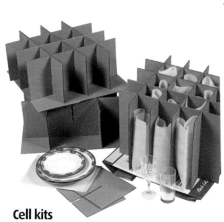

Cell kits
A cell kit, also called a partition kit, slips into a matching box to isolate glasses and other small objects. Most kits have two or more cell sizes. Small cells are typically 4½ inches square and 6½ inches deep for each section, and there are 12 sections or cell grids. Larger cells are commonly 4½ inches square but 13 inches deep. Make sure your valuables will fit loosely into the cells, so you can wrap them.

Dish barrel
This is a large box with walls made of double-thick cardboard for extra strength and cushioning. It can also be used for packing a number of small pictures and other fragile items.

Lamp box
This tall, relatively slim box is just the right size for most lamps and may accommodate the shade as well. Make sure your lamp will fit with several spare inches to allow for packing material. Some lamp boxes can also be used for golf clubs and other tall items.

Electronics and TV/monitor boxes
If you managed to save the boxes that originally housed your TV, monitor, stereo components, and other electronics components, it's always best to reuse them—especially if you have the foam packing. Otherwise consider buying boxes made specifically for electronics and small appliances. Some are designed to hold, for instance, a 19-inch TV or microwave, or standard-size CD or DVD players.

Dish saver kit
If you have especially fragile china or are unsure of your packing skills, consider buying a dish packing kit. It typically includes foam pouches of various sizes to protect saucers, salad plates, large plates, and bowls.

Laydown wardrobe box
Use this box for sweaters, coats, and other items that do not hang but need to be stored with plenty of space to avoid wrinkling. It can also be used for quilts and bedspreads.

Picture and mirror packing

To pack a large glass-framed picture or mirror, buy a two-part picture box. The upper portion slides up and down to accommodate pictures of various sizes; see pages 80–81 for instructions. If you're ordering boxes online, they are typically shipped in bundles housed in a frame box, so you may end up with one frame box as a bonus with each bundle of boxes you order.

As an alternative, buy a picture packing kit, which includes four foam corners and a strap that holds them tight. Once wrapped, the picture can be safely stored in a box.

Scavenging boxes

Of course the cheapest way to obtain moving boxes is to scavenge from local merchants. Liquor stores, copy centers, office supply, and grocery stores can be good sources. Check with the manager. Often stores have boxes available only early in the morning—before they break them down and dispose of them.

Unfortunately the hallmark of a scavenged-box move is often a hodgepodge of different-size boxes that have to be fit together like a jigsaw puzzle. As much as possible try to get groups of boxes that are the same width and length, so they can be stacked neatly. Also avoid boxes without lids, because you can't stack on top of them.

Liquor boxes are sturdy, but tend to be on the small side. Use them for small heavy items, but be sure to also look for large boxes.

Picture box

Picture packing kit

Copier-paper boxes are sturdy and have a removable lid. They are strong and big enough to be useful but not so big that they'll be too heavy to carry. Copying outlets will often set them aside for you. Some veteran DIY movers swear by banana boxes because they are strong, plentiful, and stack well. Handle holes make them easy to carry, though the openings in the lid and bottom can be inconvenient.

Boxes that hold toilet paper or paper towels are large but usually not strong enough for dishes or heavy items. They are ideal for clothing and linens.

You'll often find a stack of broken-down (that is, folded-up) boxes near a dumpster. If they have not been damaged by a packing strap, you can easily fit them into your vehicle. However it pays to be a bit choosy; check them for size and make sure they are not damaged.

Copier-paper box

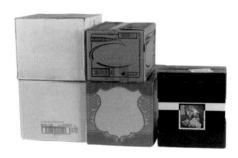

Liquor boxes

Appliance box

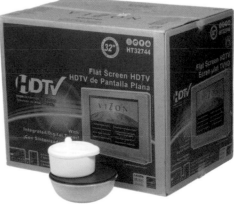

Packing materials and tools

I n addition to boxes you will need a variety of materials that cushion, wrap, and seal your goods. You'll also need tools to make it all happen. Don't skimp when it comes to buying supplies; the right materials and tools will make the job go more smoothly and will help ensure against breakage.

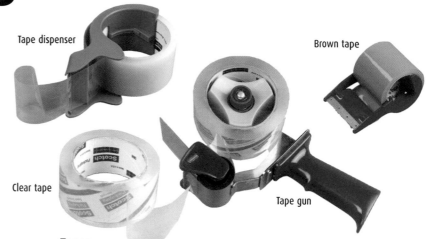

Tape dispenser

Brown tape

Clear tape

Tape gun

GOOD IDEA

GET TAPE FOR SPECIAL USES
If you are shipping some cartons, buy mailing tape, which is similar to packing tape but has lettering that clearly announces that the package is for mailing. You may also need masking tape or painter's tape to fasten down floor protection (see page 67).

Tapes

For sealing boxes buy the plastic packing tape—either clear or brown—that the pros use. It's easy to work with, seals securely, and is strong and durable. A 4-roll bundle of tape provides about 440 yards of tape—enough to seal about 100 medium boxes. If you have a small number of boxes, a simple tape dispenser will do. If you have lots of packing to do, either buy a tape gun, or learn the no-gun technique and simply work with the roll of tape (see page 69).

Packing paper

Newspaper

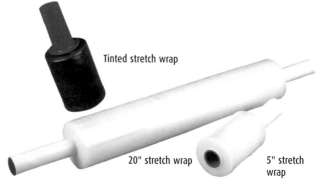

Tinted stretch wrap

20" stretch wrap

5" stretch wrap

Packing paper

Professional packing paper is sometimes called newsprint, but it is free of printing, is thicker and stiffer than actual newsprint, and has a slightly glossy surface. Use it to wrap most any breakable item. It comes in rolls, but the sheet form makes it easier to wrap an item in two or three thicknesses of paper. Many pros use packing paper almost exclusively for wrapping breakables. Paper pads are available that are large enough to let you wrap mirrors and pictures. To save money and trees, you can wrap in actual newsprint. Use several thicknesses when wrapping breakables. Beware: The ink will rub off, so avoid using newspaper on things that can be permanently stained.

Stretch wraps

Stretch wrap, also called mover's wrap, is available in widths ranging from 2 to 20 inches. For most moves it's a good idea to buy at least two widths of rolls. It sticks only to itself, so it will not leave a residue. It can wrap dresser drawers and other movable parts securely while they are being transported (see page 86). Use it to protect sofas, tables, dressers, and other furniture from dust, dirt, and scratches. Wrap it around CD racks to hold all the CDs in place.

Also buy carpet film protector, which is thicker than stretch wrap. It has a mild adhesive, so it sticks to carpet and other surfaces without leaving a residue. (See page 66.)

Bubble and foam wrap

For an extra measure of protection, use bubble or foam wrap to protect fragile items like stemware, figurines, and fine china. Both wraps can be bought in sheets or rolls. A large roll in a dispenser box enables you to tear off a piece of just the right size quickly and with one hand. When it comes to bubble wrap, the larger the bubbles, the greater the protection. Pros also use corrugated cardboard, which comes in rolls. It is useful, though usually hard to find; you can buy it most easily from an Internet moving supplies site.

Foam wrap

Bubble wrap

Moving pad

Covers and pads

When you start loading the truck, you'll need a good stack of moving pads, also known as blankets. Moving pads are filled with quiltlike batting to give them cushioning power. They can be used to protect most goods, including furniture, appliances, bicycles, and the like. Plastic mattress covers (page 87) are available in twin, queen, and king size that fit right over your mattress or box spring to protect from dust, dirt, and stains. They are vented to prevent ballooning and sealed on three sides. After you fit one onto a mattress, you need only seal the top with tape and you're ready to move. Mattress boxes are also available.

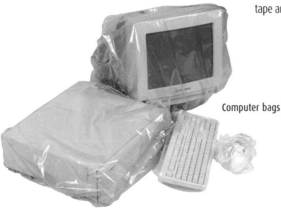

Computer bags

Organizer bag

Protective bags

You'll find a host of bags to protect small, medium, and large items. A clear organizer bag has pockets to keep important items in view. Shrinkable bags squish down and vacuum seal, so bulky clothing items like sweaters take up a fraction of their normal space. Bubble bags make quick work of bubble-wrap protection. Use computer bags to protect electronic equipment from dust and water damage.

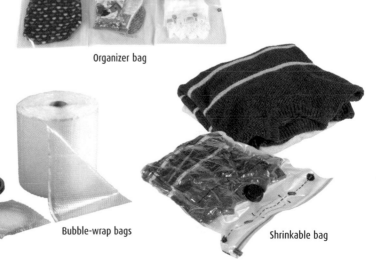

Bubble-wrap bags

Shrinkable bag

PACKING MATERIALS AND TOOLS *(continued)*

GOOD IDEA

LOCK IT UP
To keep your possessions safe from thieves at night or when you are away from the truck or trailer, purchase a heavy-duty security padlock. Make sure it will fit onto your truck or trailer's latch.

Sticker labels and markers
You can simply use a marker to write the room and other information onto each box, but many people find bright, color-coded labels easier to use and easier to spot. A typical kit will have eight or more different types of labels.

Label tape
Another labeling option is label tape. It is slightly less fussy to use than sticker labels, although you'll have to cut it every time you label a box. Wrap it around one corner of the box so the destination room is visible from two sides.

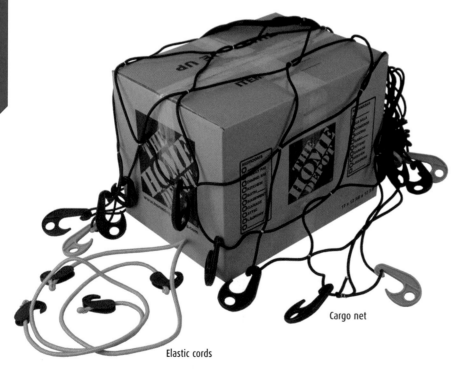

Cargo net

Elastic cords

Ropes and tie-downs
Whether you are moving in a large truck trailer or carrying things on top of your vehicle, you will need to tie things down. Often a simple tie-down rope or a set of elastic cords will do the trick. Where your possessions will be exposed, you may be better off with a cargo net or a spider strap.

Knives
You'll need a knife to open boxes and for a variety of general tasks. A utility knife (above right) works fine, but a box cutter (above left) is better, because it slips easily into a shirt pocket and you can quickly change its razor-sharp blades.

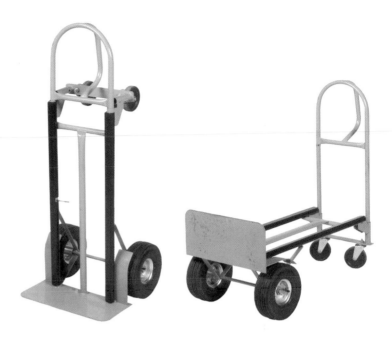

Storage bins

For items that will be stored permanently at the new home, consider buying plastic storage bins. You won't have to unpack them—just stack them in the basement, garage, or other storage area.

Hand trucks

When loading and unloading the truck, a hand truck (also known as a dolly) almost always makes the job easier. Many truck rental firms will rent you a hand truck, but you may want to buy one—it's handy to have around the house. Be sure the hand truck feels sturdy and has air-filled tires, which make for a much smoother ride than solid rubber tires. If you will be moving heavy furniture up and down stairs, consider getting a truck with a rubber track that glides easily along the stair treads. For large items be sure to have a strap or two (which may be attached to the hand truck) that can be ratchet-tightened around the box or piece of furniture. Convertible hand trucks can lie down (above right) for carrying extra-wide items.

Flip the guide like this for use on carpet.

Moving straps

Forearm straps almost magically enable you to lift things you thought you couldn't. They also help you keep your back straight, thereby helping you avoid back strain. See page 91 for instructions on using the straps, as well as on how to lift using a simple straight strap.

Furniture glides

To slide a heavy piece of furniture easily and without damaging the floor, place a glide under each leg. Use a glide with a fabric backing when sliding across a hardwood or tile floor and a hard glide when sliding across carpeting.

Protecting floors, doorways, and banisters

Carting and carrying furniture and boxes around can lead to scratched floors, railings, and doorways. Damage is especially likely when loading the truck, but it can also occur during packing. That's why professional movers take the time to cover scratchable surfaces. Sheets of cardboard—commonly, broken-down boxes—or construction paper provide enough protection for most situations. If you have easily scratched floors or especially heavy furniture, consider laying down hardboard or particleboard instead (see next page). Whichever method you use, keep these ideas in mind:

- If there is any grit under the protective cover, it will get ground into the floor when you walk on the cover. So vacuum thoroughly before covering and seal the covering tightly. If a part of the covering lifts and dirt gets underneath, vacuum it and reseal the covering.
- The covering should lie flat, with no wrinkles. Otherwise the covering could easily tear. Cover any tears with tape.
- All ends and seams should be tightly sealed, so that wheels and feet can slide across without lifting the covering or tripping someone.

Protecting a banister

Wrap a banister
Use construction paper or film protector (shown below) to cover the banister railing and perhaps the balusters (upright pieces) as well. When it comes time to move something heavy, also place a moving pad on the railing.

Using carpet film protector

 SPREAD AND TUCK
Working with a helper roll out the film protector and hold it taut as you press it in place onto the carpeting. Work to avoid any wrinkles or bubbles, which may lead to the film lifting when people walk on it. At a stairway, push the film tightly into the inside corners. Apply to several steps, then test by walking on the film. If it comes loose you may need to apply the film either more or less tautly.

2 OVERLAP AND CUT
Run one sheet over another so it overlaps by 8 inches or so and cut with a utility knife. Use your hand to smooth the film so there are no lifted-up edges.

Other options for protecting floors

Particleboard or hardboard
For maximum protection cut pieces of hardboard or particleboard to fit the room; they cannot overlap. Seal the seams and the edges with masking tape or duct tape.

Cardboard boxes
If you use cardboard boxes, open them up with a utility knife. Lay the sheets on the floor; it's OK to overlap one sheet over another. Use 3-inch-wide masking tape or packing tape to seal the edges and the seams, as well as any gaps.

Taped rosin paper
Rosin paper or kraft paper comes in long rolls. Measure and cut with a knife, leaving 2 inches or so of space near the walls for attaching the masking tape. Overlap pieces by at least 2 inches. Work carefully to avoid wrinkles. Seal all edges and seams with masking tape.

Protecting a doorway

Clip
Moving pad

Clamp and pad
A doorway is especially vulnerable to damage when carrying furniture. To protect it, purchase or rent special clips (shown) or use clamps and scraps of wood to hold moving pads in place on each side of the doorway.

Remove a door
If a piece of furniture won't fit through a doorway or if you worry about scratching a door while moving, remove the door. Have a helper hold the door at the handle, then start at the bottom hinge and remove the hinge pins, working your way up. If there's no decorative ball on the bottom of the hinge pin, center a nail set on the bottom of the pin and strike the nail set with a hammer. The pin will come at least partway out and may even fly out of the hinge. If it only comes partway out, put a screwdriver underneath the head of the pin and tap the screwdriver with a hammer until the pin comes out. If there's a decorative ball on the bottom of the hinge, drive the top ball upward. Put the screwdriver underneath the ball and against the pin as soon as there's room and tap until the pin comes out. If the hinge pins are rusted in, squirt with penetrating oil and wait a few minutes. If the hinge is hopelessly rusted, you may have to remove the screws from the door or jamb instead.

Packing boxes

Much of what you'll move will be packed into boxes. Filling and taping a box may seem a no-brainer, but packing your stuff so it survives loading, hauling, maybe some time in storage, and unloading takes technique and a knowledge of the right packing materials to use.

Set up a work area
You'll be spending plenty of time packing boxes, so it is worth the trouble to create a comfortable workstation. When packing fragile items (as in a kitchen), cushion the floor to prevent breakage. Place moving pads, drop cloths, or several layers of cardboard on the floor. A soft surface is also easy on the feet—an important consideration when you are standing for hours. An island countertop or large table where you can lay out sheets of packing paper in a flat stack will help make the job go smoothly.

Arrange your boxes so you can easily find the ones you need. If the boxes are broken down (unfolded), you can set them on end according to size in a sort of filing arrangement. Keep other boxing supplies—packing tape, bubble wrap,

foam wrap, stretch wrap—in easy reach, perhaps on a separate supplies table. Develop a system and work habits so you leave the supplies in the same place after use. That way you don't have to keep looking for them. Have several knives on hand; they tend to get lost. You may want to keep one or two retractable-blade knives in your shirt pocket.

In addition to a main packing station, set up a movable one for other rooms, such as the basement or office. While packing in bedrooms you will probably not need a station, because there will be fewer fragile items.

Working with tape
Use tape made for packing boxes; duct tape is slow to apply, and masking tape is not strong enough. Packing tape that is ribbed with strengthening strings is not necessary unless you have a box that is in danger of bursting at the seams— which should not be the case if you pack properly.

A tape gun is well worth its modest cost if it makes your work go smoothly, but many pros find it easier and quicker to work without a gun. Experiment to find the method that works best for you.

Using a tape gun

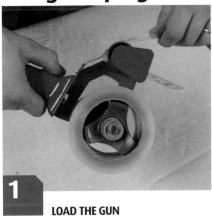

1 LOAD THE GUN

Place the roll of tape on the wheel so the sticky side will face outward and thread it through the metal tab and over the roller. Note that if the metal tab does not grab the tape, the tape may slip back onto the roll where it will lie flat—and be a real pain to lift up again.

2 APPLY THE TAPE

Press the tape onto the box, holding the roller flat against the box. Press down firmly as you draw the tape toward you; the tape should stick firmly at all points.

3 CUT THE TAPE

When you reach the end of the tape run, lift up on the handle so the flexible plastic tab bends against the box. Make sure the metal tab is contacting the tape. (Usually gravity makes this happen if you are holding the handle vertically. If not, press on the tab with your thumb or finger to make contact.) Push down fairly hard to cut the tape.

The no-gun method

1 APPLY THE TAPE

Pull the tape out about 8 inches and apply it to the box with one hand while you stretch the roll fairly taut with your other hand. With your fingers inserted into the roll, unroll the tape, set it into position, and smooth it with your other hand.

2 CUT THE TAPE

All it takes is a small nick from a retractable-blade knife to cut the tape. It is not necessary to make a clean or straight cut; you can simply push down hard to break the tape. If you have a fairly long thumbnail, poke it into the tape to make the break.

3 FOLD THE TAPE OVER

To keep the tape from lying back flat onto the roll, bend its end under to create a flap that you can easily grab the next time you use the tape.

WORK SMARTER

SHIPPING A BOX?

It often makes sense to ship a few boxes during a move—especially when you discover at the last minute that a box won't fit into the car. If you ship a box, it is usually a good idea to cushion the contents with twice the packing material shown on these pages. One effective method is to wrap each item with bubble wrap, followed by a layer of packing paper.

CLOSER LOOK

TAPING USED BOXES

If you are using a banana box, tissue paper box, or other large scavenged box, it is usually a good idea to reinforce it with at least two pieces of tape on the bottom. If a box is torn even slightly, cover the tear with packing tape that extends at least 3 inches past the tear on either side. If a scavenged box has its flaps folded over, unfold them and treat the box as you would a new box.

Box packing basics

The box packing methods shown on these two pages apply to just about any box you will pack, from clothing or books to dishes and glassware. You will find yourself repeating these tasks over and over again, so learn to do them smoothly; with practice, they will become almost second nature.

As much as possible, work in a comfortable position. For a large box this often means placing the box on the floor. You might prefer to place smaller boxes on a table.

Sometimes it is more comfortable to work while seated—but not if you have to stand up every 10 seconds or so.

Avoid the temptation to close a box by folding the flaps over in interlocking fashion—doing so does not make a secure closure nor a strong box. A box with flaps that are taped fairly tightly against each other will stand up to almost anything you load into it.

1 **TAPE THE BOTTOM**

Unfold the box and place it upside-down on the floor or a table. Fold the short flaps first, then fold the longer flaps. See that the flaps are fairly tight against each other, with their ends aligned so the box is square. Apply a strip of tape that covers the flap seam and extends at least 8 inches down on either side of the box. Then apply a strip of tape in the other direction across the middle of the box. If the box is longer than 24 inches or if it will be loaded with extra-heavy objects, apply two or three of these strips.

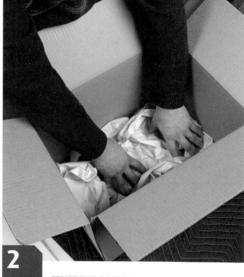

2 **STUFF THE BOTTOM**

If the box will contain any fragile items, cushion the bottom. Grab two or three sheets of wrapping paper, crumple them, and stuff them into the bottom of the box. As an alternative you could cushion the bottom using bubble wrap, foam wrap, soft clothing, or towels.

 3 **WRAP FRAGILE ITEMS**

Set a fragile item at a 45-degree angle on a stack of wrapping paper, grab the corners of two or three sheets, and roll the fragile item in the paper, crumpling the paper as you go. After the rolling is halfway done, fold the ends of the paper over and continue rolling. As an alternative you can use bubble wrap or foam wrap (see page 73).

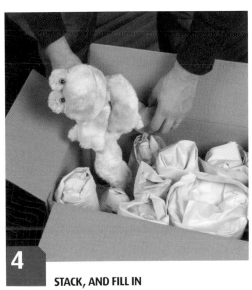

4

STACK, AND FILL IN

Aim to create a padded nest for the fragile items. In most cases they will be less likely to break if they are placed upright rather than laid flat. Push the items close together. If needed, fill spaces with crumpled paper or something soft like a plush toy. If you shake the box, nothing should jostle.

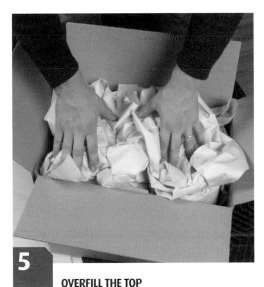

5

OVERFILL THE TOP

Unless the box is marked TOP LOAD (or DO NOT STACK ON), other boxes will probably be stacked on top, so the box as a whole needs to be structurally sound. Add crumpled wrapping paper or other soft items so it overtops the box by 2 to 3 inches.

GOOD IDEA

KEEPING TABS ON SMALL ITEMS
Small items like teapot lids or glass figurines can get lost in all the packing paper. To make them easier to find, wrap them in brightly colored tissue paper. Or wrap the items in the usual packing paper and put the bundle into a gallon-size resealable plastic freezer bag.

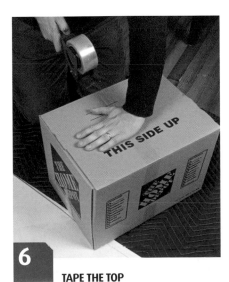

6

TAPE THE TOP

Fold down the short flaps, then the long flaps. This should require moderate pressure; if not, add or remove top packing as needed. Align the flaps, apply tape over the seam, then crosswise.

7

TEST THE BOX FOR FIRMNESS

The finished box should feel firm when you press down on the middle of the top. When you shake it, it should feel like a solid object. If the top is soft or objects rattle, open the box and repack. Or label the box TOP LOAD and make sure nothing is stacked on top of it.

8

MARK

Use color-coded labels to clearly mark where the box will go when you reach your new home. Label at least two or preferably three sides so you can see the label whichever way the box is positioned.

Packing dishes

Dishes stacked flat will easily break, especially if they are laid flat and a heavy object is placed on top. Dishes set on edge are less susceptible to damage. Make sure that when you load the truck, the box is not turned on its side with other boxes laid on top. The boxes shown on these pages—a dish packing box and a deeper box called a dish barrel—are made of thick corrugated cardboard. If you use a standard-strength box, be sure to label it TOP LOAD and do not stack another box on top.

As with plates, glasses that are stacked upright rather than lying flat will be less likely to break. Everyday glasses can be simply wrapped. Fine crystal, porcelain cups, and other fragile vessels should be further protected by stuffing the inside of the cup fairly tightly with wrapping paper; stuffing loosely will not protect against breakage.

Glasses should be packed in a dish packing box, which is extra strong and well padded. Or use a cell kit, as shown on opposite page.

3

MAKING THE MOVE YOURSELF

Individual wrapping

1

WRAP A DISH
Place a dish on a stack of wrapping paper so one corner of the paper will just cover it. Grab two or three sheets at a corner and draw them across the plate. Crumple the paper and fold the ends onto the plate. Roll the plate over and over until it is fully wrapped in a tight bundle.

2

PACK THE DISHES
In a box that is cushioned at the bottom (see page 70), place the wrapped dishes on end and crammed tightly together or placed in cells (opposite page). Position the better-cushioned sides or edges against the sides of the box. If needed, fill in gaps with wrapping paper or other soft material.

3

TOP WITH SMALL ITEMS
It often happens that there is space at the top that is not deep enough for another layer of plates. You can fill this space with small light items from a kitchen utensil or "junk" drawer.

 GOOD IDEA

OTHER WRAPPING MATERIALS
For fine china purchase foam or bubble bags specially made for your size plate. You can also wrap plates in bubble wrap or foam wrap. Kitchen towels are less effective because they do not cushion well, and using them for packing will wrinkle them, so you may need to launder them at the new house.

Wrapping bundles

1

WRAP SEVERAL PLATES AT ONCE
Set one plate on the paper, fold over two or three sheets of crumpled paper, then add another plate, and repeat for a total of three or four plates. Then roll the whole assembly over, fold over the ends, and wrap into a bundle.

2

TAPE A BUNDLE
Apply packing tape around the bundle in at least two directions. The finished bundle should feel solid, and you should not be able to feel the plates when applying moderate pressure at any point.

Using a cell kit

1 ASSEMBLE CELLS

A cell kit contains cardboard dividers that can be assembled in any number of arrangements, allowing you to pack dishes, cups, and plates of various sizes. Assemble the cells to accommodate plates that have been wrapped.

2 STACK THE PLATES

Insert the cells into a box that is cushioned at the bottom. Wrap the plates in packing paper, bubble wrap, or foam wrap, and place them in the cells.

3 ADD A FLAT PIECE

Top the first layer with the flat piece of cardboard provided with the kit. You have now effectively created another box.

4 LOAD SMALLER PIECES

The smaller cells of the top layer are ideal for packing cups, saucers, or glasses. Pack the sturdiest items to the outside.

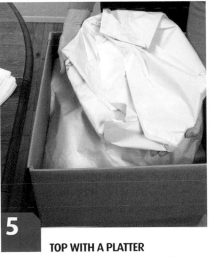

5 TOP WITH A PLATTER

If a few inches remain at the top, you could lay a large platter there. Wrap the platter well and top with a piece of cardboard. When the box is taped, test for firmness and mark it TOP LOAD if it feels at all spongy.

Wrapping with bubble wrap

You can effectively wrap plates in two to three layers of small bubble wrap, or one to two layers of larger bubble wrap. Wrap individually or in bundles of two or three. Secure the bundles with packing tape.

SAFETY ALERT

KNIVES

Wrap sharp knives individually with wrapping paper, then tape the knives together in a bundle. Label the bundle "knives" to prevent injury during unpacking and pack in a box with other kitchen items.

GOOD IDEA

POTS AND PANS

Cover nonstick pans and skillets with a plastic bag, then stack them. Put larger pans in the bottom of the box with padding between them.

Packing individual glasses

1 **ROLL AND FOLD**

Lay a glass at a 45-degree angle near the corner of a stack of packing paper. Fold two or three sheets over the glass and roll the glass about half the distance across the paper. Fold in the flaps.

2 **ROLL UP AND PACK**

Finish rolling the glass. You should end up with a fairly neat package. Pack the glasses in the box upright and tightly nested together. As much as possible, place glasses of like height next to each other.

Stack packing

1 **WRAP THE FIRST PIECE**

For small cups, or cups with lids, place two or three items on the stack of paper. Pull two or three sheets on top of the first item, and roll it up, crumpling as you go.

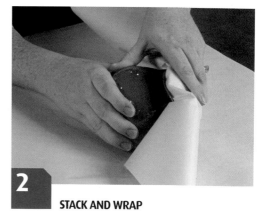

2 **STACK AND WRAP**

Stuff the first item into the second; the wrapping should fit tightly. Continue rolling, crumpling as you go. Fold over the ends and finish rolling.

Wrap stemware

For fine stemware fill the goblet tightly with a wad of packing paper or bubble wrap. Wrap the stem with several windings of bubble wrap, foam wrap, or corrugated cardboard. You may need to tape the stem wrapping to hold it in place. Finally wrap the glass with wrapping paper, as shown above.

Packing clothes and books

When packing clothes don't just stuff clean clothes into bags, or you'll end up with a wrinkled mess at the other end. Most of your nonhanging clothes can simply be left in dresser drawers (see page 86). If you have leftover dirty laundry, put it in a bag—preferably cloth rather than plastic, to ensure against mildew—and stuff the bag into an odd space in the truck. You can use the bag to pad furniture or appliances too.

For your collection of books, choose modest-sized boxes of a uniform size, if possible. Stack books of a similar size, filling around them with books set on edge. Pack them well so the books won't shift in transit.

HANG IN A WARDROBE BOX
Hang clothes in a wardrobe box as you would in a closet—not too tightly or they will get wrinkled.

USE A FLAT BOX
Use a drawer-size box like this for coats, sweaters, and other large items. Overstuff the box so it will be firm and stackable once you tape it.

PACK BOOKS NEATLY AND TIGHTLY
Take a little extra time to stack books neatly and tightly, so they won't get wrinkled or bent. Unless you are sure you will be able to use a handcart when transporting them, use small boxes so they will weigh no more than 30 pounds. First stack most of the books laid flat. As much as possible, make stacks of books that are the same width and length. Then you may be able to fill in some spaces with books laid on end. Fill gaps with wrapping paper.

Packing lamps

To safely pack a lamp, you can buy a special lamp box or simply use a long, large box. A lampshade is one of the most fragile things in a home and should be packed in a separate box marked "top load" with little or no padding. If your lamp has a glass globe, stuff the globe with a firm wad of packing paper, wrap it with paper or bubble wrap, and pack it carefully.

For a short move remove the lamp's shade and bulb, and wrap the base with a moving pad. When loading the truck place the base and the unwrapped shade at the top of the load where they will not be jostled or crushed.

Floor lamps

Tall floor lamp bases are nearly impossible to box. Remove the globe or shade and pack it separately. Plan to put the base upright next to a mattress or lay it horizontally at the top of the truck.

WORK SMARTER

WHAT TO DO WITH THE BULB
Lightbulbs break easily and are inexpensive. A used bulb may not have much life left in it anyway. Unless your move is a short distance, consider leaving the old bulbs behind and buying new ones when you reach your destination.

1 **DISASSEMBLE THE LAMP**
Remove the lightbulb. If the lamp has a shade, unscrew the ring on the socket or the fastener at the top of the harp (see opposite page) and remove the shade. If it has a glass globe, loosen the setscrews and carefully pull out the globe. Keep the shade or globe in a safe place until you're ready to pack.

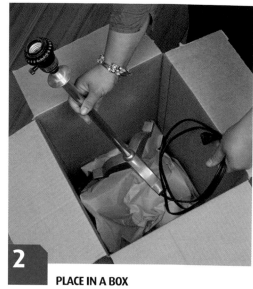

2 **PLACE IN A BOX**
Cushion the bottom of a box with crumpled packing paper and place the lamp in the center. Make sure the box is tall enough that you can add packing on top of the light socket.

3 **FILL AROUND THE LAMP**
Stuff the area around the lamp base with packing paper or other loose material. There's usually plenty of space around the lamp's stem and socket where you could put stuffed animals, a comforter, or linens as packing materials. Or consider adding paper-wrapped small items, such as trophies and action figures. It's best if they belong in the same room as the lamp.

4 **PLACE THE SHADE IN A SEPARATE BOX**
Place cushioning in the bottom of the shade's box. Even stuffed paper can sometimes rip a shade, so pack the area inside and around the shade very lightly with packing paper or tissue paper, or put nothing around the shade. Mark the box "top load" and do not stack anything on top of it.

REMOVE A HARP

Some lampshades are held by a ring at the base of the socket (see Step 1, opposite page), while others—especially older ones—have a metal harp that curves around the bulb. To remove a harp, lift the ferrules at each side, then squeeze the bottom of the harp to free it. You can usually pack the harp in the same box as the lamp.

CLOSER LOOK

IT'S FRAGILE
A lampshade can be easily ripped, bent, or separated from its wire skeleton. Many shades are inexpensive, so consider discarding a slightly damaged shade and replacing it at your new location. Finding a perfect replacement is often difficult, however.

Moving electronic items

TVs, recording and replay devices, stereo components, computers, and printers all tend to be fairly large and heavy, yet have delicate parts. A monitor or TV screen should be protected from jarring; rear input jacks should be guarded from debris that could clog them. Be sure to put manuals and other relevant literature in an easily accessible place, such as the open-me-first box (page 56).

GOOD IDEA

LARGE-SCREEN TV
If you don't have the original packing, wrap a large-screen television with moving pads or broken-down boxes and plenty of packing tape. Place the TV on the truck so its screen is well protected—perhaps facing a truck wall or a mattress. Sometimes you can fit one under a table.

REAL WORLD

REMEMBER HOW TO RECONNECT THOSE WIRES
Before disconnecting and packing electronic items, particularly the computer and the DVD or VCR, draw a diagram or take a photo showing which wire or cord goes where. You can use color stickers to color-code the wires with their respective sockets. Measures like this can save you hours of head-scratching time when you move into your new house and start setting things up.

ORIGINAL BOX
The component's original box is the ideal packing container. Its molded plastic foam packing keeps the component stable and protected, and provides ample space for the cords.

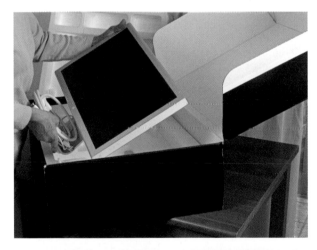

WRAP AND PACK
Use TV or computer boxes, which are extra-strong (see page 60), and fill the spaces with packing paper. Or wrap a component with a packing pad and then secure the pad with packing tape to form a tight bundle that can go into a standard box.

Moving plants

3

MAKING THE MOVE YOURSELF

GOOD IDEA

GET CERTIFIED

Some states have laws governing the types of plants you can bring in because certain varieties are known to carry plant diseases. Have available a receipt naming the plant species you are transporting. Or have a nursery provide a written document certifying that the plant is safe for import.

WORK SMARTER

SEPARATE THE DISH

If the pot has a ceramic dish under it, be sure to wrap the dish separately, or it may crack during the move.

1 f a houseplant is currently thriving, chances are good that it will survive a move with only the loss of some leaves and perhaps a branch or two. If you can pack the plant so its root system will not be compromised, the plant will soon do well again in its new home.

Most plants can recover from two or three days of darkness while in transit. If you are moving in the summer, remember that temperatures inside a truck are often about 30 degrees higher than outside temperatures—hot enough to seriously damage many plants.

The main object when packing a plant is to keep the soil in the pot. If the soil shakes out during the truck ride, the plant's roots will suffer and the pot will rattle around.

Water the plant a day or two before the move, so the soil is moist (and heavy) but not downright wet.

Small plant

1

SECURE THE SOIL

Stuff bubble wrap or foam wrap around the base of the plant to cover the soil. Wind packing tape around the bubble wrap and the pot so it will stay in place during the ride.

Bag and tie option

If the pot is large and stable and you can secure it during loading, you may not need to box the pot. To protect the foliage gently slip a large plastic bag around its leaves and pull the bag down. Wrap and tape the bottom of the bag around the base of the foliage. Secure the soil with bubble wrap and packing tape, as shown in Step 1, above right. Keep the bagged plant in a cool, shady place.

2

PACK AND LABEL

Set the pot in the middle of a box and stuff packing paper or bubble wrap around the pot only. In most cases the plant's leaves will fill the upper area, so no packing paper should be put there. Label the box TOP LOAD and do not stack anything on top of it.

Large plant

1

STUFF WITH BUBBLE WRAP

Place the pot in a box that is at least several inches taller than the pot. Stuff bubble wrap first around the pot, then on top of the soil. Mound the wrap up several inches, so it will be firm when the flaps are folded down.

2

CUT NOTCHES

Using a knife or a pair of scissors, cut triangle-shaped notches in the centers of each flap, as shown. The notches should be larger than the base of the plant so they secure the plant without damaging it.

3

FOLD OVER

Fold the flaps in interlocking fashion. If they are pressing on the base of the plant, unfold and cut larger notches. Secure the flaps with packing tape.

Packing shop tools

Power tools are usually heavy and solid, but they can be damaged if jostled repeatedly. Pack them in their original cardboard boxes or molded plastic cases if possible. Or place them in a box, crate, or plastic bin, perhaps along with other tools. Fill the area between tools with tool belts, shop rags, or packing paper. Hand tools can usually be left in a toolbox.

Packing pictures and mirrors

A picture with a plastic (acrylic) covering is not easily broken, but it is easily scratched. Pictures with glass and mirrors are quite fragile, so take the time to protect them. Always pack and load them standing upright; if laid flat, even the slightest pressure from above can break them.

Professional movers often have a roll of corrugated cardboard on hand, an ideal material for cushioning pictures. If you have a lot of pictures, consider buying a few rolls. You'll likely need to order them online if you can't find them to purchase locally.

As an alternative to the methods shown on these pages, you can wrap pictures in cardboard, as you would a tabletop (see page 84).

Short trip option

If you will travel a short distance, you can protect pictures and mirrors during transport by slipping them upright between mattresses or between a mattress and the soft side of a box spring. To quickly add a measure of protection, hold two pictures of the same size face-to-face and tape them together with masking tape or painter's tape.

Large mirrors or framed pictures

1

WRAP THE PICTURE
Lay the picture on large sheets of bubble wrap or foam padding. Wrap the picture, being careful to tape only the padding and not the picture surface.

2

PREPARE THE BOX
The sides of two-piece boxes are marked so one piece can be assembled in a way that makes it slimmer than the other. Open the bottom half of a picture box and tape one end. Stuff crumpled sheets of paper into the bottom of the box.

3

INSERT THE PICTURE
Cut a sheet of bubble or foam padding wide enough to fit into the box and long enough to wrap around the picture. Slip the padding into the box so it hangs over both sides. Slide the picture into the box, between the padding.

4

FOLD AND TUCK
Fold the ends of the padding over the picture and tuck them into the box.

5

ADD THE TOP BOX

Open the top half of the picture box and tape it closed on one end. Slide the top portion over the bottom half.

6

TAPE AND MARK

At three places wrap tape completely around the box. Then tape the seam where the two halves join. Mark the box FRAGILE or MIRROR on both sides and make sure it is kept upright during loading.

Smaller pictures

1

WRAP EACH SMALL PICTURE

Place a smaller framed picture on a stack of wrapping paper at a 45-degree angle. Fold the paper over, crumpling it as you go, then roll the picture over once or twice. Fold the flaps in, then roll the picture again.

2

SET PICTURES IN A BOX

In a cushioned box place the pictures upright and tightly nested together. Top the box with soft, light items.

Clocks

To move an antique clock, first remove its dangling parts—chimes, weights, and pendulum. Wrap them securely in wrapping paper or bubble wrap and pack them in a small box. Wrap the clock with bubble wrap or a packing pad; wrap the resulting bundle with tape (do not tape the wood or you could damage the finish). Pack the resulting bundle in a box. If the clock is a large, priceless heirloom, consider having it crated professionally (see page 50).

Packing furniture

Wrapping a sofa

A sofa may be carried into the truck without protection. However trucks may not be very clean or well sealed, so expect dust to fly around inside the truck, especially during a long ride. Vibrations in the truck can cause nearby boxes and other objects to rip fabric—especially the delicate fabric underside. Protect a couch by wrapping it with stretch wrap (shown), several moving pads or old blankets, or paper-backed bubble wrap (often called bubble craft paper).

Wrapping a chair

Chairs can also be protected by stretch wrap, but a moving pad or old blanket is faster. Drape a pad or blanket over a chair, tuck it in as much as possible, then wrap with packing tape. Make sure the tape touches only the wrap, not the frame or upholstery on the chair.

Because most furniture does not fit into boxes, you must use other techniques to make it packable. Keep these overall goals in mind:

■ Make the piece as easy to load as possible, which often means disassembling it.

■ Protect edges and finishes against the bumps that occur during loading and driving.

Often your loading plans influence how you will pack a piece of furniture. For example, a sofa that will be loaded standing upright on one end should be wrapped with pads, not just plastic wrap.

When moving furniture there is sometimes a tradeoff between time and space. Disassembling, wrapping the disassembled parts, and reassembling at the other end will save space in the truck, but may not be worth the time it takes. You may decide to simply carry a table onto the truck and pack around it, as long as the items placed on and around it will not scratch the finish.

3

MAKING THE MOVE YOURSELF

Packing rugs

Even if you've vacuumed a rug regularly, it may be dusty on its underside. Turn it over and vacuum it or take it outside for a good shake, then roll it up. Stretch wrap is ideal for securing the roll. To keep a rug from getting dusty during the trip—or to keep it from getting other contents dusty—wrap it completely in stretch wrap.

Short trip option

If you will drive only a short distance and both the truck and the rug are reasonably dust-free, you can simply roll up the rug and slide it on top of a stack of boxes or slip it under chairs.

Protecting wood furniture

If you feel confident that you can load furniture without bumping it and that only soft items (such as cardboard boxes, sofas, and mattresses) will rub against it while driving, then there may be no need to provide protection for the wood finish. However wood furniture is easily scratched; here's a sure method for protecting it.

Short trip option

Chairs are notoriously difficult to load because their legs and backs stick out awkwardly. Wrapping can be a time-consuming process, especially for a dining or kitchen set. In most cases you can stack chairs with a moving pad between them to protect against scratches. Or cut pieces of cardboard and attach them with painter's tape to the seat and the back as protection.

1
STRETCH WRAP

To make sure the tape does not touch the wood and possibly damage the finish or leave a hard-to-clean residue, first wrap the furniture tightly with stretch wrap.

2
CARDBOARD PROTECTORS

Buy preformed cardboard protectors, or cut pieces from an old cardboard box and bend them to fit. Stretch the tape taut when you attach the cardboard onto the stretch wrap.

Protecting a table

You can simply carry a table onto the truck, but you run the risk of scratching it or, if the load shifts, damaging the legs. Disassembling and reassembling a table often takes only a few minutes and it's usually worth the trouble.

Have the right tools on hand. Removing screws using a hand screwdriver is slow work. If you have a variable-speed drill, purchase a magnetic sleeve that holds screwdriver bits. With it you can easily change types (Phillips or slot) and sizes (number 2 is the most common) of screwdriver bits. Removing a screw with this setup takes only a few seconds.

Some tables have fasteners that require a wrench. You can use an adjustable wrench, but a socket wrench will make a much faster job of it. Socket wrench sets (including the ratchet handle and sockets of common sizes) are usually available inexpensively.

To protect the table's surface while dismantling it, place it top down on carpet or a moving pad or two.

1 REMOVE THE LEGS

Tip a table on its side to see how the legs are attached. In some cases you need only loosen one wingnut or screw in order to remove each leg. In other cases you may have to remove several screws or bolts. Unscrew the hardware and remove the legs. (The dog is beginning to suspect something is going on.)

2 ORGANIZE THE HARDWARE

Place the bolts, screws, or nuts in a plastic bag. Or reattach them to the leg or the table so you can easily find them. Mark where the hardware goes if it isn't obvious.

3 WRAP THE LEGS

Place the legs together in as tight a formation as possible and wrap them together using stretch wrap. For extra protection wrap the cluster with a moving pad and packing tape.

4 WRAP THE TOP

Wrap a tabletop with broken-down cardboard boxes and packing tape. Mark the box to indicate the room where the table should be unloaded.

Preparing a desk

Most desks are wider than they are tall, so you will probably need to tip a desk on its side in order to get it through the doorway. Usually dismantling a desk—or even just removing its legs—is too difficult to be worthwhile. If the desk is not too heavy, you may want to leave some or all of the drawers in place—as long as the contents will not spill out when you tip it up. If some drawers are full of heavy objects, it is often best to remove them for loading and reinsert them when the desk is on the truck.

If the desk top has a delicate finish, or if there is a chance that you will scratch it while carrying it, or if hard objects will be placed on it in the truck, protect the top by wrapping it with broken-down cardboard boxes and wrapping tape.

Short trip option

You may choose to skip wrapping the drawers in place if you are confident of your carrying skills (the drawers will likely not open when carrying the desk tipped on its side) and if you can place soft objects (such as boxes or a mattress) firmly against the desk in the truck.

1

FILL SOME DRAWERS

If a drawer will hold its contents when the desk has been tipped, fill it with light items and add crumpled packing paper. Reverse or remove the knobs or pulls if possible (see page 86).

2

WRAP LOADED DRAWERS

To ensure that the drawers won't open and get scratched or spill their contents during the move (something that can happen while carrying or during the drive), wrap them with stretch wrap.

3

EMPTY DRAWERS THAT SPILL

Some drawers—often the top middle drawer—will spill their contents when the desk is tipped. Empty these. Secure them with wrap so they won't slide out while being moved.

Preparing file cabinets

A two-drawer file cabinet with the drawers left in and filled is often light enough for two people to carry or for transporting with a dolly. A filled four-drawer cabinet can be difficult to maneuver even with a dolly. It's usually a good idea to remove the drawers, carry the cabinet and drawers separately, and replace the drawers in the truck. Some file drawers are difficult to remove from or insert into the glide when full and heavy, so you may need to remove some of the files first.

1

REMOVE A FILE DRAWER

Pull out the drawer until it stops and figure out how to disengage the drawer from the glide. With some models there is a tab that you push to release the drawer. With others you simply lift up, then pull out.

2

SECURE THE GLIDES

Unless you secure them the glides will almost surely slide out as you carry the file cabinet. Use painter's tape to hold them temporarily in place.

3

MAKING THE MOVE YOURSELF

Disassembling shelf units

Left assembled, a shelf unit wastes only a moderate amount of space in a truck; you can usually fill most of the shelf space with boxes and loose items. If a shelf unit can be disassembled easily, it may be worth your time to take it apart before loading. Some units are difficult or even impossible to disassemble, though some of the shelves may be removable.

Many inexpensive shelf units have sides and shelves made of particleboard covered with a thin veneer. Take care when disassembling and moving these, because they are easy to chip.

DISASSEMBLE
Many shelves come apart by removing allen bolts (above) or by giving a series of metal cams a quarter turn to disengage the shelves from the uprights. The unit's back may be nailed or attached with screws or sliding hooks. Remove any hardware that protrudes and place it in a resealable bag. Mark the bag and put it in the open-me-first box (page 56).

REMOVE ADJUSTABLE SHELVES AND CLIPS
If you do not disassemble the whole unit, check for adjustable shelves that can be removed. (Often a center shelf is permanently fixed in place.) Stack them on the bottom shelf or wrap them in a blanket with tape and store them separately. Remove and store the shelf clips.

Prepping a dresser

1
REVERSE HANDLES OR KNOBS
Handles or knobs can be damaged during moving and are usually difficult to replace. Use a screwdriver to remove the screw or screws inside the drawer and remove the knob or handle. Reinstall the knobs backwards, as shown, to make them easy to find.

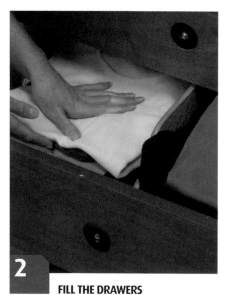

2
FILL THE DRAWERS
Add more items to your drawers, such as jewelry, knickknacks, or other small breakables that belong in the same room as the dresser. The clothing will amply protect most breakables. Fill the drawers fairly tightly.

3
WRAP THE DRESSER
Apply several windings of stretch wrap around the dresser to hold the drawers in place. The dresser can now be carried by hand or moved with a dolly.

Protecting a mattress

WRAP OR BOX IT

For most trips a plastic mattress bag provides the protection you need. Or wrap a mattress with two fitted sheets—one on each side. You can also wrap a box spring in a mattress pad or a fitted sheet. If you have a pillow-top mattress, consider buying a cardboard mattress box.

Preparing a crib

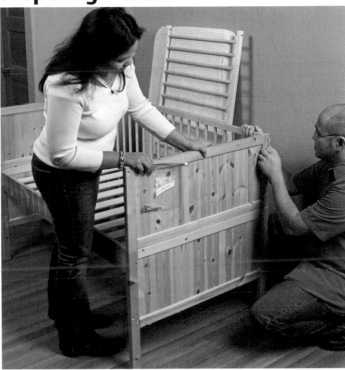

FOLD OR DISMANTLE

An unfolded crib is difficult to move through doorways and is not strong enough to support a stack of heavy boxes. Remove the mattress and disassemble at least partially. Some cribs can be folded up easily.

Dismantling a waterbed

If you do not already have one, purchase a waterbed drain kit that has fittings for hooking the drain to the mattress and to a faucet or hose bib. A waterbed will drain in a half hour or so if the drain end of the hose is 6 feet or more below the end that is stuck into the mattress. However if the drain end is only a foot or so lower than the mattress end (as may occur in a basement), draining could take most of the day.

To drain the mattress attach a drain kit's adapter to the mattress and screw the male end of the hose into it. Attach the female hose end to an outdoor hose bib or to a faucet. You will likely need to first unscrew and remove the faucet's aerator, which is at the end of the spout, then screw on an adapter fitting, then screw on the hose. To prime the hose turn the faucet on and let it run until water flows freely into the mattress. At the faucet, kink the hose, turn off the faucet, unscrew the hose, place its end into the lowest drain you can find, then unkink the hose. Water should flow from the mattress. If it doesn't, try again.

Once the water has drained out, replace the mattress's cap, carry the mattress outside (it may be heavy), remove the cap, and pick it up to drain out as much water as possible.

Use a drill with a screwdriver bit to remove the screws and brackets holding the sides of the bed to the platform pieces. Disassemble all the pieces and wrap them in blankets and packing tape. Keep all the hardware in a marked bag placed in the open-me-first box.

Moving appliances

PROJECT DETAILS

SKILLS: Shutting valves, disconnecting hoses, moving on a dolly

PROJECT: Disconnecting, preparing, and moving a refrigerator, washing machine, or dryer

TIME TO COMPLETE

EXPERIENCED: 15 min.
HANDY: 30 min.
NOVICE: 45 min.

STUFF YOU'LL NEED

TOOLS: Groove-joint pliers, screwdriver
MATERIALS: Packing or masking tape

CLOSER LOOK

AGITATOR GUARDS

For a long trip you can buy special agitator guards, which hold the agitator stable. However filling the agitator with cloth items is usually enough to stabilize it.

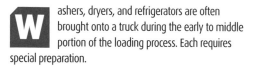

Washers, dryers, and refrigerators are often brought onto a truck during the early to middle portion of the loading process. Each requires special preparation.

Preparing a refrigerator

Remove all glass and wire shelves and wrap them with blankets or cardboard. Either remove plastic crisper drawers or fill them with soft items. You can fill the inside with lightweight boxes or linen-stuffed bags; this may be best done after the refrigerator is in the truck. Be sure to tape the doors shut. A refrigerator is often moved without protecting its sides, but you can tape broken-down cardboard boxes to its front and sides. If the handles protrude quite a bit, remove them (they are usually secured by four screws), then replace the screws into their holes so they won't get lost.

Prepping a washer and dryer

Most washers and dryers have a raised console at the rear that contains the dials. These dials are easy to break while carrying or while loading items on top. You can pull the dials off, but that will expose the metal stems which, if bent or

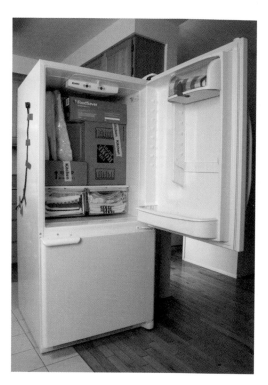

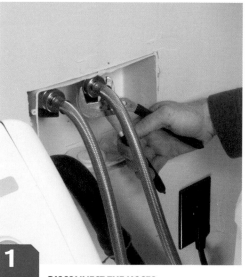

1

DISCONNECT THE HOSES

Shut off the hot and cold water shutoff valves. You can usually do this by hand, but you may need to use pliers. Use groove-joint pliers to loosen the couplings that connect the hoses to the spouts. Set the hose ends on the floor or in a bucket so they can drain completely. Disconnect the supply hoses at the machine.

2

PACK THE MACHINE

Place the hoses in the machine, along with some blankets, rags, or other soft items. Filling the agitator will stabilize it, reducing the risk of damage in transit.

3

MAKING THE MOVE YOURSELF

broken, will be even more expensive to repair. Protect the dials by taping pieces of cardboard over them. Once in the truck use a piece of plywood to protect the console (see page 96). A washing machine is heavier than a dryer, but can usually be carried by two hefty workers or transported on an appliance dolly. Unplug the cord and tape it to the side or rear of the machine—wherever it is least likely to get in the way.

Disconnecting an electric dryer is straightforward; you need only pull the plug and detach the vent (right).

A gas dryer has three connections: an electric cord, the gas line, and the vent. You will likely need to slide the dryer out as far as it will go to disengage the connections. Usually it is best to leave vent pipes behind; they are cut for a particular location and are bulky, dusty, and easily bent.

Modern plumbing codes require the installation of a coated stainless-steel flex line (shown below, right). If you have an older bare-brass flex line, replace it.

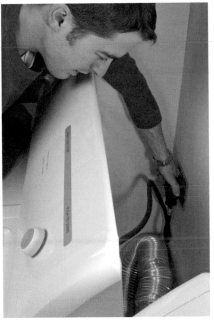

PULL THE PLUG
An electric dryer has one oversize plug and a vent to disconnect. To remove an electric dryer, unplug it and tape the cord to the side and disconnect the flue pipe.

(see page 96)

SAFETY ALERT

SHUT OFF THE GAS
There should be a gas shutoff valve behind or next to the dryer, where the flex line connects. Shut off the gas by turning the valve one-quarter turn, so it is perpendicular to the pipe. If you cannot do this by hand, use a pair of groove-joint pliers. If there is no shutoff valve, call in a plumber.

Turn valve handle to shut off gas.

DISCONNECT THE VENT PIPE
Where the vent pipe enters an electric or gas dryer, remove any duct tape, unscrew the sheet metal screws, and pull the pipe out.

DISCONNECT GAS AT THE VALVE
After turning off the gas, use a wrench or a pair of groove-joint pliers to unscrew the nut attaching the flex line to the valve. If you will leave the flex line behind, you may leave it connected to the valve, as long as you can get at the connection in the back of the dryer (next step).

DISCONNECT GAS AT THE MACHINE
To ensure against damaging the gas flex line during a long-distance move, use pliers to disconnect it from the machine. If the move is a short one and you are confident the machine will be protected, you can leave the flex line attached to the dryer, taping it to the rear or tucking it into a recess.

Carrying techniques

A pply these techniques yourself and encourage your helpers to use them as well. A large male adult in good shape should avoid lifting objects over 50 pounds, even if he can manage heavier loads. A smaller person should lift no more than 35 pounds at a time. See that the floors and doorways are protected (see pages 66–67) and clear pathways so you can carry large objects without fear of tripping and wheel a hand cart smoothly.

Using a hand cart

1 LOAD THE HAND CART

To load a box or stack of boxes onto a hand cart (also called a dolly), have a helper tilt the box back to raise one side while you slip the cart's platform under the box. Set the box back down and push it snug against the cart.

3 BRACE AND LEAN BACK

Place your foot against the back of the hand cart at the bottom, and tip the cart back until you reach the balance point—where you do not need to either push or pull to keep the load steady. You can now easily wheel the load, as long as the path is clear.

Lift with your legs

The adage "lift with your legs, not your back" is no less true for being oft repeated. Bending over and picking up even moderate-size boxes can damage your lower back. (You may not even feel it at the time, but you can wake up the next morning with pain that will take a long time to go away.) As much as possible, keep your back straight and use your legs to lower and raise your body. (You may choose to wear a weight belt to prevent hernias.)

2 STRAP THE LOAD

If the object is large or heavy or if you have to make some tricky turns, secure the load to the cart with a separate strap or (preferably) with a strap that is attached to the cart and has a ratchet for tightening. Tie it tight, so the hand cart and load are tied together to become one big object.

4 MOVING UP AND DOWN STAIRS

Always work with a helper when negotiating stairs. If the hand cart has a rubber tank-tread-like mechanism above the wheels, you can drag it up the stairs. If not, you will need to take it one step at a time. Have the helper lift on the bottom of the load while you lift on the cart handles.

WORK SMARTER

KEEP TALKING

Communication is a key element of successful hand cart use—or when two people are carrying a sofa or other large object. Take it slowly. Let your partner know when you see an obstacle or turn that he or she cannot see. If you need to slow down or speed up, be sure to communicate that as well.

Using a hump strap

1

SET THE BOX ON TOP

To carry a tall box or several boxes at once, you may want to try this technique, which takes a little practice. Lay the hump strap on the floor and place the box on top. It's important that the strap be in the center of the box. The stack should be near shoulder height; a smaller stack will not work.

2

TIE A KNOT

Wrap the strap around the box and tie a knot just below the top front edge of the box. The knot should be comfortable to hold; you may want to wrap one strap end several times around the other, then loop it under.

3

LIFT AND CARRY

Back into the box, bend your knees, and grab the knot behind your neck with one hand. Slowly straighten your legs. If the load tilts set it down and center the strap. Get a secure grip on the strap ends. Start walking when you feel comfortable with the load, which should rest on your slightly bent back.

The forearm strap

EXTEND YOUR REACH

A forearm strap is a real back saver if you are doing a major move. It extends your grab beyond your reach, effectively giving you an extra pair of hands for steadying the load. Working with a helper, place the straps under the piece of furniture or an appliance and adjust the straps so they rest at a comfortable height for your forearms. Lift together, using only your legs. As you climb a ramp, you can raise or lower your arms to keep the load upright. (Straps can be bought online from moving equipment suppliers.)

Blanket drag

GIVE IT THE SLIP

This technique is especially helpful when moving an appliance through a doorway when there is little clearance on each side. It also works well for moving inside the truck. Have a helper tilt the appliance back while you slip a blanket under all the legs. Set the appliance back down and pull on the blanket to move it.

Renting a truck

Take the time to visit the rental lot in advance so you can choose the truck that exactly suits your needs. (See page 58 for guidelines on how to choose the right size truck.) When it comes time to pick up the truck, do so as early as possible—many companies overbook their trucks (to make sure they rent them all) and they may not have the truck you want.

Features to look for

The rental company will have a chart with recommended truck sizes for various sizes of homes. When in doubt choose the next size up; it will probably not cost much more. Also review the loading strategies on pages 94–96. Here are the features to look for:

- Look at the truck's floor space, not just its capacity in cubic feet. A very tall truck will have plenty of cubic feet, but will be more difficult to load than a shorter truck.
- One of the most common complaints is that some trucks do not have adequate tie holds along the sides—places where you can loop a rope or strap in order to tie down (or more accurately, tie back) your stuff (see page 96). Look for a truck that has tie holds near the top, as well as in the middle, of the wall. The best trucks supply straps with ratchets that can be easily tightened. These are easier to use and more effective than tying with a rope.

- Most trucks today have automatic transmissions, but if you have difficulty operating a manual transmission, check to be sure.
- If you are driving in the summer, be sure the truck has air-conditioning; a tinted windshield is nice too.
- Make sure the company has a roadside assistance plan so you will not be stranded for long periods if the truck breaks down.
- Make sure it has a ramp or a lift gate.
- Learn which type of fuel to use (it might be diesel fuel) and clarify whether you should bring the truck back with its tank empty or full.
- To make the time pass more pleasurably on a long trip, ask for a CD player or a tape player.

Inspecting the truck

Ask to look inside the truck before you sign for it. If that is not possible, at least inspect the truck before you leave the rental lot; you may be able to go back and make an exchange if the truck is not satisfactory.

- The truck should be reasonably clean. Dust will seep into plush furniture, mattresses, and any boxes that are not sealed with tape. This is especially true on a long trip.
- Test the lights, including turn signals and emergency flashers, and the air-conditioning.

GOOD IDEA

RENT AN EXTRA AFTERNOON
Consider booking the truck for pickup the day before your move, to allow time to practice driving and to get a start on loading, so you can finish the loading earlier the next day and drive off at a reasonable hour.

- Does the truck have a slide-out loading ramp like the ones the pros use? Pull out the ramp to be sure it is strong and attaches securely to the truck.
- Make sure the seatbelts work.
- Test the seat for comfort. An older truck may have a worn-out seat that is lumpy or has springs that poke you. This is not a problem on a short move, but can be a real annoyance if you will drive 4 or more hours.
- Find out how the lift gate works and test it.

Questions to ask
Before you sign with a company, clarify these details:
- What mileage charges may be assessed in addition to the standard free miles? Is there a drop-off fee?
- Where is the fuel filler? For planning stops, how many miles should you expect to travel on a tank?
- Will you have to go to a truck stop for fuel?
- How many days can you keep the truck?
- What is the telephone number for roadside assistance? Is the number answered at all times of day and night?
- How much does insurance cost and what is covered? Most automobile insurance policies will not cover you while you're driving a moving truck; find out about coverage from the truck rental company. Check with the rental company or your insurance agent about load insurance.
- Is it possible to tow a car behind?
- Are any moving pads included? Make sure you get plenty of moving pads. You may have to pay extra for these.

Hooking up a trailer
To tow a trailer, you need a solidly attached trailer hitch. Most rented trailers hook up to a 1⅞-inch, 2-inch, or 2⅛-inch hitch ball. If you do not already have a trailer hitch, arrange for the rental company to install one for you. They will probably install a permanent hitch; it is no longer common practice to rent a temporary trailer hitch.

It is important to have a strong enough van or truck to haul whatever is connected to the trailer hitch. The truck must have enough power; a dealer for your vehicle make can help you determine towing capacity.

The rental company should help you hook the trailer to the hitch. Here is the basic process:

1 Back your tow vehicle as close as possible to the trailer; it's easier and safer to do this than to pull the trailer to your car or truck.

2 Release the coupler locking device. Raise the front end of the trailer coupler directly over the hitch ball; then lower it until it is seated on the hitch ball, covering it

completely. Check under the coupling to ensure the ball clamp is below the ball and not riding on top of it.

3 Latch the coupler to the hitch ball. Make sure it's locked in place by lifting up the trailer tongue. If the coupler comes loose from the ball, unlatch it and start again. If you have a weight-distributing hitch with spring bars, attach the spring bar chain to the trailer and tighten it until your trailer and car are in a normal level position. If your trailer has a surge brake, breakaway cable, or chain, attach the cable or chain to your tow vehicle, allowing enough slack for you to make tight turns.

4 Attach the safety chains and crisscross them under the ball mount to ensure they do not drag.

5 Connect the trailer wiring harness to the lighting system of your tow vehicle. In most cases this simply means plugging two parts together. Test that all the lights work—nighttime lights, brake lights, turn signals, and flashers. Take care to distribute the weight correctly in a trailer, or the trailer will either pull up or press down on your trailer hitch, which could damage your vehicle and affect handling. Check the rental company's manual; most recommend that you place about 60 percent of the weight in the front part of the trailer.

Auto-transport trailer
You can tow a car with two of its wheels on the ground, but the best way is to rent an auto transport that carries the entire vehicle so none of its wheels are on the ground. Have a rental employee guide you as you drive the car onto the transport, then tie its wheels firmly in place with the ratcheted straps on the trailer.

REAL WORLD

ROADSIDE ASSISTANCE: READ THE FINE PRINT
Make sure assistance is offered for the route you will be taking. Check whether in the event of a breakdown the driver is responsible to arrange and pay for repairs, and then submit papers for later reimbursement by the company—a lot more hassle and time.

3

MAKING THE MOVE YOURSELF

Loading a truck

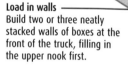

Start thinking and planning how you will load even before you rent the truck. Once you have packed your boxes and prepared the furniture and appliances, you can make a pretty good estimate of how much space your things will take up in a truck.

Unless you have a lot of extremely heavy items—say, four or five full file cabinets or a library of books—there is usually no need to worry about balancing the weight in a truck from front to back. It is a good idea to make sure that one side is not much heavier than the other side.

Boxes first

Among professionals there are a variety of ideas about loading strategies. Some believe that you should load all the large objects—such as appliances and furniture—first, then fill in with boxes and smaller items. While it is important to make sure you have room for the large items, for most household moves it makes the most sense to begin by loading boxes. That way you can pack them tightly in the front of the truck.

Next load the large and the awkward items (such as appliances, sofas, tables, and chairs), preferably on either side of the truck. Fill in under and on top of them with small boxes and oddly shaped items. After that you have a good space remaining in the middle for finishing the loading of boxes and smaller items.

Build walls

As much as possible load the truck with "walls" that are fairly stable and can be strapped off (secured with straps; see page 96). In the illustration on these pages, two stacks of boxes in the front form a solid wall. On either side of the truck there is a wall that is not as clearly defined, but that can be strapped off.

Especially for a long move, each wall should be secure and stable on its own, without having to lean on the next wall. Here straps with ratchets are used. If your truck does not have them, you can use rope instead; do not use elastic cords—they are not strong enough.

MAKING THE MOVE YOURSELF

Load in walls
Build two or three neatly stacked walls of boxes at the front of the truck, filling in the upper nook first.

🕐 TIMESAVER

WHO'S IN CHARGE?
When working with helpers make sure someone is in charge of the loading strategy. It often works best to have the brains of the outfit on the truck doing the actual stacking and arranging while others bring things into the truck. If two or three people, each with their own ideas, carry things onto the truck and stack on their own, you may end up with a hodgepodge arrangement and less-than-tight packing.

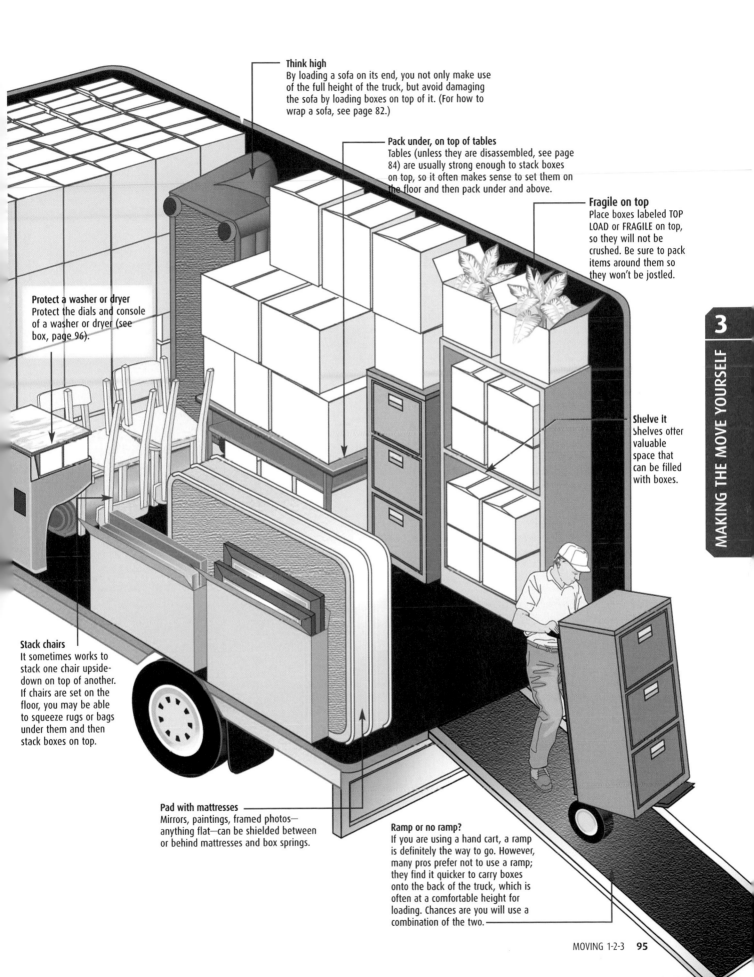

Think high
By loading a sofa on its end, you not only make use of the full height of the truck, but avoid damaging the sofa by loading boxes on top of it. (For how to wrap a sofa, see page 82.)

Pack under, on top of tables
Tables (unless they are disassembled, see page 84) are usually strong enough to stack boxes on top, so it often makes sense to set them on the floor and then pack under and above.

Fragile on top
Place boxes labeled TOP LOAD or FRAGILE on top, so they will not be crushed. Be sure to pack items around them so they won't be jostled.

Protect a washer or dryer
Protect the dials and console of a washer or dryer (see box, page 96).

Shelve it
Shelves offer valuable space that can be filled with boxes.

Stack chairs
It sometimes works to stack one chair upside-down on top of another. If chairs are set on the floor, you may be able to squeeze rugs or bags under them and then stack boxes on top.

Pad with mattresses
Mirrors, paintings, framed photos—anything flat—can be shielded between or behind mattresses and box springs.

Ramp or no ramp?
If you are using a hand cart, a ramp is definitely the way to go. However, many pros prefer not to use a ramp; they find it quicker to carry boxes onto the back of the truck, which is often at a comfortable height for loading. Chances are you will use a combination of the two.

GOOD IDEA

PROTECT A WASHER OR DRYER
To protect the dials on the console of a washer or dryer, place a piece of plywood on top, supported by strong boxes resting on top of the appliance. If a stack of boxes will be placed on top of the plywood, it should not actually rest on top of the console.

1

LOAD A COUPLE OF WALLS OF BOXES
Start by building a wall of tightly packed boxes at the front. Place the strongest, heaviest boxes at the bottom. If the truck has an upper nook, fill that first. As much as possible stack boxes that are the same width and length on top of each other. Use rope or straps to hold the walls in place.

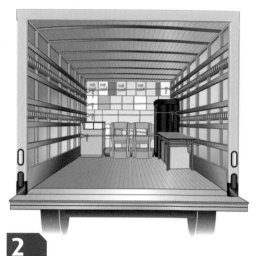

2

ADD SOME LARGE OR AWKWARD PIECES
With the wall of boxes in place, add some heavy items and pieces that are large or odd shapes. Put to good use any voids—like the areas beneath the stacked chairs and the table. Use the height of the truck as much as possible.

3

ADD MATTRESSES AND BOX SPRINGS
Mattresses and box springs can be used to protect fragile pictures or wood shelves and tabletops. Because you cannot stack very heavy objects on top of them, it usually works best to place them upright. Place fragile, slim objects between a mattress and box spring or next to the truck wall.

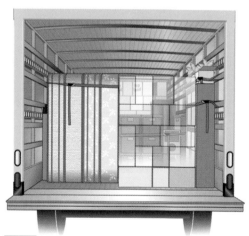

4

COMPLETE THE LOAD
Complete the loading by adding tall and heavy objects along the sides of the truck, securing them with straps. Place lighter boxes and objects highest. Place top-load items (see page 76) highest of all and secure them from jostling. Fill in with more boxes and tie them off.

Driving tips

 GOOD IDEA

FUEL ECONOMY
You'll use less fuel if you:
- Gradually accelerate to reach your desired speed.
- Ease off the accelerator early when approaching a stop.
- Keep the truck speed under 65 miles per hour.
- Park in a secure, well-lit area to avoid fuel theft.
- Drive cautiously and obey posted speed limits.

You don't need a commercial license to drive a moving truck, but it does call for some new driving skills. Rental truck drivers have the greatest chance of an accident in these situations:
- backing up
- driving a tall vehicle into low-hanging branches, bridges, and overhead structures
- turning in traffic with a long vehicle

With careful attention to the task at hand and a bit of practice, you can avoid these and other mishaps.

If parking is tight in your neighborhood, plan ahead before you pick up the truck. If you need to stake out a space ahead of time, ask the company for the truck's dimensions—the length, width, and height. Check for tree clearance and make sure the truck won't be so wide it will block a narrow street.

Make sure you know the correct procedures in case the truck breaks down. Reflective triangles or other warning devices should be under the seat, and an emergency phone number should be printed on the dashboard or in the glove compartment.

Take a test drive
Before you leave the rental location, ask the dealer any questions you may have. Familiarize yourself with the truck before driving it. Adjust the seat and mirrors. Know the location of all controls and switches, including lights, turn signals, windshield wipers, and the horn. Then go for a test drive. Start in an empty parking lot to get a feel for how the truck handles.

Heads up
If you are driving a tall truck on roads other than interstate highways, be sure you can fit under the bridges. Some larger trucks are as tall as 12 feet, and some bridges as low as 11 feet. To avoid a disaster know your truck height and read clearance signs carefully.

More often you may encounter problems with overhanging branches or low-hanging telephone or power wires. Have a helper watch as you drive on residential streets and as you

Safety tips for driving a truck

- Since you are driving a truck, heed signs that pertain to trucks: weigh stations, restricted lanes, overhead clearance, parking restrictions, and so forth.
- Drive more slowly than you normally would.
- Decelerate and brake sooner. Since you're carrying a lot of weight, it will take longer to come to a complete stop. Sudden stops can damage your possessions. If the truck has a manual transmission, slow down by downshifting into lower gears; be sure to downshift when going down hills.
- Don't tailgate. Trucks weigh three to ten times more than cars and must have more time and room to stop when traveling at any speed.
- Avoid sudden stops or lane changes.
- Be careful with turns. Use the vehicle mirrors and allow plenty of room. The additional width and length of a truck requires more turning area and more room for lane changes. Checking mirrors will help you stay clear of other vehicles and reduce the risk of a collision.
- Pass with care. Do not attempt to pass a vehicle moving faster than 40 mph. Never pass on hills or curves.
- Set the parking brake every time you park. Turn the wheels away from the curb when parking with the truck faced uphill. When parking with the truck faced downhill, turn the wheels in toward the curb.
- Obey the traffic laws. Use your turn signals, use headlights, and buckle your seatbelt.
- Stop for gas when the tank gets to the one-quarter level.

park near a house. Gently brushing against tree leaves is not a problem, but avoid bumping into branches—and stay well away from wires.

Gas stations that are designed for cars and pickup trucks may have overhead structures as low as 10 feet. To be safe go to a truck stop with a higher overhead, or use gas stations that do not have overheads.

Truck length. Practice right- and left-hand turns in a parking lot before you venture out onto the road. Be aware that the truck is a good deal longer than a car, and take steps to avoid hitting curbs, poles, and other vehicles with the rear of the truck. Pull the truck forward farther than you're used to before making a turn. On a large truck the back of the truck—the portion behind the axle—is longer than on a car, and it can swing into oncoming traffic when you make a turn.

Blind spots. Get to know your side-view mirrors. Often there is a blind spot to the left or the right side of the truck where you will not be able to see another vehicle—especially a motorcycle. If your mirrors have convex inset mirrors, they will help you see the blind spots. Practice using them.

Backing up a truck

Most accidents in large vehicles occur when backing up. It's best to avoid it altogether if possible. But if it's necessary, follow this procedure:

CLOSER LOOK

D.O.T. RULES ABOUT REST

The Department of Transportation (D.O.T.) has strict regulations governing how long professional truckers can stay on the road and how much rest they should get. It is a good idea for you to follow these rules. They include:

- A rest break must be at least 10 hours long. You need a good night's sleep, and it usually takes a few hours to eat, get settled in a motel, and get ready to go again in the morning.
- A driver can operate a truck no more than 11 straight hours between rest breaks. Driving for longer than this can cause you to lose concentration or become drowsy—either of which is dangerous.
- A driver must not be on duty more than 14 straight hours. "On duty" refers to any type of work—including loading the truck. If you spend all day loading the truck, get rest before setting out on a long drive.

- Get out of the vehicle, walk around, and check for obstacles both high and low.
- Make sure you have plenty of maneuvering room.
- Ask someone to help. Agree on hand signals and ask the helper to stay within sight of your side-view mirror.

Backing up a trailer

If you haven't done it before, backing up with a trailer can be difficult. Be sure to have a helper positioned so you can see him or her in a side-view mirror, and move slowly. You want to avoid jackknifing, which occurs when the trailer is at too small an angle to the towing vehicle. If you do jackknife, stop and drive forward for 10 feet or so. Then try again.

When driving in reverse turn the towing vehicle's front wheels in the same direction you want the trailer to go (from your point of view as you face forward) or in the opposite direction (from your point of view if you turn around and face backward). The rear of the vehicle should go in the direction opposite the way you want the trailer to go. Once the trailer is going in the direction you want, immediately turn your front wheels in the opposite direction, so the vehicle will follow the trailer.

Get plenty of rest

You'll be safer if you're on your toes every minute of the trip. Driving a huge truck over a long distance is more wearing than you may realize. Add to that the fact that nearby vehicles may make risky moves to get around your truck. Fatigue can put you at risk for an accident, so start your trip well rested and make frequent stops to take a break and refill your coffee mug.

Plan the route

The best route for a large truck may be different than the one you would normally take in your car because of size and weight restrictions or obstructions such as low bridges or overhanging trees. Plan ahead as much as you can. If possible, drive the route before moving day arrives, watching for obstacles and noting the time it takes to travel the route at a reasonable pace. If you can't drive the route, buy a good map or visit a mapping website and chart the route. Motor clubs provide maps, suggested routes, alternate routes, and rest-stop information. With membership these organizations may also offer roadside assistance and additional insurance coverage. If you are driving a long distance, consider booking a motel before you leave.

GOOD IDEA

PHONE ADVICE

Take a cell phone. If you don't have one, consider borrowing one, or buying a phone with a limited number of prepaid minutes. If you'll be driving through remote areas, check that the service provider has a good record for reception.

- If you won't be traveling with a cell phone, carry a telephone credit card or extra change for pay phones.
- Be careful about using the phone while driving; make calls at rest stops or when pulled over to the side of the road.
- Keep your personal phone list close at hand, together with the truck rental company's emergency phone number.

Things to bring

Prepare for your drive by gathering these items:

- Sunglasses, for everyone traveling, and reading glasses if needed for maps.
- Rental and insurance documents. These may be needed along the way and are essential when you return the truck at the end of the move.
- A cell phone and phone numbers (see above), including the rental company roadside assistance number.
- Extra cash. Bring change for tolls and extra cash for the unexpected. In remote locations, some places do not accept credit cards, and gas will be high since you may be getting only 10 miles per gallon for a loaded truck (see page 11).
- Prescriptions. Before you leave, refill medical prescriptions for everyone riding in the truck and keep them handy during the trip.
- A first-aid kit. Keep first-aid supplies in the truck cab or glove compartment.
- A few creature comforts such as bottled water, snacks, tissues, hand cream, tapes or CDs.

Perform routine maintenance checks

At every stop walk around and inspect the truck. Check the tires, lights, and cargo door. If you're towing a trailer, check the trailer tires, door, hitch, and hitch security chain. Follow the truck rental firm's recommendations for how frequently you should check the oil.

Secure the truck at overnight stops

Park in a well-lighted area and lock the truck cab. Lock the cargo door with a padlock. If you're towing a car, also padlock the safety chain from the towing device to the towed vehicle. Ask motel security to keep an eye on your truck to avoid theft of contents or fuel.

Keep a log for long trips

If you will drive more than a day, keep a simple log—perhaps in a spiral notebook—detailing when you left, how long you (or your partner) drove, and how long you rested. You are not legally required to do this, but a log provides valuable information in case you get into an accident.

What to do in case of a breakdown

If your truck breaks down, drive it off the highway and into a parking lot if possible. If that is not possible, ease it onto the shoulder, but not so far that the truck starts to lean; doing so puts you in danger of tipping the truck over. If the truck starts to lean, gently drive back toward the road.

Turn on the emergency flashers, then set out triangular reflectors or electric flares. The D.O.T. recommends that you place three warning devices on the traffic side of the shoulder or the lane in which the truck has stopped.

- Place one 10 feet (about 4 paces) from the truck in the direction of approaching traffic.
- Place another 100 feet (about 40 paces) from the truck in the direction of approaching traffic.
- Place a third 100 feet (about 40 paces) from the truck in the other direction.

If the truck is stopped within 500 feet of a hill or curve so that approaching vehicles cannot see it, place warning devices so the oncoming vehicles have ample warning.

SAFETY ALERT

MOVING IN WINTER WEATHER
Winter weather adds an extra challenge. Whether you're moving to or from a cold climate, stay safe by making these preparations:

- Stay tuned to weather forecasts. While loading the truck and during the drive, keep track of weather developments.
- Be prepared. Have shovels and other ice and snow removal tools handy for clearing walks for loading and unloading.
- Drive slower.
- Choose a company that offers 24-hour emergency assistance.

3

MAKING THE MOVE YOURSELF

Preparing your new home

When considering a new home, one of the smartest steps you can make is getting it inspected. For a relatively modest cost, you'll come away with renewed confidence in your purchase (or some bargaining points for getting a better price on the house) and a clear idea of what repairs and improvements you'll need to do after you move in. This chapter will explain what to expect from a competent home inspector and how to get the most benefit from the inspection.

Doing it yourself

You can often make those needed repairs and upgrades yourself. With your first project you'll begin to understand how things go together. You'll learn something that will help you make the next repair. Replace an outlet and you'll know how to replace a switch. Put in a deadbolt and you can fix a broken lock.

This chapter will help you learn how to make the basic connections and repairs you may run into. You can learn about more complicated

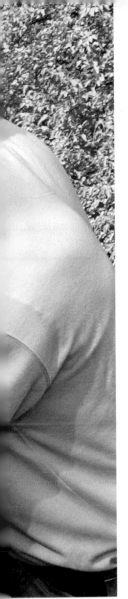

Chapter 4 highlights

GETTING THE MOST FROM A HOME INSPECTION

What to expect when you choose an inspector and how to assess the results.

102

MAPPING ROOMS

Make settling in faster and easier by planning in advance where the furniture will go.

112

KNOW YOUR SHUTOFFS

Learn where your water, gas, and electric cutoffs are and how to use them when you need to make a repair or handle an emergency.

113

THE ELECTRICAL SYSTEM

From service head to light switch, here's how the power gets distributed throughout your home.

115

ELECTRICAL REPAIRS AND UPGRADES

Inevitably, your new house is going to require a new fixture or two as well as some minor repairs.

118

THE PLUMBING SYSTEM

Here are the essentials about the pipes and fixtures that make up your home's plumbing system.

124

PLUMBING REPAIRS AND UPGRADES

Here are some of the plumbing projects you are likely to encounter after you move in.

127

HEATING SYSTEMS

Here are the basics you need to know about how your home will stay comfortable—no matter what the weather is like outside.

138

REPAIRING AND PAINTING WALLS

Nothing makes a room look better as quickly or inexpensively as patching and painting walls.

141

REPAIRING AND UPGRADING FLOORS

Here's how to repair and clean wood, ceramic, resilient-sheet, and carpeted flooring.

148

REPAIRING DOORS AND WINDOWS

Broken windows and sticking doors are among the nagging chores you'll want to get out of the way.

155

projects at home centers. Vo-tech schools offer night classes on carpentry, plumbing, and wiring taught by people who do it for a living. If you've got friends that know what they're doing, help them with one of their projects. You'll learn twice as much.

The right tools for the job

This chapter also outlines the specific tools you'll need for each job. Choose tools that last a lifetime and you'll still be reaching for them when you're working on the house 20 years from now. (Choose a cheap one and you may end up replacing it next week.) How much you spend is a personal matter. On the one hand, a $40 tool is more than twice as good as a $20 tool. It's made better, easier to use, and more reliable. On the other hand, $40 is a lot of money for a tool that you're only going to use once. The simplest advice is to buy the best you can afford, or a little better. If you have to replace it 10 years from now, it's going to be a lot more expensive.

Getting the most from a home inspection

Wouldn't it be nice to be able to look up customer reviews on the Internet before buying a house to be sure you weren't getting a lemon? Unless you're purchasing a new home from a well-known builder, it's difficult to know exactly what you are getting into with a house purchase. Your best recourse is to hire a home inspector to help you answer important questions about the condition of your prospective home.

A home inspector will take you on a guided tour of the house and provide you with detailed information about its condition. Based on a two- to three-hour visual assessment, he'll describe the home's positives and negatives, explain how its basic systems work, and provide advice about areas that currently need or will soon need repairs or replacement. The inspector will not, however, make a buy or no-buy recommendation. To make the most of your home inspection, follow the inspector around and ask about things you don't understand.

A home inspector typically will examine the home's heating, ventilation, and air-conditioning systems; the interior plumbing and electrical systems; the roof, attic, and visible insulation; the walls, ceilings, floors, windows, and doors; and the foundation, basement, and visible structures of the home.

Usually you'll pay extra for an inspection of your septic system, a termite inspection, a swimming pool inspection, testing for allergens, or testing for the presence of toxic substances like radon, lead, asbestos, and carbon monoxide.

Choosing an inspector

Ask your real estate agent or the local building department to recommend an inspector. You can also look in the yellow pages under "Building Inspection" or "Home Inspection," or check with the American Society of Home Inspectors (ASHI). ASHI is a nonprofit association for independent home inspectors. To be a member an inspector must have performed a minimum of 250 professional fee-paid home inspections. The ASHI website (www.ashi.org) can provide a list of inspectors in your area.

When you call to book an inspection, ask a few questions to be sure you have found someone you will be comfortable working with. You'll want to know the following:

- Does the inspector have experience with houses similar to your prospective home, for instance, a Victorian-era home or a contemporary type?

- Can you tag along? If the inspector is not welcoming, look for a different inspector. Most inspectors are comfortable in the presence of a prospective homeowner and happy to share knowledge. (Expect the seller or the seller's real estate agent to also be present.)
- What will the home inspection consist of and how long will it take? (It should take about 2–3 hours for a four-bedroom house).
- Is the inspector an ASHI member?
- What additional testing services does the inspector offer (environmental and termite testing, for example)?
- How long is the written report, and when will it come back to you? (A thorough report is often 16–18 pages long and should be available in several days.)
- Is the report written so a homeowner can understand?

Once you find an inspector that you feel comfortable with, ask about the fee. It is typically between $300 and $400 (or more for a large house) and is set when you book the inspection.

How to tag along

Around the time the home inspection comes into the equation, most buyers are overloaded with concerns: the loan approval, the move, the new adjustments for family members. Many are tempted to just let the inspector do his job, thinking they will skim through the report later. But skipping out of the inspection means wasting a valuable opportunity. Make it a priority to follow along. Even if you are making a long distance move, it can pay to fly out just for the inspection. Not only will you be able to see firsthand potential deal breakers (one homeowner learned of a needed roof replacement that was otherwise invisible from ground level), but you'll have the chance to visit the house again and get room measurements for furnishings.

The inspection is a good time to learn how things work in your house. Bring along pencil and paper and a list of questions. You can learn the following information:

- what kind of systems (heat, water, electrical, etc.) the home has
- how the systems work
- what kind of maintenance requirements the home has so that everything stays in good working order
- how to turn off power, fuel, or water in case of an emergency (see pages 113–114 for more information)

Don't panic

No home is perfect. It's the inspector's job to list all flaws, but not all flaws need to be fixed right away—or even at all. The report is meant to give you a clear idea about the condition of the home. If it does indicate serious problems, you may need to negotiate with the seller about either the purchase price or the terms of the contract.

If work needs to be done, it's generally better to focus on negotiating a change in price rather than demanding that the seller fix the problems. Sellers are overloaded with their own concerns. They will not be motivated to pay for quality work; nor will they have time to supervise workers to be sure a job is done right. You'll likely get better results if you arrange for the repairs yourself after you take possession of the home.

4

PREPARING YOUR NEW HOME

Inspection checkpoints

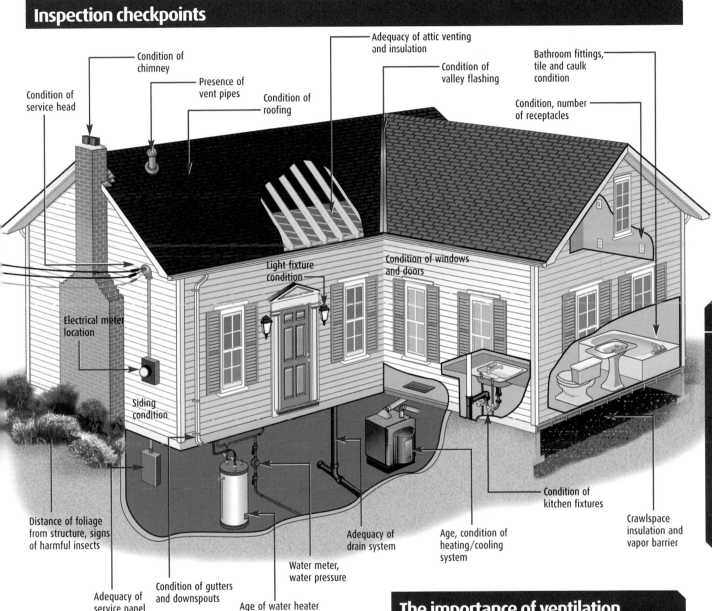

Condition of
service head

Condition of
chimney

Presence of
vent pipes

Condition of
roofing

Adequacy of attic venting
and insulation

Condition of
valley flashing

Bathroom fittings,
tile and caulk
condition

Condition, number
of receptacles

Electrical meter
location

Light fixture
condition

Condition of windows
and doors

Siding
condition

Distance of foliage
from structure, signs
of harmful insects

Adequacy of
service panel

Condition of gutters
and downspouts

Age of water heater

Water meter,
water pressure

Adequacy of
drain system

Age, condition of
heating/cooling
system

Condition of
kitchen fixtures

Crawlspace
insulation and
vapor barrier

There are a number of tips you can pick up. For instance, if you've never owned a home with a fireplace, you'll find out how to open and close the flue and how often to have the chimney cleaned to avoid a dangerous buildup of creosote, a major cause of chimney fires.

The following pages present some of the most common issues encountered during a home inspection. However don't be surprised if your inspector finds different sorts of problems—every house is unique.

The importance of ventilation

The inspector will check what he can see of the attic's ventilation, including insulation and vapor barriers, as well as the ventilation system and its exhaust pipes. He will also check out the foundation areas. One common problem is an accumulation of moisture in the attic due to inadequate attic ventilation. Another is bathroom exhaust fans that partially or completely vent moisture into the attic. If the inspector finds such moisture problems, he will describe the reason the moisture is accumulating and advise you what to do about it. Sometimes the solution is as simple as clearing away insulation that is blocking eaves vents. Other times, you may need to have additional vents or even fans installed in the roof or the gable ends.

Outside your house

Typically an inspection will begin with the home's exterior, including the garage. The inspector will check whether your house does a good job keeping the elements out, especially at windows and doors. He or she will also check the siding and trim, roof and flashing, any steps, driveway, porch, balcony, and deck.

If there is damage—for instance, a window frame that is cracked, split, or decayed—the inspector will let you know whether the window needs to be replaced or whether it can be repaired. If there are unpainted surfaces that are vulnerable to water damage, the inspector will use a moisture tester to check whether moisture is getting into the home's interior. Exterior walls are meant to shed water and shield framing and interior walls from seeping moisture. They face a lot of abuse from the elements—glaring sun, freezing cold, and driving rain. A home inspection will check for the effects of wear and tear.

An inspector typically will not look at seasonal items like screens, shutters, or awnings, and may not inspect fences, play structures, sheds, retaining walls, garden paths, and other landscape features.

Siding

The inspector will identify any gaps due to loose, damaged, or missing siding, and will check for areas of rot (above) and make repair recommendations where sections should be replaced, repaired, or caulked. Even a small opening can allow in enough moisture to cause expensive damage, so take care of these problems as soon as possible. The inspector will also check exterior wood trim and note where paint has worn away, look for loose trim, and inspect caulking where different cladding materials meet (right).

Masonry

Brick or block usually makes a durable exterior material, but can deteriorate in time. The most common problem is cracking or crumbling mortar between the bricks (above). If this is a general problem, the entire masonry surface may need to be repointed (or tuck-pointed) by a masonry contractor. If bricks themselves have lost their protective sheen, they will likely start to flake off, a condition known as spalling. Correctly sealing these bricks is a job for the pros.

Termites

These ant-size winged insects live in soil and eat wood from the inside out. A wooden timber that has been consumed by termites looks like a bundle of hollow tubes. Young termites swarm in the spring to new breeding grounds, usually not far from where they hatched.

In many areas a termite inspection by a licensed pest-control contractor is required before a home is sold. If the inspection uncovers a problem, a licensed exterminator will

need to be hired. Insecticide is usually applied to the soil where the termite colony is living and may also be sprayed in areas where there appears to be termite activity. The seller is usually responsible for the expense of curing the problem.

Chlordane was used to exterminate termites until 1988, when it was banned by the EPA. Newer pesticides are not as potent or as long-lasting as chlordane, and since early termite damage is not visible, an annual termite inspection is often recommended, especially in areas where the winters are mild. The cost is modest. To avoid harboring termites, avoid piling firewood—as well as other wood that may provide a damp, dark place to attract young termites seeking a new home in the spring—near the house (below). For additional information about safety of pesticide products, see the Environmental Health Coalition website at www.environmentalhealth.org.

Roofing, flashing, and gutters

An inspector will look at the roof covering—the shingles, shakes (above right), or tiles. The inspector will also check the roof's drainage systems (the gutter and downspouts) and the flashings (the metal pieces placed at joints where roofing material meets structural elements of the house).

Asphalt shingles may last from 15 to 25 years, depending on the quality of the shingles. If shingles show wear to the granular surface or if cracks appear, you likely need new shingles. If the roof has only one or two layers of shingles, you may only have to pay to add a new layer on top. If there are three layers, you will likely need to pay more for a tear-off job, in which the old shingles are removed.

Roof leaks often originate not at the roofing but at the flashing. Metal flashing is most commonly found at a valley, around a chimney, at the eaves overhang, and where roofing

meets vents and flues. If gaps develop in the flashing, water can get in and cause leaks. Flashing can be tricky; even pros make mistakes, and sometimes the wrong type of flashing is used or it is installed incorrectly.

Gutters must be free of gaps or holes and slope properly toward downspouts. Downspouts should be attached securely and should drain water well away from the house. If there is damage to the gutter system, the inspector will describe it and make recommendations.

Railings and decks

Posts, decking, and joists will be checked for signs of rot. A poke with a screwdriver often tells the tale—if the tool sinks in, there's rot. A moisture sensor (below) will tell if a framing member has soaked up excessive moisture. If the damage is not deep, the solution may be to seal a joint or add a piece of hardware. Where a piece is seriously compromised, it will have to be replaced. Often if one piece is rotted, adjoining pieces may also be rotted.

4

PREPARING YOUR NEW HOME

Septic system

If you're buying a home in a rural area, it may have a septic system—a private sewage treatment system on the home's property. If so, you will need to pay for a separate inspection.

In a septic system the home's wastewater travels through pipes to a large tank buried somewhere in the yard. Tanks need to be pumped out on a regular basis. Once every four years is the average, but a small tank may need to be pumped once a year.

Tank inspections are generally performed together with pumping service. An inspector will assess the physical condition of the tank and its components and check for broken baffles and cracked pipes. At the same time he will measure the depth of the scum and sludge layers to determine if pumping is needed.

In older established communities where septic tank access lids are buried 6 to 24 inches below grade, locating and gaining access to the tank for inspection can be expensive. In newer developments septic tanks have access ports that are flush with or above the existing grade, making inspection easier.

Be sure to get as much information as you can from the previous owner about where the tank is located, when it was last pumped, and which service provider was used.

4

PREPARING YOUR NEW HOME

CLOSER LOOK

CHECKING ENERGY EFFICIENCY
If there are adjustments you can make to improve your home's energy efficiency, the inspector will discuss that with you (and include it in his or her report). If the inspection is done during warm weather, you will not get a complete heating inspection; have a heating company check out your system once cold weather sets in.

Inside your house

Indoors the inspector will examine your crawlspace or basement, the living areas, and any accessible attic or roof spaces. If you follow along the inspector can give you plenty of useful information about maintaining your home, for instance, how to turn off water, gas, and electricity in an emergency and how to maintain your furnace for maximum heat efficiency.

In the living areas the inspector will examine walls, ceilings, floors, and a representative sampling of, but not necessarily all, doors and windows. Evidence of plumbing problems will receive special attention.

An inspector typically does not look at the washing machine and its connections, central vacuum system, and water softening equipment.

Water heater and flue

The inspector will check the condition of your home's water heater and its fuel source to see if they are installed safely and correctly. If the water heater has a flue (above), it is important to know that it draws fumes out of the house efficiently. An inspector will test the draw, perhaps by holding a lighted match near the flue to see whether the flame is drawn upward by the flue pipe.

Exposed pipes

Your home's plumbing system has pipes that bring water in (supply system), and pipes that carry both water and gases out (the drain/waste/vent system). To the extent that pipes are visible, the inspector will check whether they are properly installed and in good shape so there are no leaks. Fixtures, faucets, and sump pumps will also be checked, along with the home's water pressure. He can show you how to shut off water for individual sinks and fixtures and how to

shut off the fuel supply to the water heater. An inspector cannot examine pipes hidden in walls or floors, only those that are exposed.

Galvanized pipes develop rust that can lead to leaks. They also collect minerals inside that clog the pipe and reduce water pressure. The inspector will let you know whether you should expect to replace such pipe. Copper pipes are usually corrosion free and will give many decades of reliable service. Plastic pipes also do not rust, but some types have joints that are unreliable.

Plumbing under sinks

Moisture on the floor under a sink likely indicates a leak. An inspector may turn on the water and perhaps the garbage disposer and check for the source (above). Leaks coming from a bathroom in the floor above are usually the result of inadequate caulking or sealing around the bathtub or the bathroom floor. Leaks from showers, tubs, or toilets are also common bathroom problems. The inspector will check whether there is any evidence that moisture is accumulating

in the bathroom. He may use a moisture detector (bottom of opposite page) to examine key spots in the bathroom and will check ceilings underneath fixtures for water stains.

Boiler or furnace

If your home has a furnace (below), the inspector will check the vent systems, the flues, and the chimneys. The inspector will follow the heating system from the furnace in the basement or utility room up to the roof where flue pipes carry exhaust out of the house. A home's system of vents and vent connectors carries dangerous exhaust and will be checked for proper installation and signs of leakage or blockage. The inspector does not look at interiors of flues beyond what is visible nor examine electronic air filters or solar space heating systems. If your home has a boiler that provides hot water for radiators or baseboards, the inspector will check pipes by the boiler, which are especially prone to

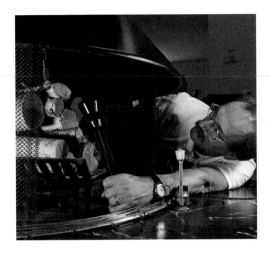

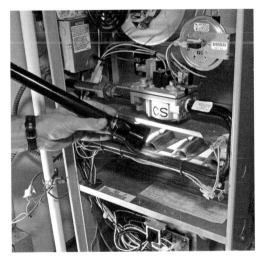

leaking and rusting. Often a timely pipe repair will prevent more expensive damage to the boiler.

Fireplace

A typical house inspector is not an expert on fireplaces and does not have the equipment to fully examine the inside of the chimney. The inspector will look at the fireplace (above right) or woodburning stove and describe the condition based on visual clues, will examine chimneys and flues in the same way, and will tell you if your fireplace needs a more thorough examination. For instance stains above the fireplace on the inside of the house could indicate that smoke is coming in (a carbon monoxide hazard). Other inspection points are to look for gaps in the mortar between the firebricks and check the inside of the chimney for signs of creosote, a fire hazard.

Electrical service panel

The inspector will check your home's service entrance wires and the service panel (below). Some of the things to look for are improper wiring (for instance, too many wires on one breaker), frayed wires, and evidence of scorching or corrosion. The inspector will often recommend appropriate repairs. The inspector will also note whether the amperage capacity of the home's electrical system is adequate for today's heavy electrical needs and will let you know if an upgrade is in order. (Most homes need at least 100-amp service; some need 200-amp service.)

Visible wiring and connections throughout the house will be checked for signs of shoddy electrical work. Amateur repairs—which may indicate other amateur work hidden behind walls or ceilings—will be reported. The inspector will check whether your service is grounded and can show you how to test GFCI receptacles (see page 116) and shut off circuits at the main panel and any subpanels.

A home's electrical receptacles provide connection for an ever-growing array of electrical products: computers, appliances, and more. Receptacles often handle more abuse than other components in a home's wiring system. The inspector will take a look at the physical condition of the receptacles. Cracked switches or receptacles should be replaced. He or she will also test receptacles, using either a two-pronged voltage tester or a plug-in receptacle analyzer, to see whether the receptacle is correctly wired so it is grounded and polarized (see page 115).

Reading and evaluating the report

The inspector's written report (right) will usually come back to you within a few days after the inspection. If you tagged along on the inspection, it will be interesting to read and easy to understand. At some point it's a good idea to methodically list the maintenance suggestions made by the inspector on a log. Divide the work that needs to be done according to the time frame in which the work should be finished. Some things may need to be taken care of within a month or two—getting the furnace or fireplace cleaned, or the gutters repaired, for instance. Other things might be able to wait—replacing windows for better energy efficiency or upgrading the heating system or the water heater for better efficiency, for example.

Some inspectors' reports (below) even include pages of digital photos of problem areas with captions explaining the deficiency. Such reports may include bonus items like seasonal checklists, record keeping guides for tracking home improvement and energy costs, and sometimes even a free CD-ROM version of a home improvement book.

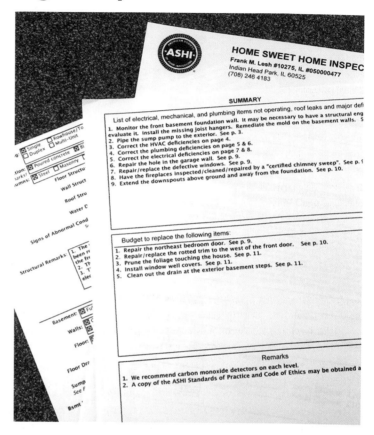

Assessing potential dangers in your home

You can pay extra for a number of tests to ensure your home is safe and healthy. The home inspector may provide some of these testing services for an extra fee. For others you will need to hire other trained professionals.

Mold

A home with mold has a moisture control problem. Look for these signs of excess moisture:

- mildew in the bathroom
- peeling, cracking, or blistering paint
- efflorescence (a whitish powder) on indoor plaster or brick (typically in the basement)
- mold growing in the corner of a closet, kitchen, or bathroom

Many common activities produce moisture: cooking, bathing, breathing, dishwashing. Other contributors include gas appliances, leaky plumbing, lots of rain or snow, and ground moisture.

Relative humidity is the amount of air moisture in relation to the temperature. Problems arise when inside relative humidity exceeds 50 percent. Some people develop allergies or respiratory problems caused by mold. A relative humidity of 30 to 45 percent is considered healthy and comfortable, for the home and for people.

To combat moisture problems, find the source and take measures to dry it out.

- Find what's causing excess humidity.
- Install a fresh air return on the furnace to draw fresh air into the home when moisture levels get too high.
- Install a bathroom exhaust fan (or check that the one you have is in good working order).
- Have your home's ventilation systems inspected to ensure that moisture can escape.
- Install a kitchen exhaust fan.
- Crack a window so moisture can get out.
- To prevent structural damage to your home and to prevent moisture from getting into exterior walls, have vapor barriers installed.
- Cover cold surfaces, such as cold water pipes, with insulation.

The EPA has not yet established safe limits for mold or mold spores, but you can call professionals who have specific experience in testing mold

samples and interpreting results. Sample analysis should follow analytical methods recommended by the American Industrial Hygiene Association (AIHA), the American Conference of Governmental Industrial Hygienists (ACGIH), or other professional organizations.

For more information check out the EPA's National Service Center for Environmental Publications (NSCEP) (www.epa.gov/ncepihom/) website; the site shows a number of publications you can order.

Carbon monoxide

Appliances that burn fuel—gas, oil, wood, coal, propane, or kerosene—are potentially hazardous if they are not properly installed and in good working order. When fuels burn they produce carbon monoxide (CO), a colorless, odorless gas. Heating systems that are properly vented and leak-free provide a safe escape for CO outside the home. Problems occur when blockages (for instance, in chimneys) or leaks (in vent pipes) develop so CO collects inside the house. A CO inspection should include furnaces, boilers, fireplaces, water heaters, space heaters, and vents. Chimneys and flues should also be regularly inspected. They can become blocked by debris—sometimes from nests built by birds or other animals in the spring and summer.

A little bit of CO in the air leads to flu-like symptoms (with no fever), including headache, fatigue, shortness of breath, nausea, and dizziness. High levels of CO can cause death. Each home should have a CO alarm (above right) in the hallway near bedrooms.

Lead in paint

Many homes built before 1978 have lead-based paint; after 1978 lead was banned for interior paint. Lead becomes a problem when paint deteriorates and chips, peels, or flakes. Opening and closing painted doors and windows can send lead dust into the air, and construction work can kick up dust. Lead is particularly hazardous for children.

To be sure an older home does not have a problem, you should have it tested by a trained professional. (According to the EPA, home test kits

for paint are not always accurate.) Contact the National Lead Information Center (NLIC) at http://www.epa.gov/lead/nlic.htm for a list of professionals in your area.

There are two types of lead professionals: those who can be hired for an inspection and those who do a risk assessment. Some are certified or licensed for both.

- A paint inspection will tell you the lead content of every painted surface in your home, but won't say whether the paint poses a hazard or how you should deal with it (cost: $300 to $500).
- A risk assessment will provide information about lead content of deteriorated painted surfaces and options for reducing the hazard. It should also tell whether lead is in dust and soil around the home (cost: $25 to $40 per paint chip assessed).

A paint inspection includes:

- visual inspection of paint condition and location
- use of a portable X-ray fluorescence (XRF) machine
- lab tests of paint samples
- surface dust tests

If lead abatement work needs to be done, it should also be handled by qualified professionals to ensure it is done safely, reliably, and effectively.

Assessing potential dangers in your home *(continued)*

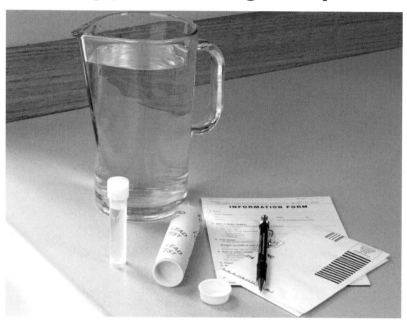

Lead in water

Homes built in the early 1900s often used lead pipes for interior plumbing, but even when a home has no lead pipes, lead in water may be a problem for various reasons:

- Many communities installed lead for service connections—the pipe that carries water from the water main to residential property lines—and have not yet replaced the old lead pipe.
- When copper pipes replaced lead pipes, lead solder was commonly used to join the pipes. Lead solder is a major cause of lead contamination in drinking water today.
- Homes with plastic drinking water lines, which are glued rather than soldered, should not have problems. But chrome-plated faucets, generally made of brass, contain 3 to 8 percent lead. Corrosive or hard water eats away at these fixtures so that lead gets into the water.
- Private water supplies or wells can contain lead in the plumbing or the fixtures or both.

Fortunately many municipalities now treat water with a trace element of phosphate, which effectively coats lead surfaces and keeps the lead from leaching into the water. Check with your building department to see if your town has taken such measures.

You can't see, smell, or taste lead in water. Testing at the tap is the only way to measure lead levels. Moderately priced kits (left) are available from your home center. Some cities and counties conduct tests for free or for a modest charge. Private laboratories charge fees ranging from $25 to $75.

Radon

Radon is a cancer-causing, radioactive gas that, like carbon monoxide, is colorless and odorless. The U.S. Surgeon General calls radon the second leading cause of lung cancer (behind smoking). It is produced as part of the natural breakdown of uranium in soil, rock, and water, and travels up through the ground into the air, entering homes through cracks and holes in the foundation. Radon can also be found in well water.

Any home can have a radon problem—new or old, well-sealed or drafty, with or without a basement. Radon has been found all over the United States, and it is estimated that 1 out of about every 15 homes in the U.S. has an elevated radon level.

Before you buy a home, you should know what the indoor radon level is. If the seller has had the home tested, ask to see the test results. If the home has a radon-reduction system, ask for information about the system.

If the home has not yet been tested, you should have it tested. If your property has a well, you should also have it tested. Call your state radon office for a list of qualified contractors in your area. If a problem is found, a contractor will describe the problem and recommend a treatment method. Often the solution is fairly simple: sealing gaps and cracks in the foundation or siding. If you as the buyer are doing the testing, be sure you agree with the terms of the testing ahead of time. For instance, the EPA recommends that a testing device be placed in the lowest level of the home (such as a basement) that will be used as a common living area; avoid less commonly used areas, such as the laundry room, hall, or bathrooms.

Your state radon office can provide you with several pertinent EPA publications: *Home Buyer's and Seller's Guide to Radon; A Citizen's Guide to Radon: The Guide to Protecting Yourself and Your Family from Radon;* and *Consumer's Guide to Radon Reduction.*

Checking your home's security

An inspector does not inspect alarm systems or their components, but will most likely check to see that locks and outdoor lights are operating correctly.

Outdoor lighting

Good exterior lighting helps eliminate an unoccupied look. Lighting deters burglars best when it illuminates all entry points and has been installed so it's difficult to disable simply by removing or breaking bulbs. The lighting pattern should not have areas with deep shadows, which make detection of burglars difficult. Newer systems provide two levels of illumination—a low level that comes on at dusk via a light-sensitive photocell and stays on all night, and a high level that comes on via a motion detector.

Locks

Law enforcement officials say a common way of breaking into a house is to simply kick down the front door. To safeguard against this the front door should be solid and heavy and secured with a deadbolt lock. Since locks work together with the door and the frame to resist a physical attack, the area around the lock should be reinforced too: The door frame should be solid and the area around the strike plate should be reinforced. If not, the lock can be pried open by bending the frame, or the door can be kicked in. If you want to upgrade the locks in your home, ask a locksmith to describe some of the options and explain what needs to be done for proper installation.

Doors with glass should have burglar-resistant glazing so the burglar can't simply smash the glass and unlock the door. Sliding patio doors should have a bar that fits into sockets and locks the doors in position. Garage doors, including the door leading into the house, should have secure locks.

Windows should have effective locks equipped with latches and pins. Basement windows should have a reinforced frame and break-resistant glass.

Hinges should be on the inside so a burglar cannot easily remove the pins to enter the house.

 GOOD IDEA

INSPECTING A NEW HOME

If you are buying a brand-new home, you can benefit from more than one inspection. Hiring an inspector to take a look at the house just before the drywall goes up is a golden opportunity to visually check out the house systems, the framing, and the roof to ensure that everything is in good working order. Even if you have every confidence in your builder or contractor, you know that he cannot be present at all times to supervise the work. Good builders are amenable to having an inspector check things out (as long as he's not unduly picky). A second inspection can follow at the usual time before signing the final papers. Some people feel it's worthwhile to pay for a third inspection just before the one-year warranty expires to check for any deterioration.

Mapping rooms

One of the cardinal rules of moving is to label each box and piece of furniture with the name of the destination room so you can carry it directly into its rightful place. If you neglect to do this, unpacking will be disorganized and inefficient, and you may find yourself living amid boxes for weeks rather than days. It's clear from the start where many items go: plates and glasses in the kitchen, sofa in the living room, and so on. But many cases are not clear-cut. For instance, will the bookcase fit in a bedroom or should it go in a den? Which bedroom is the best size for each family member's beds, dressers, and end tables? And how should the bed and dressers be arranged in the master bedroom?

If you have the opportunity to measure the rooms in your new home, you can make many of these decisions before you move, thereby saving yourself plenty of hassle. The process is simple, but it should be done systematically and carefully. Often a piece of furniture will be just 2 inches too long to fit where you want it, so it is important to measure the room and the furniture to within an inch or so.

1 MEASURE THE ROOM

You can usually measure a room accurately without moving furniture. A standard 25-foot tape measure will do the job. First measure the width and length of the room and make a rough sketch (you will make a more accurate drawing later). Include every possible obstruction to furniture. Keep in mind that you need the door to swing freely open. Windows may or may not be high enough to place a sofa or bed under them. Include the locations of heat sources—radiators, convectors, or vents. If you block them with furniture, they will supply heat or air-conditioning much less efficiently.

2 MEASURE THE FURNITURE AND MAKE CUTOUTS

When you measure furniture keep in mind the desirable clearances. Dressers and bookcases may be placed tightly together, but stuffed furniture should not be crammed against a wall or other piece of furniture. Using sheets of graph paper, cut out little pieces that accurately represent the sizes of the furniture pieces. In most cases it works fine to use graph paper with ¼-inch squares and to have each square equal 6 inches (that is, 2 squares to the foot).

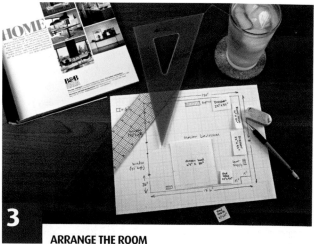

3 ARRANGE THE ROOM

Draw the room dimensions on graph paper and double-check for accuracy. You can now easily experiment with furniture arrangements. Keep in mind the sorts of clearances that you find comfortable. Having at least 16 inches of space on either side of the bed makes it easier to change sheets and make the bed. Once you have decided on an arrangement, glue-stick scale rectangles representing furniture to the plan drawing and put the drawing in the open-me-first box. When you get to the new home, tape the drawing to a window in its room so you can quickly arrange at least some of the furniture as you unload it.

Know your shutoffs

Teenagers and adults in your family should know how to shut off the electrical, water, and gas lines in your home. These pages show the most common types of shutoffs; yours may look different. If you are unsure how to shut off utilities, ask the home inspector or a professional electrician or plumber to show you how.

Keep shutoff valves free of obstructions, so you can easily reach them during an emergency. At the same time make sure children cannot reach an electrical service panel.

Shutting off the gas

If you smell a strong gas odor, get the family out of the house and call the gas company with a cell phone or from a neighbor's house. Shut off the gas at the meter outside.

Valve

GAS SHUTOFF

Before removing a stove or dryer, or before working on a furnace or other gas appliance, shut off the gas at a nearby valve. Follow the gas line from the appliance back to a valve, often red-handled. Turn the handle so it is perpendicular to the pipe (as shown). Wait 5 minutes before doing any work. When you disconnect the pipes or flexible line, you will smell a little odor from the gas left in the lines.

MAIN GAS SHUTOFF

To shut off gas to the entire house, find the main valve located just next to the gas meter, usually outside the house. Use a wrench or pliers to turn the valve perpendicular to the pipe. To ensure that the gas will not be turned back on, padlock the valve.

Shutting off electricity

Whenever you work on an electrical fixture or device, be sure to follow these steps:

1 Shut off electricity at the service panel.

2 Use a voltage tester to make sure power is off.

3 Lock the service panel shut or at least put a KEEP AWAY sign on it, so nobody will mistakenly turn power back on while you are working.

In most cases you will shut off power to one circuit only. In an emergency shut off the main disconnect.

To turn off power open the service panel's door. If your panel has an index indicating which breakers or fuses control which circuits, it can help you determine which fuse to unscrew or breaker to flip.

If a fuse has blown or a circuit breaker has tripped, shutting off power to part of the house, you will want to restore the power. You can usually identify a blown fuse by looking at its little glass window. The blown fuse will either have a broken metal tab or the window will be darkened. If you have a blown fuse, unscrew it and replace it with an exact replacement. Never replace a fuse with another of higher amperage; doing so may cause wires to overheat and perhaps cause a fire inside your walls.

A tripped breaker may have a little square button that has popped out or its switch may be partially turned toward the off position. Restore power to the circuit by pushing in the button or by flipping the breaker off, then on.

To shut off power to the entire house (see page 117), turn off the main breaker, usually located at the top of the panel. Or remove the main fuse, which is often housed in a square block that you pull out.

4

PREPARING YOUR NEW HOME

KNOW YOUR SHUTOFFS (continued)

Shutting off water

Most homes have a number of ways to shut off the water to all or part of the system. Newer homes tend to have more shutoff valves than older homes. If you are replacing a faucet or working on the system and you encounter a sink with no stop valves underneath, or no shutoff where one should be, install a stop or shutoff valve to make it easier to react to leaks or work on your system in the future.

 CLOSER LOOK

SIMPLER OUTDOOR MAIN SHUTOFFS
In some areas, especially where winters are not freezing, the main shutoff may simply be a valve located on the outside of the house, in the garage, or in a PVC pipe buried upright in the ground.

MAIN INDOOR SHUTOFF
Some homes have a shutoff valve indoors that controls water to the entire house. Usually it is near the point where a large-diameter water pipe brings water into the house—perhaps in the crawlspace or basement. The valve may be near the water meter. Be sure you understand how the valve works. Some must be turned clockwise a number of revolutions until they stop. Others (like the one shown) shut water off when you give them a quarter turn so the handle is perpendicular to the pipe.

MAIN OUTDOOR SHUTOFF
In addition to the indoor main shutoff, there is usually a valve located outside the house. Often it is between the house and the street. The valve may be located underground, in a plastic or concrete enclosure. The cover may be hidden by foliage or even soil; you may need to have the utility company help you find it. Once the cover is removed, there may be a hand-turn valve or there may be a valve that requires a special long-handled key. If so buy a key and keep it handy.

INTERMEDIATE SHUTOFFS
In utility areas such as a basement, garage, or laundry room, you may also find valves that shut off water to one or several rooms in the house. These intermediate valves are typically found in pairs to shut off both hot and cold lines. Close the valves and test to find which fixtures they control.

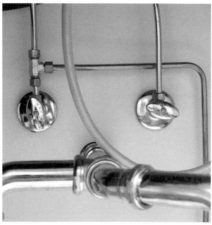

STOP VALVES
Also called fixture shutoff valves, these control water running to one fixture only. In newer homes you'll find two—one for hot and one for cold—for each faucet, and one for the cold-water supply to a toilet. Many stop valves corrode open, so handle with care. If a stop valve does not completely turn the water off, you may need to also close an intermediate or main valve.

INTEGRAL SHUTOFFS
To shut off water to a tub and shower valve, remove the faucet's cover and look to see if there are integral shutoffs like the ones shown. Turn the screws clockwise to shut the water off. If your shower does not have in-valve shutoffs, look for a removable access panel on the opposite side of the faucet in an adjoining room or closet.

4 PREPARING YOUR NEW HOME

The electrical system

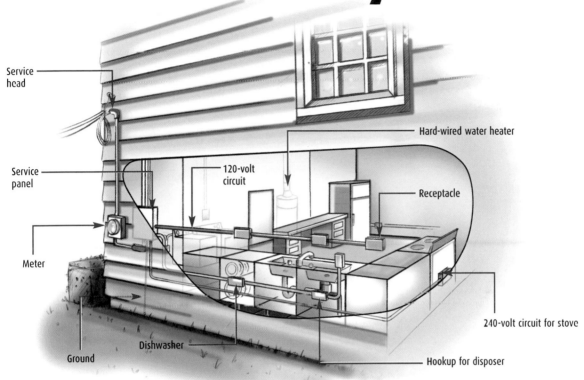

Service head

Service panel

Meter

Ground

120-volt circuit

Dishwasher

Hard-wired water heater

Receptacle

240-volt circuit for stove

Hookup for disposer

Electricity always travels in a loop, called a circuit. In most cases power travels out to a fixture or device through a hot wire—usually coated with black or red insulation (or another color except green)—and back through a neutral wire, which has white insulation. When the circuit is broken at any point, power ceases to flow.

Electrical power flows from the utility via overhead or underground wires and enters the home at a service head or underground entrance. The wires then travel through a meter, which for billing purposes records how much power a home uses. The wires then enter the service panel, which divides power into branch circuits.

Grounding

Almost all homes built after World War II are grounded. Grounding connects all outlets to the earth and is an essential safety feature. Grounding minimizes the possibility that a short circuit will cause a shock. A grounded device, fixture, or appliance is usually connected to a grounding wire—either bare or green—which leads to the neutral bar in the service panel. This bar is connected to the earth by means of a thick wire that leads to a cold-water pipe or grounding rods driven deep into the ground. In some older systems metal sheathing or conduit around the wires acts as the ground path to the service panel. Ungrounded receptacles—which have only two slots and no grounding hole—lack this safety feature. An ungrounded system can be basically safe however.

Polarization

Polarization is a way of making sure that electricity goes where you want it to go. Because a polarized plug has one prong wider than the other, there is only one way that the plug can be inserted into a polarized receptacle. If the receptacle is wired correctly, the hot wire, and not the neutral wire, will always be controlled by the appliance or fixture switch. If the receptacle or plug isn't polarized, the neutral wire might be connected to the appliance switch and power would be present in the appliance even when it is switched off.

Other protection

For further protection against shock, there should be ground-fault circuit interrupter (GFCI) receptacles in areas that might get wet. A GFCI shuts down power in milliseconds when it detects the tiniest change in current flow. Codes require GFCIs in bathrooms, in kitchens, near sinks, outdoors, and in garages. GFCIs are inexpensive and simple to install.

Recent codes require that bedrooms and other areas be protected with special arc-fault circuit interrupter (AFCI) circuit breakers. An arc fault most commonly occurs when a lamp or appliance cord's insulation is damaged, so that bare wires touch or come near each other and create an arcing spark. The AFCI quickly shuts down the circuit when it senses an arc fault.

With the aid of a book like Home Depot's *Wiring 1-2-3,* you can perform most repairs and installations. But do not touch wires leading to the service panel or wires upstream from the main shutoff. If your service head or other outside connections look like they might be insecure and unsafe, call the utility company. They are responsible for all connections prior to the service panel.

Inspecting your system

Your house inspector will check much of your electrical system for unsafe conditions, but will not be able to look at everything. On this page you'll find some common problems that, with some basic testing devices, you can look for as well.

If you encounter any wiring or installation you do not understand and that might be unsafe, don't hesitate to call an electrician for evaluation.

A RECEPTACLE ANALYZER
When you plug this analyzer into a receptacle, the glowing lights will tell whether the receptacle is working, grounded, and polarized (page 115). The analyzer shown will test a GFCI receptacle as well as a standard receptacle. Note that the analyzer often shows only one problem at a time, so be sure to test again after the wiring has been repaired.

TEST A GFCI
Just because a ground-fault circuit interrupter (GFCI) receptacle is supplying power doesn't mean it will protect against shock. Over time a GFCI can lose its protecting capacity. Test each GFCI by pushing the test button. The reset button should pop out. If it doesn't, replace the GFCI receptacle.

DETERMINE IF THE BULB WATTAGE MATCHES THE FIXTURE
It is easy to overlook the stickers inside light fixtures that state the maximum allowable wattage. Bulbs with too-high wattage will overheat fixtures. At best you'll have to change bulbs more often; at worst overheating can cause a fire. If you need more light, install a new fixture with a higher wattage rating.

CHECK EXPOSED BOXES FOR OPENINGS
Cable and wire must be held firmly, because vibration can cause rubbing—which can harm insulation. Metal boxes in particular have sharp edges that can nick insulation. Plus an exposed box with an opening like this invites children to poke in their fingers—a very dangerous situation. The cable shown here should be attached to a cable clamp. Other openings may need to be covered with special plugs, or the box itself may need to be replaced.

CHECK OLD WIRING
If you see exposed wiring that looks old, ask your inspector or an electrician to verify its safety. The knob-and-tube wiring shown here can be used as long as the wires are completely undisturbed and the wire insulation is in good shape. But the insulation can become brittle and easily damaged. This wiring also lacks a ground wire or metal sheathing, so the receptacles will not be grounded.

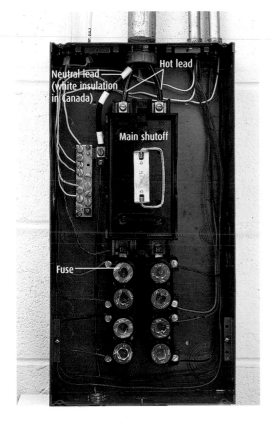

Neutral lead (white insulation in Canada)

Hot lead

Main shutoff

Fuse

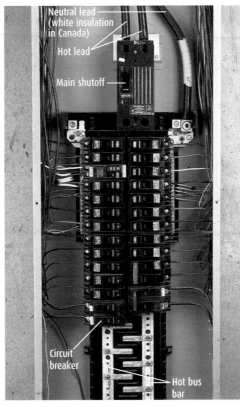

Neutral lead (white insulation in Canada)

Hot lead

Main shutoff

Circuit breaker

Hot bus bar

⊘ **SAFETY ALERT**

BARE BULBS ARE DANGEROUSLY HOT

Often light fixtures in closets and utility areas don't have protective globes. Sweaters, comforters, cardboard boxes, and other flammables placed too near bare bulbs can catch fire. The best solution is to replace the fixture with one that has a globe covering the bulb. Or replace the bulb with a screw-in fluorescent lamp, which stays cool.

4

PREPARING YOUR NEW HOME

UNDERSTANDING AND INSPECTING A SERVICE PANEL

The service panel is the nerve center of a residential electrical system. Find your home's service panel and learn how it works so you can be prepared to solve problems. The service panels shown on this page (a fuse box above and a breaker panel above right) have their covers removed to show how wires are run through them, but you likely will only need to open the panel door to access the breakers or fuses.

Power from the utility company enters the panel through three thick main wires—two hot wires and one neutral. The main neutral wire connects to a neutral bus bar, and the two hot mains connect to the main power shutoff—either a large circuit breaker or a pull-out fuse. From the main shutoff, two hot bus bars run down the panel; each carries 120 volts. Circuit breakers or fuses connect to the hot bus bars and each controls a circuit.

Most household circuits carry 120 volts. There also may be several 240-volt circuits. Circuits are rated according to their amperage. A 120-volt 15-amp circuit usually serves a number of outlets; it may supply power to a series of lights, a series of receptacles, or some of each. Heavy-use items, such as dishwashers and refrigerators, may have their own dedicated circuits.

If a circuit overloads and is in danger of overheating or if there is a short circuit, the fuse will blow or the circuit breaker will trip, disconnecting power to the entire circuit. If the circuit shuts down frequently, you may have a faulty appliance or device, but most likely the circuit is overloaded with too many electrical devices of too high an amperage. The solution may be as simple as plugging an appliance into a receptacle on another circuit, or you may need to hire an electrician to install a new circuit.

Electrical repairs and upgrades

Replacing a switch

If your switch pops when you turn it on, if it seems loose, or if your light fixture doesn't switch on even with a new bulb, it's time to replace the switch. Switches are easy and quick to test and install.

If the switch has two insulated wires connected to it (it might also have a ground wire) and a toggle marked ON and OFF, it is a single-pole switch—the most common type—and simple to replace. If three wires connect to it (not counting the ground wire), it is a three-way switch and you should consult an electrician or wiring book. If you choose to replace your switch with a dimmer, the dimmer will have wires coming out of it. Wire it the same way as a regular switch, but connect the wires to those in the box with wire nuts.

If a switch is used constantly, pay a little extra for a device labeled "commercial" or "spec-rated." It has stronger contacts and is more durable.

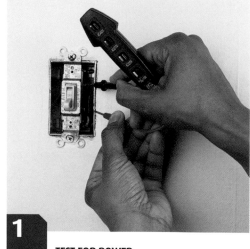

1

TEST FOR POWER
At the fuse or breaker panel, shut off power to the circuit supplying the switch. Remove the two screws holding on the cover plate to remove it. (If is painted over, first score around it with a utility knife.) **Test with a voltage tester to make sure that the power is off.**

Replacing a receptacle

Replacing a receptacle is much like replacing a switch. Start by turning off the power. Test to make sure it's really off. Test twice: Make the first test by putting the leads of a voltage or multitester in the receptacle. If the power seems to be off, remove the faceplate and touch the tester probes to the screws on opposite sides of the receptacle.

Once you're sure the power is off, remove the receptacle from the box and detach the wires from the sides of the receptacle. Snip off damaged wire ends and restrip them (see opposite page). First screw the bare copper wire to the green screw on the outlet. Attach the white wire to the silver-colored screw and the black wire to the brass-colored screw and tighten.

Wrap electrical tape around the receptacle to cover the terminal screws (see Step 7, opposite page). Fold the wires back into the box, screw it to the wall, and reattach the cover plate.

2

INSPECT THE WIRING
When you're sure the power is off, remove the two screws holding the switch to the box. Gently pry out the switch. Pull on the wires to ensure that they're firmly connected to the terminals. If a wire is loose or broken, you've probably found the problem.

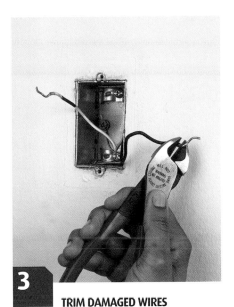

3 TRIM DAMAGED WIRES

Unscrew the terminal screws on the switch about ¼ inch (stop when it gets hard to turn the screw) and remove the wire. If a stripped wire end appears nicked or twisted, snip off the damage with side-cutting pliers.

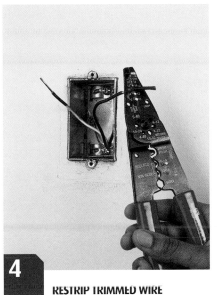

4 RESTRIP TRIMMED WIRE

Using combination strippers, strip about ¾ inch of insulation from the end of any wires that you snipped. If you strip a white wire that has been painted black or marked with black tape, remark it.

5 MAKE A LOOP

Twist the end of each wire into the shape of a question mark using the tip of combination strippers. Make the loop tight enough so that it just fits around the shank of the terminal screw.

6 ATTACH THE WIRES

On new switches the terminals are screwed down tight. Unscrew each until it gets hard to turn. Slip a looped wire end under each screw head with the end of the loop pointing clockwise. Squeeze the wire end tight around the terminal screw with long-nose pliers or the tip of combination strippers. Tighten the screw.

7 WRAP THE SWITCH (OPTIONAL)

Some electricians wrap the switch body with electrician's tape so the terminals and bare wires are covered. Before you do this make sure local codes allow it and your electrical inspector will approve it. Some inspectors will not approve a wrapped switch because they cannot see if the wires are securely attached to the terminals.

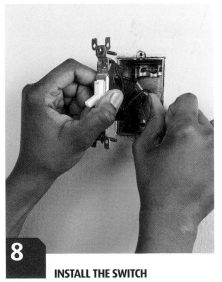

8 INSTALL THE SWITCH

Gently push the wires back into the box as you push the switch back into position. Aim the mounting screws at the screw holes. Tighten the screws and check that the switch is plumb (straight up and down). The elongated holes allow for adjustments. Replace the plate, restore power, and try the switch.

Running telephone wire

Adding a new telephone jack is straightforward work. Just run cable and connect wires to terminals labeled with their colors. When you buy cable spend a little more for "24-AWG" (American Wire Gauge) cable with solid-core wires. Cheaper cable has wires that are more difficult to strip and splice.

All connections for the low-voltage wiring shown on these pages should be made in a jack or junction box. Plan cable paths so as little of the cable as possible can be seen. For instance, going through a wall saves you from running unsightly cable around door moldings. Use these same techniques to run speaker wire.

1 TAP INTO A PHONE JACK

Unscrew the cover from a phone jack or a phone junction box. Strip about 2 inches of sheathing and ½ inch insulation from each wire. (Standard phones use only two of the wires, but it doesn't hurt to connect all four.) Loosen each terminal screw. Bend the wire end in a clockwise loop, slip it under the screw head that holds the matching color, and tighten the screw. Some jacks have terminals that clamp onto the wire so you don't have to strip it. Push the wire into the slot until it snaps into place (see inset).

Running cable through a wall

To go through a wall, drill a hole using a long ¼-inch drill bit, then insert a large drinking straw. Fish the cable through the straw. When you're finished remove the straw.

2 HIDE THE CABLE

Use any trick you can think of to tuck away unsightly cable. Pull carpeting back one short section at a time, run cable along the floor behind the tack strip, and push the carpet back into place. Or pry moldings away from the wall, slip the cable in behind, and renail the molding.

3 STAPLE EXPOSED CABLE

When there is no choice but to leave cable exposed, staple it in place every foot or so along the top of the baseboard. Use a round-top stapler or plastic-shielded staples that hammer in. (Square-cornered staples can damage the cable sheathing.)

Installing a phone on the wall

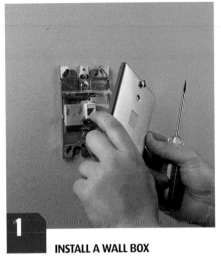

1 INSTALL A WALL BOX

To connect a wall phone, you can use either a low-voltage ring (as shown) or an electrical remodel box at the height of the phone. Start by cutting a hole in the wall and installing the ring, then tie a small weight to a string and lower it through the hole until you feel it hit the floor.

2 PULL THE CABLE

Drill a ⅜-inch hole at the bottom of the wall below the box. Bend a piece of wire into a hook, slip it into the hole, and pull out a loop of the string. Tape the string to the cable and pull the cable up through the box you installed. Install a wall jack and make connections. Install the cover plate.

Installing wires for computers and stereos

Installing wire for computers is just like installing phone cable, except that you use a cable designated "CAT 5e" and matching jacks. If you need to put a connector on the end that plugs into a jack or computer, buy a crimping tool designed for RJ 45 CAT 5e cable connectors .

Stereo wire is even easier to run, because there are no jacks involved. You can buy stereo cable at a stereo store, or you can use lamp cord sometimes called "zip cable." It's available at home centers, where it is pulled off a large spool and cut to the length you need.

Running coax for cable TV

1 ATTACH THE CONNECTORS

Cable companies may charge extra for long runs of cable. Make your own using RG6/U cable and an F-connector. Use combination strippers to strip ¾ inch of insulation, exposing the bare center wire. With a knife, carefully strip ⅜ inch of the thin outer sheathing—don't cut the metal mesh. Twist on a screw-on F connector or, for a better connection, attach crimp-on connects with a crimping tool.

2 SPLIT A LINE TO REACH ADDITIONAL ROOMS

Cut the line you want to tap into. Install male ends on both cut ends of the old line and on the end of the new line. Screw a signal splitter to the wall and attach all three connectors onto the splitter.

3 INSTALL A JACK

Cut a hole in the wall and run cable the same way you would telephone wire. Feed the cable through the box (it can be metal or plastic, though plastic is preferable) and attach the box to the wall. Attach the cable to the back of the jack and screw the jack in place.

Upgrading a light fixture

Often you'll want to upgrade a light fixture in a new home. An important part of upgrading is something you don't see—the hanging hardware. There are four different kinds—flush mounted, swivel strap, center stud, and old installation. Each works slightly differently; the new lamp you have your heart set on may not work on the hardware in your house. Fortunately new lights usually come with the necessary hardware, which is easy to install. An antique light or one you've brought from your old home may not have the hanging hardware. Compare your light with the types of hardware shown here and buy what you need from your home center.

Turn off the power when removing or installing a light fixture. Use a multitester to confirm the power is off (see page 118). When installing a fixture have a helper support the light. Twist the white wires together and screw a wire nut over them. Do the same for the black wires. For grounding attach a short length of bare wire to the green screw on the mounting strap and then twist all the bare wires together, covering them with a wire nut.

Install the fixture as described on these pages depending on the type of hardware you need. Always push the house wires into the box. Never place them in the fixture's canopy, where they may be harmed by heat from the light.

Flush-mounted fixtures

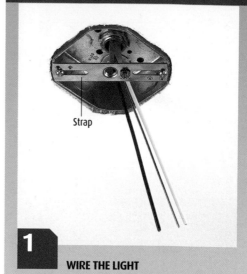

Strap

1

WIRE THE LIGHT

Tug on the hardware to make sure the box is firmly attached. Screw the strap to the ears in the corners of the box. Working with a helper rest the fixture on a stepladder or make a hook from a wire coat hanger and temporarily suspend the fixture from the strap. With the power off attach copper to copper (or the fixture's green wire), white to white, and black to black wires using wire nuts. Tuck the wires up into the box.

2

MOUNT THE FIXTURE

Slide a mounting screw through the fixture and up into the threaded hole in the strap. Start one mounting screw, running it halfway in, and then start the other screw. Tighten the mounting screws with a screwdriver.

Moving a chandelier

Chandeliers are sold with the house, unless otherwise specified. If you have a chandelier you want to keep, take it down before you show the house and replace it with another fixture. Turn off the power at the fuse or breaker box. Have a helper support the fixture while you remove the mounting screws or furled nuts that hold the canopy in place. Gently lower the fixture. Unscrew the wire nuts, but just to be safe, work as if the wires are hot. **Test that the power is off by connecting a multimeter or voltage tester to the wire.** Cut the exposed copper section of the wire and work with the helper to lower the chandelier and move it somewhere safe. Install and wire the new light as described on these pages, depending on the type of hardware involved.

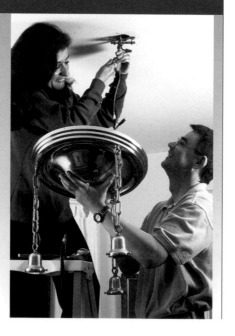

Swivel straps

Swivel strap

1

USE A SWIVEL STRAP TO ALIGN THE CANOPY

A swivel strap (also called an offset crossbar) allows you to twist the canopy for alignment. This is often necessary when the canopy isn't round. Screw the swivel strap in place the same way you screw in a flush-mounted strap.

2

HANG THE LIGHT

Wire the fixture and tuck the house wires up into the box. Screw both mounting bolts into the threaded holes of the strap. Line up the holes in the light with the bolts and attach the fixture, using the decorative mounting nuts.

Center studs

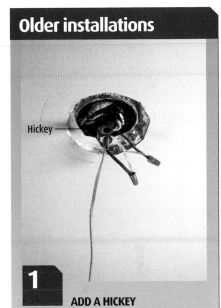

Center stud

1

USE A CENTER STUD FOR CENTER-MOUNTED FIXTURES

A center stud, sometimes called a nipple, may have wires running through it (for a pendent fixture) or around it (for a center-mounted fixture). A variation uses a center nipple, which screws into the strap.

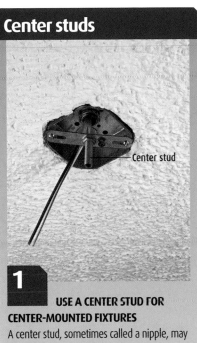

2

INSTALL THE FIXTURE

The center stud should be long enough to go through the strap and the fixture, but not so long that it pokes into the box or hits the globe. Attach the wires and fold them into the box as you slide the canopy up and over the stud. Snugly secure the canopy with the nut.

Older installations

Hickey

1

ADD A HICKEY

An older home may have a ⅜-inch pipe running through the middle of the ceiling box. To install a pendent fixture, add a hickey and nipple to make the transition from the pipe to a fixture. Feed the fixture leads through the hickey and the house wires up into the box.

2

ADD A MEDALLION

Hickeys are found in old houses with plaster and lath ceilings. The fixture canopy usually won't cover damaged plaster around the ceiling box. Adding a medallion saves you the trouble of patching and painting, and adds a decorative feature.

The plumbing system

Plumbing seems mysterious, mostly because so much of it is hidden inside walls. However it will likely take you no more than a couple of hours to gain a good basic understanding of your home's system. Read this section, study the illustration below, and follow the instructions on page 114 to find the valves to shut off your water. Then perform a basic inspection of your home's plumbing system.

Household plumbing consists of a supply system, which brings water to the house and distributes it to various faucets and fixtures; a drain-waste system, which carries wastewater away from the house; and a vent system, which carries away noxious gases and enables wastewater to freely exit through drain pipes. In addition you probably have gas lines and you may have a septic system.

Supply system

Supply pipes are pretty straightforward. In most cases a single supply pipe, usually an inch or larger in diameter (sometimes ¾-inch in older homes), runs through a main shutoff valve (see page 114) and a water meter to the water heater, where it branches into cold and hot water pipes.

Home plumbing system

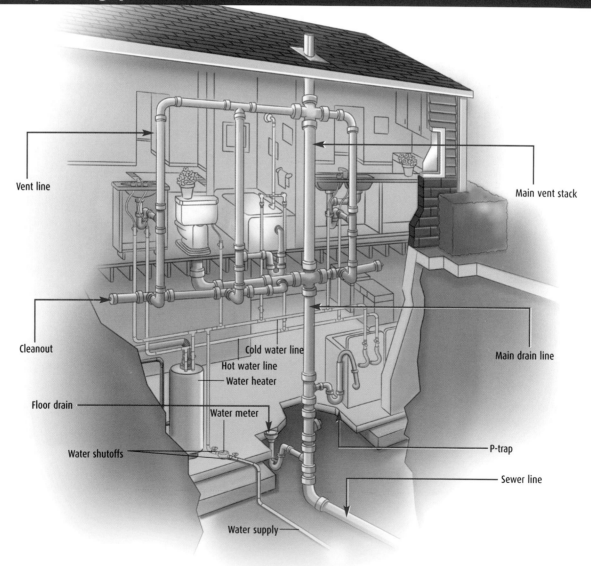

Vent line

Main vent stack

Cleanout

Cold water line

Hot water line

Water heater

Floor drain

Water meter

Water shutoffs

Main drain line

P-trap

Sewer line

Water supply

Hot and cold water pipes travel in pairs toward the various plumbing fixtures in the house. Vertical pipes are called risers. Supply pipes in an older home are likely made of galvanized steel, which corrodes and becomes clogged with deposits in time. Most newer homes use copper pipe, which reliably supplies good water pressure. Some newer homes use rigid plastic pipe such as CPVC, or flexible or cross-linked polyethylene (PE or PEX) pipe, but these materials are approved only in some locales.

After entering the house supply pipes usually reduce in diameter. The larger the pipe diameter, the better the water pressure. Ideally pipes that run to rooms will be ¾ inch, and only the pipes inside a room will be ½ inch. However, in many homes nearly all the pipes are ½ inch. This can be a problem, especially if the pipes are made of galvanized steel; they can clog with mineral deposits and limit water pressure.

Each fixture should have a stop valve—also called a fixture shutoff valve—for the hot and cold lines. From the stop valve flexible supply tubes (sometimes called risers) usually lead to the faucet or toilet. A shower or tub valve is usually connected directly to the supply pipes without flexible tubes.

Drain system

Drainpipes are more complicated, especially when you include the vent pipes (see opposite page). Drainpipes must be installed according to exacting specifications. Never install drainpipes without consulting your local building department and getting a permit.

Older homes often use cast-iron drainpipes. These typically last for many decades, but they sometimes rust or corrode in places. Newer homes use plastic pipe—either white PVC or black ABS. Plastic pipe is more reliable and easier to install as well. In some cases copper pipe is also used for some drains. In an older home some of the smaller drainpipes—typically the horizontal runs from a faucet to the main drain—are made of galvanized steel.

The main stack is usually a pipe 3 or 4 inches in diameter that runs straight down to the sewer line and up through the roof, where it serves as a vent. Many homes also have one or two secondary stacks, typically 2 or 3 inches in diameter; these usually provide drainage for a specific room—most often the kitchen.

Branch drainpipes usually travel horizontally from a fixture to a stack. These pipes are often 1¼ to 2 inches in diameter—1½ inches in the case of a bathroom sink. Horizontal branch drainpipes must slope at a rate of at least ¼ inch per foot at all points. Plumbing codes specify the use of certain types of fittings to ensure smooth flow of drain water. In general a fitting that makes a slow sweeping turn is preferable to one that makes a sharp turn.

A good drain-waste system has cleanouts located in places that are easy to access. These cleanouts allow access to the pipes so you can auger the pipes to clear away clogs.

Between a sink and the drainpipe in the wall, you will usually find a trap made of plastic or plated brass that can be easily disassembled for cleaning and augering. Traps are usually P-shape, so that water forms a seal at the bottom to prevent gases from entering the room.

Vent system

For drain water to flow freely, there must be air behind or above the water. If water completely fills the diameter of a drainpipe and there is no source of air behind it, the water will gurgle and flow sluggishly. In some cases water that fills a pipe can actually start a siphon, causing wastewater to back up into a toilet or sink. In a plumbing system vent pipes supply the air that makes wastewater flow smoothly.

Vent pipes also allow methane and other noxious gases to escape out the roof, rather than into the house. Such gases are both unpleasant and dangerous, so it's important that the vent system works well.

The portion of a main or secondary stack that extends out the roof is called a main or secondary vent. Branch vents lead to these stacks. Plumbing codes specify how and where these pipes should run and what size they should be.

One important venting consideration is the diameter of the drainpipes. If a drainpipe is large enough, it will never fill completely with water at any point and so it acts as its own vent.

Every plumbing fixture must be connected to a vent of some sort, and it must be connected in a way that meets local plumbing codes. In some cases a special fitting called an air admittance valve (AAV) is allowed to augment or even take the place of a vent that runs through the roof.

Inspecting a plumbing system

If you have a general idea of where your pipes are and where they go, it will help you find leaks in case of an emergency or auger clogged pipes. Note that pipe size is given as nominal inside diameter; the outside diameter will be larger.

ACCESS PANELS

Bathtub and shower plumbing is usually hidden in a wall. In many cases there will be a removable access panel that allows you to get at the pipes. Look in an adjacent room (or closet) on the opposite side of the shower faucet wall. The panel's cover may pop out when you pry it, or you may need to remove some screws first.

PIPES AT THE WATER HEATER

The water heater is where the main supply pipe branches off into hot and cold pipes that run through the house. Often you can find clues to the overall supply system here. If you have low water pressure in part of the house, it may be because you have old galvanized pipes that are clogged or because there are long runs of ½-inch pipe. A better arrangement is to have ¾-inch pipes for the long runs, which reduce to ½ inch only when in the kitchen or bathroom.

GATE, GLOBE, AND BALL VALVES

Older gate or globe valves have round handles. These valves have parts that can wear out in time, reducing their ability to fully shut off water and sometimes causing leaks below the handle. Plus their inner parts partially block the flow of water, thereby reducing water pressure. If you experience problems see if you can replace a problem valve with a newer ball valve, which is a full-bore valve, meaning that when opened, water flows through it as freely as through the pipe. To turn off a ball valve, turn the handle one-quarter turn.

MAIN STACK

The main stack is a vertical pipe 3 or 4 inches in diameter that runs all the way up through the roof. It will be visible in a basement or crawlspace. Often the interior wall it runs through will be 6 inches thick or thicker to accommodate the stack and connecting pipes. Shown here is an older cast-iron stack; a newer home will have a stack made of plastic pipe, either white PVC or black ABS. The cleanout plug is removable so you can run an auger through the pipe in case of a major blockage.

SECONDARY STACK

Many homes also have one or more secondary stacks. A secondary stack typically supplies drainage and venting for the kitchen alone, or for one or two bathrooms located away from the main stack.

4

PREPARING YOUR NEW HOME

Plumbing repairs and upgrades

TIME TO COMPLETE

EXPERIENCED: 20 min.
HANDY: 40 min.
NOVICE: 1 hr.

STUFF YOU'LL NEED

TOOLS: Putty knife, adjustable wrenches, basin wrench, screwdriver, groove-joint pliers
MATERIALS: Faucet, plumber's putty or silicone caulk, O-ring

CLOSER LOOK

BEFORE YOU START
Turn off the water before you remove the old faucets. Newer homes will have shutoff valves right under the sink. In other homes you may have to turn the water off using a valve at the meter, which will probably be in the basement, utility room, or outdoors. Once the water is off, drain the lines by turning on a faucet that is lower in the house than the one you're working on.

A faucet that is dripping doesn't need to be replaced—it just needs to be fixed. Often you can make the repair with only a few tools and some inexpensive parts. Sometimes a faucet is so old or ugly that it is time to replace it. Putting the new faucet in is a relatively simple job if you have a basin wrench. Taking out the old faucet can be frustrating—rust and age can make it hard to loosen nuts and pipes.

Faucets come in different sizes. Bathroom faucets usually have controls (called valves) that are 4 inches apart, center to center. Kitchen faucets are twice as wide. When you shop for a new faucet, make sure you know how many holes are in the kitchen sink before you buy. Four holes are for faucets with sprayers; three holes are for faucets without sprayers. Faucets with a single handle fit on either three- or four-hole sinks, depending on whether or not they have sprayers.

Installing a center-set faucet

1 **SEAL AROUND THE OPENING**
Scrape off any residue and scour clean the location for the new faucet. Apply a bead of silicone caulk or plumber's putty around the faucet opening.

2 **PLACE THE GASKET AND FAUCET**
Slip the gasket, which comes with the faucet, onto the threaded tailpieces of the faucet. Check the gasket; some have a front and back.

Installing a center-set faucet (continued)

GOOD IDEA

CULTURAL MATTERS

Use silicone caulk instead of plumber's putty when installing faucets on cultured marble or other composites. Putty is fine on stainless-steel and enamel sinks, but it will stain cultured marble.

WORK SMARTER

CAULKING TUBS AND SINKS

As long as you're looking at the faucets, look at the caulk around them, as well as around sink and tub. Gaps in the caulk, or even small pinholes, let water work down into the countertop, cabinet, or wall and could lead to expensive damage. Recaulk any holes you see. Around sinks and faucets the caulk sold in squeeze tubes will probably be enough. Around the tub you may want to use a caulk tube and gun. Use a smooth continuous motion when applying caulk. Put on a disposable latex glove when finished and run your finger along the caulk to smooth it.

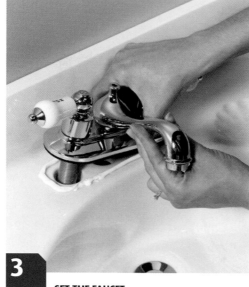

3 SET THE FAUCET

Slide the tailpieces into the holes in the sink. If they don't fit, the faucet is the wrong size and you'll need to return it.

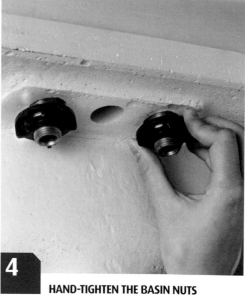

4 HAND-TIGHTEN THE BASIN NUTS

Thread the nuts over the faucet stems, alternating between them to draw the faucet body evenly over the gasket.

TOOL SAVVY

A BASIN WRENCH MAKES THINGS EASY

Getting to the supply riser nuts on an old faucet can be a real knuckle buster. A basin wrench is a handy wrenchlike tool that reaches up under the sink to grasp and twist off hard-to-reach retaining nuts. It takes a little practice to learn how to use, but it is well worth the effort.

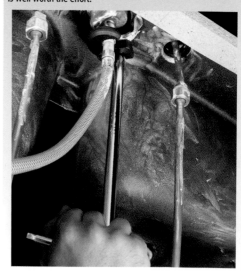

5 CENTER THE FAUCET BODY

When the nuts are a turn or two short of snug, center the faucet on the sink and then finish tightening. Connect the water lines, turn on the water, and test for leaks.

Repairing a compression faucet

Compression faucets have been around for more than a century and have a very simple mechanism. Turning the handle forces a rubber washer against a valve seat to stop the flow of water. If your faucet leaks the washer is worn. Disassemble the faucet and take the parts to your local home center so you can buy an exact replacement.

Screw

Handle

Packing nut

Spindle

O-ring

Washer

Bib screw

Valve seat

CLOSER LOOK

REPLACING THE VALVE SEAT
Sometimes a faucet leaks because the seat that the washer presses against has worn. Stick your finger down into the faucet body and feel if the valve seat is rough. If it is, use a seat wrench to remove it. They're designed to fit seats of differing sizes. Select an end that fits snugly into the seat. Tap the arm of the wrench with a hammer to loosen the seat. Once it's loose turn the wrench counterclockwise and remove the seat. Take it to your home center to get the right replacement seat.

1

UNSCREW THE STEM

Turn off the water supply. Pry off the cap in the middle of the handle that covers the handle screw. Remove the screw and lift the handle up and off the stem. Removing corroded handles usually calls for a handle puller (see page 132). Unscrew the nut at the base of the stem with groove-joint pliers.

2

TAKE OFF THE WASHER

Remove the screw that holds the washer in place. Pry out the worn washer and set it aside to take to the store later. The bib screw, which holds the washer in place, can deteriorate and should also be replaced when a faucet is repaired.

3

PEEL OFF (DON'T CUT) THE O-RING

Slip the O-ring from its groove and peel it from the housing. Keep the ring whole, if you can, to help you find an exact replacement at your home center; the tip of a screwdriver can help release it. Take the washer and the stem for reference when you go to buy parts. Buy a new washer, O-ring, and bib screw, and reassemble the faucet.

Repairing a cartridge faucet

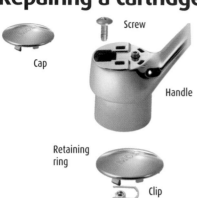

Cap
Screw
Handle
Retaining ring
Clip
Cartridge
Spout
O-ring

Cartridge faucets channel the water through passageways inside a cartridge to control flow. The handle moves the cartridge, regulating the amount of hot and cold water that flows to the spout. If your faucet leaks the O-ring seals are probably worn or the cartridge itself may be damaged.

Make the repair by disassembling the faucet and taking the cartridge to your local home center or hardware store to find out if you need a new cartridge. (You probably don't.) While you're there, get O-rings that fit in the cartridge groove. The O-rings are most likely the cause of the problem.

1

REMOVE THE FAUCET HANDLE

Turn off the water at the shutoff valves or the main shutoff valve. Pry off the handle cap. Remove the faucet handle screw. Lift the handle from the faucet assembly.

2

UNSCREW THE RETAINING RING AND REMOVE THE RETAINING CLIP

Spin the spout out of the way and use groove-joint pliers to remove the plastic retaining ring. Lift the faucet spout straight up from the faucet body and remove. Pull out the cartridge retaining clip with long-nose pliers.

3

PULL OUT THE CARTRIDGE

Slip the O-ring from its groove and peel it from the housing. (See inset.) Try to do so without breaking it so you can find an exact replacement. Use the tip of a screwdriver to help release it. Grip the exposed end of the cartridge stem. Most can be removed by pulling straight up and out of the faucet body. (If gentle pressure doesn't do the job, check the manufacturer's website for instructions.)

4

CLEAN AND REASSEMBLE

Clean the faucet body to remove debris. Coat the new O-ring with silicone grease to lubricate it, then seat it into the faucet body O-ring groove. Insert the new cartridge. Replace the faucet spout and reassemble the unit. Turn on the water. Check the hot and cold water to make sure they are not reversed. If reversed, disassemble the faucet and rotate the cartridge 180 degrees.

Repairing a ceramic disk faucet

Ceramic disk faucets channel water through holes in a disk to give you the right mix of hot and cold. Replaceable neoprene seals, set in the bottom of the disk, ensure a tight water seal. If water drips from the spout or pools around the top of the faucet during use, replace the seals.

To work on the faucet, first **shut off the water supply.** Turn on a faucet that is on a lower level than the one you're working on to help drain water before you begin. Most ceramic disk faucets come with a lifetime warranty for some of the parts. Check with the manufacturer for information on how to order.

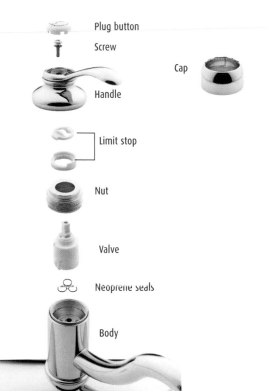

Plug button

Screw

Cap

Handle

Limit stop

Nut

Valve

Neoprene seals

Body

1

TURN OFF THE WATER AND REMOVE THE FAUCET HANDLE
Use a hex key or screwdriver to loosen the setscrew. Lift off the handle and dome housing.

2

LIFT OUT THE DISK
Unscrew the disk cartridge screws. Lift the disk up and out. Inspect the disk for cracks and set it aside to get a replacement if it's damaged. Remove the seals and take them to your local home center to find the right replacement parts.

3

CLEAN THE SEATS
Gently clean the seal seats with an abrasive pad. Insert the replacement seals.

4

ASSEMBLE THE FAUCET
Install the escutcheon cap and handle and tighten the setscrew. Air rushing through a ceramic disk can crack it, so remove air from the line before opening the supply valves fully. First open the faucet in the center position to balance the flow of water, then gradually open the shutoff valves to bleed out the air. Don't turn off the faucet until water flows freely and all the air is out.

Repairing a rotary ball faucet

Rotary ball faucets have a metal ball that rotates in the socket of the faucet body when the faucet handle is moved. Grooves in the ball pass over or away from water inlet valve seats that control the amount and mixture of hot and cold water supplied to the spout.

Leaks at the spout or the handle can be easily fixed by tightening the housing or adjusting the ring. If this doesn't work, disassemble the faucet, take the parts to your home center, and buy a replacement kit.

 **TOOL SAVVY**

HAMMERING AWAY
Unable to budge that corroded old handle? Save the day with a handle puller. With the screw removed from the top of the handle, clamp the side extensions of the puller beneath the handle. Set the shaft of the handle puller on top of the faucet stem and tighten. Continue tightening until the handle releases.

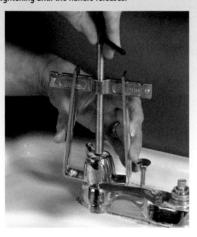

 Handle

 Setscrew

 Adjusting ring

 Cap

Spout

 Washer

 Cam

 Washer

 Metal or plastic ball

Seat and springs

O-ring and body

1

UNSCREW THE CAP
Turn off the water supply at the shutoff valves or the main shutoff valve. Use a pair of groove-joint pliers to remove the cap. Wrap the jaws of the pliers with masking tape to prevent damage to the cap.

2

REMOVE THE CAM
Lift off the cam that holds the ball in place. (You may have to gently pry it off.) Check the cam, seal, and ball for damage.

3 **LIFT OUT THE SEATS**

Use tweezers to remove the valve seats and springs. The springs are cone-shape, with one end larger than the other. Note how the springs are installed before you lift them out— you must install the replacement springs in exactly the same order or the faucet won't work properly. Remove the spout by twisting and lifting at the same time.

4 **PEEL OFF THE O-RINGS**

Remove the O-rings without breaking them so that you can find exact replacements at the store. If you must pry them off, do so gently—don't scratch or score the faucet body.

 5 **REASSEMBLE THE FAUCET**

Note the faucet brand and take the old parts, including the cam ball, to your home center to find the right replacement. Coat the new O-ring with silicone grease and seat it in its groove. Push the spout over the O-ring and faucet housing. Install the new valve seats and springs. Make sure the seats and springs are installed correctly—they will only work if installed properly, so read the repair kit instructions carefully. Place the cam ball in the housing. The tab on the cam fits into the notch in the body. Screw the cam housing onto the threads of the housing using the wrench that comes with the kit. Screw on the cap and install the handle. Turn the water on and check for leaks. Tighten the adjusting ring firmly to prevent leaks.

Repairing a toilet

If the water in your toilet runs constantly, the problem is with the flapper that releases flush water into the bowl from the tank or the tank fill valve. The flapper is easy to replace (see below).

If water is running down the overflow tube because the water level in the tank is too high, adjust the water level. If the toilet has a float ball in the tank attached to a brass arm, bend the arm slightly to lower the level of the ball. Some toilets have a valve like the one shown on the opposite page. Adjust it as explained in Step 6.

If the toilet still runs, replace the fill valve. The type of valve shown here is the one most commonly sold and will work to replace several kinds of fill valves.

Replacing a toilet seat

To remove the old toilet seat, pry open the bolt caps behind the seat. Remove the bolts by turning the bolt with a large screwdriver while holding the nut with an adjustable wrench. Lift off the old seat. Clean around the mounting holes with a scrub pad. Measure the seat to see if it's the round style that measures 16 inches from front to back or the elongated type, which is 18 inches front to back.

To install a new seat, align the hinge bolts of the seat with the holes of the toilet. Drop the bolts through the holes in the bowl. Fasten the nuts hand-tight and adjust the seat so it's centered properly. Tighten (but don't overtighten) and snap the bolt covers closed.

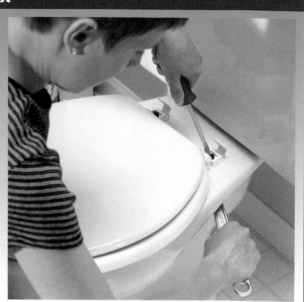

Replacing a flapper

1
DRAIN THE TANK
Shut off the water supply at the stop valve below the tank or at the main shutoff. Flush the toilet. Completely dry the inside walls and base of the tank with a sponge. Have a bucket handy to wring out the sponge.

2
REMOVE THE OLD FLAPPER
Pull the flapper from the pivot arm. For ball-style toilets grip a loop of lift wire and unscrew the old tank ball. Clean the surface area of the opening with a scrub pad to remove the sediment.

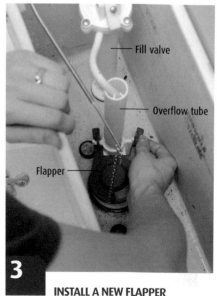

Fill valve
Overflow tube
Flapper

3
INSTALL A NEW FLAPPER
Line up the flap or ball with the valve seat by straightening the lift wire or adjusting the guide arm. This will provide a sufficient seal and keep the tank from leaking.

Replacing a fill valve

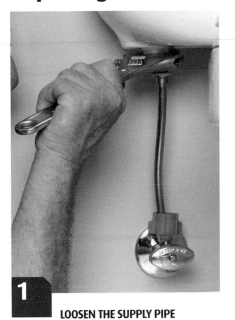

1 **LOOSEN THE SUPPLY PIPE**
Once you've turned off the water, flush the toilet to drain the tank. Sponge out any remaining water, then loosen the nut below the tank and remove the old fill valve, as shown at right.

2 **ADJUST THE HEIGHT OF THE VALVE**
Adjust the height so the marking on the top of the new valve is at least 1 inch above the overflow tube that's in the center of the tank.

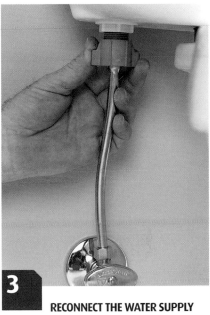

3 **RECONNECT THE WATER SUPPLY**
Push down on the valve shank and tighten the locknut one-half turn beyond hand-tight. Reconnect the water supply.

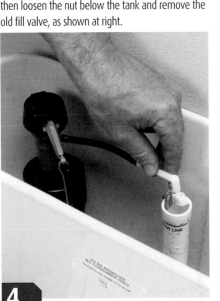

4 **ATTACH THE REFILL TUBE**
If necessary, trim the refill tube so there aren't any kinks in it when attached to the overflow. Push the refill tube into the angle adapter. Clip the adapter to the overflow.

5 **REPLACE THE TOP VALVE**
Remove the top valve. Hold a cup over the uncapped valve and turn on the water supply to flush the system of rust and debris. Turn off the water. Replace the top valve by engaging the lugs and rotating one-eighth turn clockwise. Make sure it's firmly locked into position.

6 **ADJUST THE WATER LEVEL**
Turn on the water supply to the toilet. Adjust the water level by squeezing the adjustment clip and moving the float cup up or down.

Installing a dryer and clothes washer

Connecting the dryer

The best way to hook up a dryer vent is the old-fashioned way, with 4-inch diameter rigid sheet metal vent pipe. Flexible vinyl, which is sold widely for use as dryer vent pipe, droops when installed. The lint that builds up in the low spots reduces efficiency and can be a fire hazard.

To connect the dryer to the vent, first put an elbow over the exhaust pipe on the back of the dryer. Apply foil tape around the joint to seal and secure it. Put a pipe long enough to reach the dryer elbow into the elbow that comes out of the wall vent and tape it in place. With a helper push the dryer into place, guiding the pipe into the dryer's outlet. Tape it in place.

Electric dryers have a three-or four-pronged plug which fits in a special outlet. Gas dryers need to be connected to the gas line (see page 89). Have a plumber or utility company do this work for you.

Connecting the clothes washer

Washing machines are easy to install. All you have to do is hook up the drain and supply lines, level the machine, plug it in, and you are ready to wash a load of laundry.

Washing machines aren't particularly heavy but they are awkward, bulky, and very likely to be installed in a basement or some other out-of-the-way corner. If you're moving yourself, you'll want to have a helper or two. Use a hand truck (see page 65) or slide the unit (see page 91) to make the work a little easier on your back. Before starting to haul in the unit, make sure you've walked the delivery route and measured openings so there won't be any surprises .

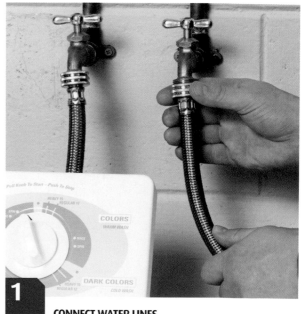

1 CONNECT WATER LINES

Connect hot and cold water lines using either reinforced rubber or stainless-steel braided hose to protect against bursting. Tighten the connectors securely. Turn on the water shutoff valves. If there are any leaks, tighten the connections with groove-joint pliers.

GOOD IDEA

WATER HAMMER

Air in your pipes can cause them to bang when you turn on the washer. Water hammer shock absorbers will solve the problem. To install turn off the water shutoff valves. Disconnect the supply hoses from the valves, screw on the shock absorbers, and reattach the hoses.

2 LEVEL THE WASHER

Once the machine is in place, check that it is seated securely on the floor and is level to keep it from "walking" and banging loudly. Place a level on top the washer. Level by turning the feet on the washer up and down with a pair of pliers until you get a level reading. Some washing machines are self-leveling; follow manufacturer's instructions.

3 HOOK UP DRAIN HOSE

The drain hose is the large diameter hose that doesn't have a hose fitting on it. Put it in the standpipe—the pipe that runs straight up and down and which connects to a nearby drainpipe. In some cases you may need to hook it into a nearby utility sink. Make sure to secure the drain hose so it won't leap out as the washer begins to drain. Plug the washer into an outlet.

Heating systems

The following three pages show general information about the major types of heating systems—forced-air and hot-water, as well as an introduction to gas and oil burners. To learn how to maintain and repair these systems, consult Home Depot's *Home Improvement 1-2-3*. No matter which heating system you have, it is a good idea to have a heating pro check out your system at the beginning of each heating season and advise you how to best maintain your system.

How a forced-air system works

If air vents deliver heat to the rooms in your house, you have a forced-air system. An oil or gas flame heats a chamber inside the furnace, and a fan sends the air throughout the house. In addition to the fan, you should understand a few important controls.

Once the thermostat on your wall tells the furnace to send heat, the furnace starts a fire in the firebox. Before the heat reaches you, two more controls must do their jobs.

The first is the blower relay, which turns the fan off and on. The thermostat, operating at 24 volts, is connected to one side of the relay. The fan, connected to the other side, operates at 110 volts. With the help of the relay, the 24-volt thermostat starts (and later stops) the 110-volt blower motor.

Meanwhile the fan-and-limit control is monitoring the temperature of the air heated by the flame. The fan-and-limit control prevents the fan from starting until the firebox reaches a prescribed temperature, usually around 115 degrees Fahrenheit. When the air does start flowing, the fan pumps it into a large central box, called a plenum, to which the ducts are attached. The air flows through the house and then returns to the furnace through the cold-air return. Without the return vents the furnace would heat dank basement air and send it through the house. With no cold-air vent pulling air back out of the rooms, they would become slightly pressurized and resist the new hot air coming out of the vents. So the return vents allow the flow of air that maintains comfort.

When the house warms up and the thermostat turns off the heat, the fan-and-limit control is still monitoring the firebox. When most of the residual heat has been pumped into the house, the control lets the fan turn off. When the thermostat calls for heat again, the cycle starts over.

REPLACE A FILTER

A clogged filter inhibits air flow, reducing the efficiency of your furnace. Change or clean your filter every two months during heating or cooling season, or as recommended by the manufacturer or dealer.

CLEAN A THERMOSTAT

A thermostat is a heat-sensitive switch that turns a boiler or furnace on and off as needed. If you have a low-voltage thermostat like the one shown, you can work on it without shutting off power. If you have a line-voltage thermostat, which connects to a 120-volt electrical box, call in a pro for repairs. Often a malfunctioning thermostat can be fixed by gently cleaning the contacts with a brush. If that doesn't solve the problem, replace the thermostat with an inexpensive round model or purchase a programmable thermostat, which allows you to adjust heating and cooling several times a day.

How a hot-water heat system works

When the thermostat calls for heat, the furnace starts a fire in the boiler of a hot-water system. While it's heating, a thermometer called an aquastat measures water temperature. When the temperature reaches a set point, the aquastat activates a switch and the circulator starts pumping water through the slim convectors in a newer home, or through more bulky radiators in an older home.

The circulator is really a three-part device. First is the electric motor, which provides power once the aquastat turns it on. Second comes the coupling that connects the motor to the last element, the pump. If any of the three parts fail, water won't flow, no matter how hot the boiler gets.

Fortunately the aquastat guards the system against this situation. If the water in the boiler gets too hot, it shuts down the furnace before too much pressure can build up in the boiler.

Because water expands as it warms, pressure builds in the system. During normal operation—when the pump is working and the water temperature is neither too high nor too low—water flows into an expansion tank. As the water flows into the tank, it compresses the air inside and creates the pressure that the system needs to run once the water has reached its final density.

Old steam system

If you have old radiators with only one pipe leading to them and they alternate between very hot and then cold during the heating season, you have steam heat. A steam system requires more maintenance than a hot-water system. Have a heating pro show you how to check and maintain the correct water level and pressure.

GOOD IDEA

GETTING THE MOST OUT OF RADIATORS OR CONVECTORS

Do not place furniture or other obstructions in front of a radiator or convector; if you do you will direct heat at the back wall rather than into the room. A convector's cover is precisely designed so that cool air flows under it and warm air comes out the top. If you add carpeting or other flooring to a room, be sure to raise up the convectors or you will inhibit the flow of heated air.

At least once a year, remove the cover and dust the fins of a convector or a radiator. One simple way to increase the efficiency of a radiator is to place a piece of sheet metal behind it, against the wall; it will reflect warmth into the room rather than absorbing it, as a wall would.

BLEED A CONVECTOR

At the beginning of the heating season, bleed your radiators or convectors, starting with the one farthest away from the boiler. While the boiler is running, hold a cup under the valve and open it. Air may hiss out or water mixed with air may spurt out. Once you get a clear flow of water, close the valve.

How an oil furnace works

When a modern oil furnace starts, a pump draws oil through a filter and forces it inside the firing assembly. There the oil is pumped through a nozzle, creating an oil spray. A transformer on top of the assembly provides power to an electrode that sparks and ignites the oil spray. One of two systems ensures that the oil has ignited—an electric eye senses the flame or a sensor in the chimney notes a temperature rise. If they detect nothing, the furnace shuts down.

An oil furnace needs filter replacement at least once per heating season. For greatest efficiency use a small brush or cloth dipped in mineral spirits to clean the blower, strainer, and sensors. Clean the heat sensor with soapy water. These are all messy jobs, so you may want to hire a heating service pro to do them.

How a gas furnace works

On a modern furnace when the temperature falls below the one the thermostat is set to, a call for heat goes to the furnace, which turns on the igniter. The igniter is usually what's called a hot surface igniter, a piece of metal that glows bright red when electricity is fed to it. After about 20 seconds the igniter is warm enough to open a valve, letting gas flow into the furnace. The gas flows through a pipe called a manifold and then into tubelike burners attached to it. Each burner has an adjustable opening, called an air port, that mixes air with the gas to control how efficiently the gas burns. The burner ends inside a firebox, which heats up to provide heat for the house. The heat is distributed through either a forced-air or hot-water system (discussed on pages 138–139). When the house reaches its set temperature, the thermostat cuts off the gas. The fire goes out until the thermostat calls for more heat. Older furnaces have a constantly burning pilot light instead of a hot surface igniter. On these a thermocouple monitors the heat created by the pilot light. If the pilot light goes out, the thermocouple senses a drop in temperature and shuts off the flow of gas.

If natural gas isn't piped to your home, you can use propane, or bottled gas, though you'll need to change the nozzle in the burner to do so. Talk to your propane dealer to see what's involved in having a bottled-gas system installed.

REPLACE A THERMOCOUPLE
If a pilot light will not stay lit even though you have followed the lighting instructions, you likely need to replace the thermocouple. **Shut off the gas valve.** Remove the thermocouple where it attaches near the pilot flame, and unscrew it from the other end. Buy an exact duplicate and replace it, making sure that the end is positioned so the pilot light touches it. Relight the pilot light.

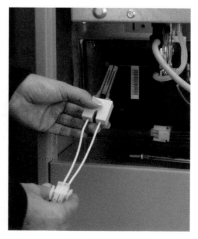

REPLACE AN IGNITER
Newer units have electric igniters rather than pilot lights and thermocouples. If the igniter fails to glow when the thermostat calls for heat, **shut off the power to the circuit.** Remove the old igniter and buy an exact duplicate. Handle the new igniter only by the porcelain part or the bracket; touching the heating surface may shorten its life.

4 PREPARING YOUR NEW HOME

Repairing and painting walls

PROJECT DETAILS

SKILLS: Measuring, cutting drywall with a drywall saw and knife, applying joint compound
PROJECT: Repairing holes in drywall

TIME TO COMPLETE

EXPERIENCED: 15 min.
HANDY: 20 min.
NOVICE: 30 min.

STUFF YOU'LL NEED

TOOLS: Framing square, drywall saw, utility knife, electric drill or screw gun
MATERIALS: 1×3, 1×4, or ¾-inch plywood scrap wood, 2-inch drywall screws, drywall scrap, self-adhesive fiberglass drywall tape, setting-type drywall compound, fine-grit sandpaper

Y ou may be able to fix a small hole in your drywall with one of the drywall repair kits sold at home centers. If the hole is much larger than the size of a quarter, it may be time for more radical surgery. To repair these larger holes in drywall, you begin by making the hole even larger so it spans from the center of one stud to the center of the next. Then you cut a patch from a piece of drywall—most home centers will sell you a piece of scrap pretty cheaply—and screw the patch to the exposed section of the stud. Don't expose the entire stud when you cut away the damage. The existing wall needs it for support and to keep from cracking.

Pipes or wiring may be hidden in the wall cavity. Probe for obstructions with wire or a bent coat hanger.

When you repair a crack (right), give the patch something to hold on to. Enlarge the crack by pulling a screwdriver along it. Then fill the crack with joint compound, if the wall is drywall, or with plaster patch, if it's plaster.

Fixing nail pops

Some drywall is held in place by nails, which can pop out as the stud holding them dries out. Nail pops, as carpenters call them, may expose the head of the nail or may appear as if a small disk has been slipped under the drywall paper. If you have a nail pop and can remove the nail from the wall without damage, do it. Then drive in 1¼-inch drywall screws about 1 inch above and below the pop to attach it.

If the nail won't come out, drive it into the wall with a hammer. Drive the nail just far enough that the last tap of the hammer puts a slight dent in the drywall without tearing the paper surface. Fill the dents or screw holes with joint compound. When the compound is dry (usually 24 hours later), sand or wipe the patch with a damp sponge to smooth it out. Prime and paint.

$ BUYER'S GUIDE

GET THE RIGHT COMPOUND FOR FIBERGLASS TAPE

If you use fiberglass tape, shown on page 143, use a setting-type joint compound instead of the ready-mix that comes in buckets. Setting-type compound is a powder that mixes with water and quickly dries to a hard surface. Because it dries quickly you can apply three coats in a single day. Combined with the fiberglass tape, this forms a strong patch. If you use regular compound with fiberglass tape, the mesh in the tape will show through the compound, so use paper tape instead. When working with paper apply the first coat of compound directly on the wall and the patch to hold the tape in place.

Patching drywall

1

OUTLINE THE DAMAGED AREA

Draw lines about 1 inch above and below the damage. Use a square to keep the lines straight and parallel. Check for any pipes or wiring inside the wall cavity.

2

CUT ALONG THE LINES

Push a drywall saw, which has a pointed tip, into the line and start cutting. When the saw blade runs into the studs, measure over ¾ inch and draw in the sides of the cutout. This is the center of the stud, and the patch should overlap it for support.

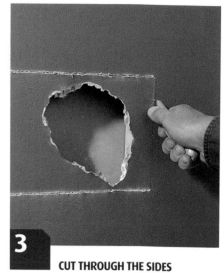

3

CUT THROUGH THE SIDES WITH A UTILITY KNIFE

Don't try to cut through the drywall in one pass. Make several cuts along the line, each one slightly deeper than the previous cut.

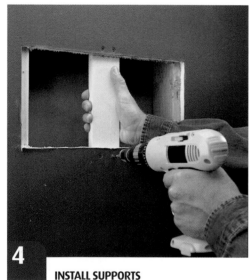

4

INSTALL SUPPORTS

To keep the patch from flexing then cracking at the seams, screw a 1× or ¾-inch plywood support across the opening. Cut it about 2 inches longer than the patch is tall. Hold the support in place and drive drywall screws through the drywall and into the wood.

5

CUT THE PATCH TO SIZE

Carefully measure the hole you've made and use the framing square to lay out a same-size rectangle on a scrap of drywall. Mark so the patch is ¼-inch smaller in both dimensions. Cut out the patch with a utility knife.

4

PREPARING YOUR NEW HOME

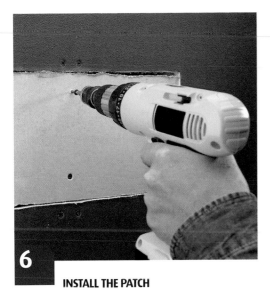

6

INSTALL THE PATCH

Attach the patch to the studs and support with 1¼-inch drywall screws. Position the screws as far as possible from the edges of the patch to avoid splitting the supports or causing the drywall to crumble.

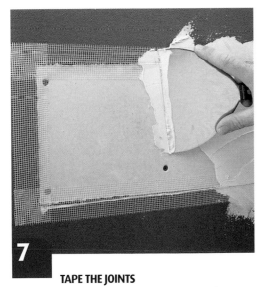

7

TAPE THE JOINTS

The seam between the patch and wall will crack unless reinforced. Run strips of fiberglass drywall tape around the patch, then spread setting-type joint compound across the patch and wall to create a smooth flat surface. (Do not use regular joint compound; the fiberglass tape will show through.) Let the compound dry and spread on a second coat with a 9-inch knife. Let the second coat dry, then spread a third coat with a 12-inch knife and sand when dry.

Hanging pictures and mirrors

Don't hang pictures from nails unless you want to damage the walls you've just repaired. Picture hangers provide better support, are less likely to fail, and are less likely to damage the wall. Each of the hangers shown here comes in several sizes, based on the weight of what you're hanging. It's a good idea to weigh your pictures before you go to the home store. A lightweight hanger will pull out of the wall if you put a heavy picture on it.

Traditional hangers (A) have a nail that runs at an angle through the top of the hook. They work in both drywall and plaster, but tend to chip plaster. Apply a small cross of tape over the spot where you'll drive the nail to minimize chipping.

Hangers sold as professional picture hangers (B) also work in plaster and drywall. They have a thin, sharp, hardened nail that is less likely to chip plaster. Taping the spot is still a good idea.

Wallboard anchors (C) are large nylon screws that house metal screws. Drive the pointed end of the plastic into the drywall with a hammer, then screw the anchor into the wall with a Phillips screwdriver.

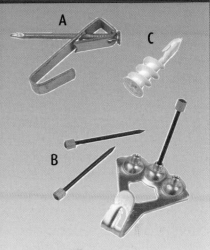

Drive the screw into the anchor and hang your picture or mirror.

To hang heavy pictures or mirrors at a point where there isn't a stud, run two wires between the screw eyes in the back. (Cut the wire about 50 percent longer than the width of what you're hanging. Run it through the eye and then wrap it around itself.) Put two hangers on the wall at least half the picture's width apart, and hang one wire from each hanger.

Hanging curtain rods

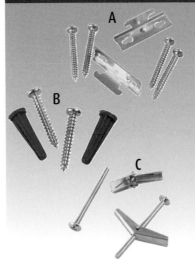

There are countless kinds of curtains and ways to hang them. Lightweight expandable rods (the white ones) have brackets (A) that attach with small brads or screws. If you lose the brackets during the move, you can buy replacements. (If you'd rather not hit your thumb while driving the brads, hold them in place with long-nose pliers and use a tack hammer.)

Heavier brackets need heavier hanging hardware and screws. New brackets come with the appropriate fasteners, but if you're moving, you probably had to leave the screw anchor in the wall of the old home. For lighter curtains use screws that come with a plastic sleeve, called conical anchors (B). For heavier curtains use toggle bolts (C), which have wings that open behind the wallboard as you tighten the screw.

Priming and painting walls

A good paint job depends on good prep work—washing and repairing the walls, sanding chips in painted woodwork, applying a stain sealer, and applying a good primer. Painters say the prep can take twice as long as the actual painting, but the results are worth it.

There's nothing complicated about prep work: Wash the walls with TSP (trisodium phosphate) to remove dirt that might otherwise bleed through the primer. Apply spackle over scratches and dents with a flexible putty knife. Repair larger holes as explained on pages 142–143. Let the repairs dry, then sand them smooth with 120-grit sandpaper. Sand the chips in the paint on the trim to remove the sharp edges.

Unless your walls are clean and spot free, you may need to apply a stain sealer, a special coating that covers stains caused by water, smoke, and almost anything else. The sealer keeps the stains from bleeding through the primer and paint and marring the final paint job. The best stain sealers are oil-based.

Good primers, on the other hand, are a must. They are formulated to stick well to a variety of surfaces and also provide some protection against stains. The finish coat sticks more effectively to a primed surface than it does to drywall, wood, or an earlier coat of paint. Applied right out of the can, primers are white, but they can be tinted to the same color as your top coat, although it will be a lighter shade—primer will accept only about one-third as much pigment as the top coat. A tinted primer often saves you from having to roll on a second top coat. You can use either oil or latex primer, though latex is easier to work with.

WORK SMARTER

QUICK TIPS FOR A QUALITY PAINT JOB

■ Time sometimes matters more than anything else when you're moving. You can save a lot of time by painting both the trim and the walls the same color—this cuts down considerably on the time taken by masking.

■ A dark color often covers an existing dark with just one coat.

■ Tinting the primer the same color as the top coat usually makes a second top coat unnecessary.

■ If the paint is in good shape but is bland, paint one wall in the room an accent color and leave the others alone.

■ Don't cut back on prep work to save time. Dirt can show through or shorten the life of your paint. Sand chips and bubbled paint; a coat of paint won't make them go away.

Priming the room

1 MASK THE WALLS

If any areas of the walls are stained, apply an oil-based stain blocker over them. Let any repairs dry. Brush primer on the repairs, on any areas of bare wood, and over the stain blocker once it's dried. Mask the top of the walls and all of the trim with blue painter's tape, which removes easily.

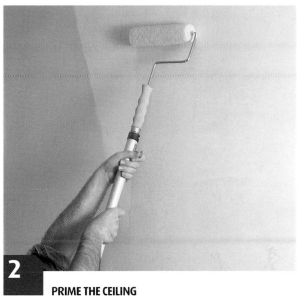

2 PRIME THE CEILING

Start on the narrow side of the room and do what painters call cutting in. Paint a strip about 2 inches wide and about 5 feet long along the edge of the ceiling. Then roll paint onto the ceiling, working the roller into the cut-in area to remove as many brush marks as possible. Roll with diagonal strokes and move from the edge toward the middle of the room. Continue cutting in and rolling until you've finished the ceiling.

3 CUT IN A SECTION OF WALL

Wait until the ceiling dries and put masking tape along the ceiling where it meets the wall. Cut in the corner, about 5 feet of wall at the ceiling, and along any nearby trim.

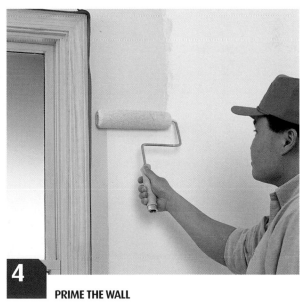

4 PRIME THE WALL

Roll paint as close as possible to the corner and to the masking tape to remove brush marks left by cutting in. Move along the wall in 3- to 5-foot sections, cutting in and rolling until the job is done. Work in sections small enough to cover with a single load of the roller and always roll up on the first stroke. Wait until the primer is thoroughly dry and sand the room lightly with 120-grit sandpaper.

Applying paint

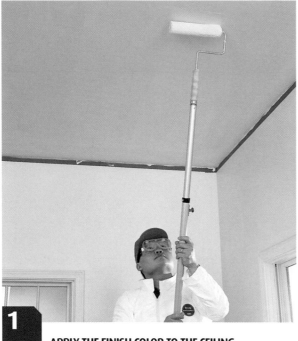

1 **APPLY THE FINISH COLOR TO THE CEILING**

When the primer is dry, mask around the ceiling. After cutting in a section, start rolling. Roll diagonally, as before, to avoid creating visible rows across the ceiling. An extension pole allows you to reach more with the roller without leaning dangerously from a ladder. Remove the masking tape while the paint is wet to avoid chipping. Remask and apply a second coat if necessary.

2 **CUT IN THE WALLS**

After you've painted the ceiling, remove the tape from the top of the walls and allow the ceiling to dry thoroughly. Then mask off the ceiling edge and trim to paint the walls. Start painting in a corner and cut in a few feet along the ceiling, as well as a few feet along the baseboard, and along the starting corner.

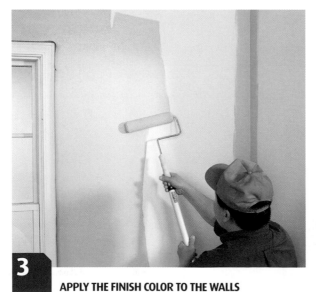

3 **APPLY THE FINISH COLOR TO THE WALLS**

Remove the masking from the walls and allow the paint to dry thoroughly. Remask and apply a second coat if necessary. When the paint is dry, mask off for the trim.

4 **PAINT THE TRIM**

Control dripping by pouring the trim paint into a small bucket and dip the brush about halfway into the paint. Tap the brush against the sides (instead of scraping it around the rim) to remove excess paint in the tip of the brush; this will leave paint in the body of the brush where you need it.

Painting doors

1 REMOVE THE DOOR

Insert long screws in the top and bottom edges of the door and suspend it between sawhorses. Remove the hardware. Fill dings, apply stain sealer over knots, and sand the door as necessary with 80-grit sandpaper. Follow with 120-grit sandpaper.

2 PRIME THE DOOR

Use a tinted, stain-blocking primer to prime the door. When the primer is dry, sand it lightly and then apply the finish coat. Let it dry and apply a second coat if necessary.

 WORK SMARTER

ORDER OF WORK

Painters paint doors in a particular order so that the brushstrokes automatically end where one piece of wood meets another. Paint the edges (1) first and then paint the panels (2). Paint the middle stiles (3) next and then paint all the rails (4). Finish by painting the outer stiles (5).

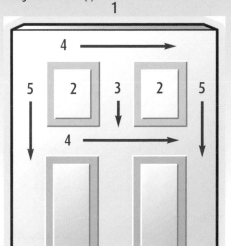

 TIMESAVER

WASH INSTEAD OF PAINT

If you have a gloss or semigloss paint on your walls, you may be able to save time by washing instead of painting. Gloss and semigloss paints have a shiny surface and are often used in the

kitchen and bath precisely because they clean easily. Any soap will work, but a nonsudsing cleaner, such as ammonia, is easiest to rinse. Mix 1 cup of ammonia with 1 gallon of water. Make sure it won't damage the paint by testing it in an inconspicuous spot. Protect floors from water with a fabric drop cloth. (Plastic is too slippery.) Wash the wall with a sponge, working from the bottom up; water running over dirty walls can leave streaks. Work in small overlapping sections. Rinse thoroughly with clean water before the wall dries. If the woodwork is painted with gloss or semigloss paint, wash and rinse it too.

Flat and eggshell (nonglossy) paint can be spot cleaned with standard nonabrasive household cleaners. Often, washing around light switches, doorways, and other high traffic areas cleans the wall to the point that painting is unnecessary. Don't try to clean the entire wall; it will end up looking blotchy.

Repairing and upgrading floors

Repairing wood floors

Because of its warmth and beauty, wood is often the flooring of choice for much-used areas of the house such as family rooms, great-rooms, and even kitchens. While wood floors and molding often get rougher treatment than anything in the house, refinishing them should be a last resort. There are many treatments for floors short of sanding and refinishing—try them first.

First determine what kind of finish is on the floor or trim. Some floors were finished with a coat or two of wax and no varnish. Trim and other floors get a surface finish—varnish, shellac, or lacquer to name a few. (Polyurethane is a varnish.) To find out what is on your floor, scratch an out-of-the-way spot with your fingernail. If the finish smudges it's wax; if there are flecks of clear finish on your nail, it's a surface finish. If it's a floor with boards that have beveled edges, the finish was most likely factory applied and is a surface finish.

Removing problem stains

PROBLEM	TREATMENT
Dried milk or food stains	Remove material with razor blade. Rub with damp cloth. Reapply finish.
Dark spots and ink stains	Remove finish over spot and surrounding area with #2 steel wool. Wash with vinegar. Let dry. Reapply finish.
Mold or mildew	Remove with wood floor cleaner and #1 steel wool. Refinish if mold is under surface of finish.
Chewing gum, crayon, candle wax	Scrape the majority off with a razor blade. Apply ice until brittle enough to break off. Pour floor cleaner around the problem to help loosen it.
Cigarette burns	Refinish if burn is in wood. If in finish, scrape burn with razor blade. Apply wax or finish over affected area.
Grease stains	Clean with trisodium phosphate (TSP). If wax finish, apply more. If surface finish, buff with clean towel.

Refreshing a wood floor

Any finish can be repaired, but no repair will be invisible. Even if you know the exact finish used, the old finish will have aged and a new coat will be a different color. If the wood has been stained, your repair work will remove some of the original stain and you'll have to find a color that matches.

If a surface finish is damaged, the quickest repair is to buff it with #000 steel wool and put a coat of paste wax over it. For a more permanent repair, sand through the damage with fine-grit (220) sandpaper. Sand with the grain so the sandpaper doesn't leave scratches when it breaks through the surface. Sand a bit of the surrounding area as well and feather the edges, so that there's no abrupt line where the finish ends. If the wood is stained, apply a matching stain, following the directions on the label. Brush on a new finish. Let it dry and brush on second and third coats, allowing the finish to dry between coats.

The finish on a waxed floor can often be repaired too. For small areas rewax and buff by hand. For large problem areas use a liquid wax stripper and a commercial buffer with a steel-wool pad. Apply more wax and buff with the machine and a buffing pad. Do not use water-base products on wood floors.

Sanding and refinishing a wood floor

1 **REMOVE THE BASE MOLDING**

A floor sander can mar the quarter-round molding that runs along the floor. Pry it off as shown, protecting the baseboard with a piece of scrap wood. If there is no shoe molding, either remove the base molding or be extremely careful.

Check the entire floor for protruding nails by sliding the blade of a putty knife across the floor. Set the nails and fill the holes with latex wood putty.

2 **ROUGH SAND THE FLOOR**

When drum sanding start with the coarsest sandpaper grit—typically 20-grit for hardwoods and 36- or 40-grit for softwoods. Sand to remove the damage, then switch to 60-grit. Finish with 80- or 100-grit. As you work move the sander so it travels along the length of the boards with the grain of the wood. Work the drum sander forward and back over 3-foot to 4-foot lengths of floor, overlapping the strokes by at least one-third of the belt.

Sanding and refinishing a wood floor (continued)

TOOL SAVVY

VIBRATING OR DRUM?
There are two types of sanders. If the finish is in bad shape but is undamaged, use a vibrating sander, as shown in Step 4, for the whole job. If the floor itself is in bad shape with noticeable knicks, gouges, and scrapes, use a drum sander. It will remove the finish and about ⅛ inch of the wood. It is usually best to have a professional sand a floor.

3 SWEEP AND VACUUM BETWEEN PASSES

The sanding dust eventually gets in the way of the sanding process and must be swept up and vacuumed. Always sweep and vacuum before moving on to the next grit of sandpaper. Doing so not only cleans the floor, it picks up any debris left by the sandpaper that would scratch the work of the finer-grit paper.

4 FINE SAND WITH A VIBRATING SANDER (OPTIONAL)

These sanders level minor unevenness left by drum sanders. If you choose to use both tools, use the drum sander for the two coarse grits (20 or 36 and then 60) and then use the vibrating sander for the medium and fine grits (80 and 100). If you use only the vibrating sander, start with 60-grit, then sand with 80-grit and, finally, with 100-grit.

5 SAND CORNERS AND EDGES WITH AN EDGE SANDER

Use 80-grit sandpaper to reach areas that the large sanders fail to reach: in corners, under radiators, in small closets, etc. Edge sanders can be difficult to control; practice on a hidden area, such as the inside of a closet, until you get the hang of it. When the sanding is done, vacuum up all the dust and follow up with a tack cloth.

6 APPLY A FINISH

Apply wood stain if desired, following the directions on the can. Allow the stain to dry as recommended before applying polyurethane with a lamb's-wool applicator. Let it dry, then sand the floor lightly with 220-grit sandpaper or #000 steel wool. Vacuum up the dust. Apply three coats of oil-based polyurethane or four coats of water-based polyurethane, sanding between coats.

Repairing stone or ceramic tile floors

Sometimes the ceramic or stone tile in a newly acquired home is mildewed, discolored, and stained. But even if it looks terrible, it often needs only a good cleaning. If you're working on ceramic tiles, start with a combination ceramic tile-and-grout cleaner. Combination cleaners are designed to remove soap scum, grease, and stains. Applying these cleaners is usually a matter of spraying the cleaner on and wiping it off. If you're working on marble, granite, or other stone, get a cleaner designed for stone. Ceramic cleaner might discolor stone.

Cleaning grout

On ceramic floors the biggest complaint is stained grout, which you can either clean or cut away and reapply. Combination cleaners (above) almost always clean the tile, but sometimes not the grout. If this happens buy a grout cleaner and use the applicator tip to apply it to the grout, but not the tile. Scrub, then rinse clean. If the stains persist there are progressively stronger cleaners that may do the trick. If none of them work, remove the grout and replace it

If you need to replace a tile, whether it's stone, ceramic, or vinyl, your biggest problem won't be the labor—it will be finding a tile that matches the existing tile. Patterns change, colors go out of fashion, and tiles fade. Before you remove a damaged tile, search for matching substitutes. In some cases it might be better to live with the damage than to make a repair that calls attention to itself.

1 **REMOVE THE GROUT**

Cut out the grout from the damaged area with a carbide-tooth grout saw. The cut must be at least $\frac{1}{16}$ inch deep to hold the new grout—the deeper the better. Vacuum up the debris and clean the remaining grout with a grout cleaner recommended for the grout you're using.

Replacing a tile

To replace a tile, first cut out the surrounding grout with a grout saw (see above). Put a straightedge across a diagonal of the tile. Guide a scoring tool along the straightedge, scratching a line in the tile until the line is at least $\frac{1}{16}$ inch deep. Repeat on the other diagonal. Put on some safety glasses and strike the center of the tile with a hammer and center punch until the tile begins to break up. Hold a cold chisel at an angle near the center of the tile and strike it with a hammer. Repeat along the entire length of both diagonals until you've removed all of the tile. Chisel away the mortar with a bricklayer's chisel. Replace the tile, using a thinset mortar made specifically for repair work. Apply grout as explained in Step 3, page 152.

Repairing stone or ceramic tile floors (continued)

2 MIX NEW GROUT

Using a mortar paddle and a ½-inch drill running at a slow speed, mix new grout in a plastic bucket. Choose a grout designed for repair work and one that has latex in it. Mix in latex admix if there's none in the initial mix. Without latex, the grout will eventually fail. After you've mixed the grout, let it rest, or slake, for 10 to 15 minutes, then remix.

3 APPLY THE GROUT

Spread the grout with a rubber grout float. Hold the float at a shallow angle and press the grout into the joints to fill them, working three or four tiles at a time. Grout has a long pot life, so it probably will stay moist in the bucket as long as you keep stirring it. Do not water it down if it hardens—it will have lost most of its strength.

4 CLEAN THE GROUT

Wait about 15 minutes or until you can press your thumbnail into the grout without leaving an impression. Then sponge off the excess. Wipe up the grout residue with a damp sponge until the water runs clear. Buff the tiles with a soft cloth to remove the haze. Some grouts need to be kept damp while curing. Others air cure. Follow the directions on the container.

Renewing vinyl floors

You can do little to repair a damaged vinyl tile. But if you can find a matching tile, you can replace a vinyl tile with a few low-tech tools. The first is an iron—you may want to buy one at a thrift store solely for this purpose. Set the iron on medium to high and put a rag over the tile you're replacing. Iron the rag for 10 or 15 seconds to warm the tile and the adhesive that holds it in place. Keep the iron away from the neighboring tiles to avoid ruining the glue beneath them. Once the tile is warm, slip a wide putty knife under it and try to pry it up. If it won't budge, iron a bit more and try again. If you damage a neighboring tile, remove it after you remove the first tile. Scrape away any adhesive with a putty knife.

Clean the area thoroughly and spread tile adhesive in the opening with the trowel recommended by the adhesive manufacturer. Let the adhesive cure for about 15 minutes or as recommended on the can. Just before you put the new tile in place, put the rag over it and warm it with the iron to make it more pliable. Then set—don't slide—the tile in place.

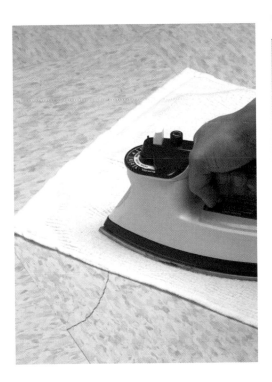

Getting to know no-wax floors

If the vinyl floor in your new home is shiny, don't wax it. Unlike wood, vinyl cannot absorb wax. To give no-wax vinyl its shiny look, it's made with a shiny top layer that only looks like wax. If you try to put wax over it, the wax will build up, collect dust, and look terrible. If you want to put a nice shine on the floor, apply a finish made by the floor manufacturer. It's usually available in two sheens—matte and high gloss. Buy some while you're buying the tile so you're sure to get the right one for your floor. Apply with a mop as directed.

 **WORK SMARTER**

MAINTAINING VINYL

Vinyl is even easier to care for than most people think. As a result it tends to be overmaintained. When you wash it simply use a nonrinsing cleaner that leaves no film. Most products sold as vinyl cleaners fit the bill.

- Avoid flooding the floor with water. Water will work into the seams and edges of the floor, causing the glue to fail and the edges to curl.
- Never use abrasive cleaners, whether spray or powder. Abrasive cleaners scratch the floor. There is no way to undo the damage.
- Don't use dishwashing soap. It may leave your crystal sparkling bright, but it will leave a film on your floor.
- Don't use oil-base floor cleaners. The film they leave will be worse than whatever dirt is on your floor.

 **CLOSER LOOK**

PREVENTING PROBLEMS

Here are a few simple things you can do to lengthen the life of your vinyl floor:

- Put felt pads under chair legs, table legs, and other furniture to avoid scratching the floor.
- Don't put rubber-backed rugs on the floor— the rubber causes stains.
- Put a heavy-duty doormat at the door and encourage all entering to wipe their feet. This is especially important if you have an asphalt driveway. The chemicals in asphalt cause vinyl flooring to yellow.
- Run the air-conditioner if the temperature rises above 100 degrees. Heat causes the vinyl to expand and the adhesive to melt. Extended exposure will ruin the floor. To protect the floor in a vacation home, set the air-conditioner on its lowest setting and let it run while you're away.

Cleaning your carpet

If the carpet at the new place needs to be cleaned, you can clean it yourself or hire a pro. Cleaning the carpet yourself will probably save you money, but make sure it doesn't void the warranty, if the carpet is covered by a manufacturer warranty.

If you choose to do it yourself, rent a carpet cleaner. Most cleaners are steam or hot-water cleaners, which pump hot water and cleaner into the rug, then suck it back out. Follow the directions carefully. Start by using your regular vacuum to remove all the dirt you possibly can. When you're cleaning avoid pumping too much water into the carpet—water can cause the backing or seams to separate. Go easy on the soap; more soap doesn't necessarily result in cleaner carpet. Extra soap can cause the carpet to get dirty more quickly next time.

Once the carpet is clean, you should have it dry within 4 hours. Use fans, open the windows, or turn on the air-conditioner to do the job. Don't walk on the carpet until it is dry.

Clean the carpet roughly every 12 to 18 months. Clean it before it starts to look obviously soiled; dirt not only takes the luster out of a carpet, it has sharp edges that shorten the carpet's life.

Vacuum to keep your carpet new

Vacuum twice a week if two people live in your house. Give the carpet an additional weekly vacuuming for every additional two people in the house. Ground-in dirt is harder to remove than surface dirt, and your best bet is to get the dirt before it's too late.

Before you vacuum find the grain of the carpet: Rub it with your hand to see which direction causes the yarn to stand up and which causes it to lie flat. When you vacuum, slowly push the vacuum forward in the direction the pile lays flat, then pull it back. The pass back across the pile will remove more dirt than the initial trip going with the pile, but make both passes.

The better the vacuum, the better the job. Use a vacuum that has adjustable, rotating brushes and is strong enough to pull air through the carpet backing. The brushes loosen ground-in soil; the airflow removes it.

 **BUYER'S GUIDE**

VACUUM CLEANER INDOOR AIR QUALITY TESTING PROGRAM

ID #:

Meets Carpet Industry Standards for

✓ Soil Removal
✓ Dust Containment
✓ Appearance Retention

For Program Information
Carpet and Rug Institute
800-882-8846
www.carpet-rug.com

YOUR NEXT VACUUM

The next time you buy a vacuum, look for one that sports the Carpet and Rug Institute's green label. A vacuum with this label meets standards for removing soil, keeping dust out of the air, and maintaining appearance without damaging the carpet.

- An approved vacuum must be able to clean up a specified amount of soil in four passes over a test carpet.
- Vacuums release some of the dust they collect into the air. A vacuum that has the green label will release no more than 100 micrograms of dust per cubic meter of air, an amount well below National Ambient Air Quality Standards.
- Regular vacuuming will eventually change the appearance of any rug. Approved vacuums cause only minor changes in a rug's appearance after a year's worth of vacuuming.

Repairing doors and windows

Solving door latch problems

When a door won't latch, it's usually because the latch bolt fails to pass smoothly into the center of the strike plate. Turn the door handle back and forth and watch to see where the problem is. If the latch meets the strike plate above or below center, try correcting the problem by shimming a hinge (see Step 2 below) to change the angle at which the door hangs. If the shim solves the problem, but the door then binds, sand the edge by hand (see page 156). If the alignment seems fine, but the door won't latch or must be pushed firmly to latch, the door is probably warped. Suspending the door between two sawhorses and weighting down the center may counteract the warp, but it's unlikely the door will completely straighten. Think about buying a replacement door. If the door does straighten enough to use, make sure the edges, top, and bottom of the door are properly finished; this will help minimize future warpage.

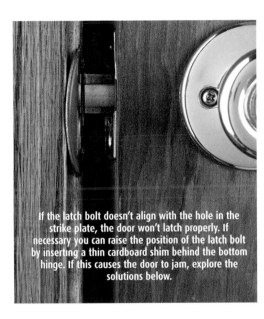

If the latch bolt doesn't align with the hole in the strike plate, the door won't latch properly. If necessary you can raise the position of the latch bolt by inserting a thin cardboard shim behind the bottom hinge. If this causes the door to jam, explore the solutions below.

Aligning the latch bolt and strike plate

1

TIGHTEN LOOSE HINGE SCREWS AND TEST THE DOOR
If the door continues to sag, replace the hinges. If the latch bolt still doesn't catch, you can fix minor problems by filing the strike plate until the latch bolt fits smoothly.

2

CHECK THE DOOR FOR SQUARE FIT
If the problem is too extreme to solve by filing, check to see if the gap between the door and frame changes as you move it from top to bottom or side to side. If so, the door is crooked in its opening. Remove the door and shim either the top or bottom hinge with an index card or playing card.

3

ADJUST THE STRIKE PLATE IF NECESSARY
Remove the plate and mark where the latch meets the door jamb. Move the strike plate to this point, chiseling away wood behind it if necessary. Fill in gaps around the plate with wood filler and paint or stain to match.

Freeing a sticky door

Doors will stick when the hinges sag, the door frame shifts, or humidity causes the door to swell. If your door seems to sag within the frame, make sure the hinge screws are tight. If it continues to stick once you have tightened the hinge screws, sand the door edge at the sticking point with 80-grit sandpaper wrapped around a scrap of wood. When the door no longer sticks, sand with 120-grit sandpaper to remove the scratches left by the 80-grit sandpaper.

Don't sand during a period of high humidity, as you may remove too much of the surface. Wait for dry weather, test to see if the door is still sticking, then start sanding. Varnish or paint the sanded edges to minimize the effects of humidity in the future.

Doors get a lot of attention because they're central to the finished look of a room. When working on a door, be careful not to scrape, gouge, or scratch the door. Try not to damage the finish on the hinges.

1

IF THE DOOR SAGS

Typically a door sags because one or more of the screws is loose and won't tighten. Drive out the hinge pins with a screwdriver and hammer, and remove the door. Remove any loose hinges.

WORK SMARTER

EASY DOES IT

If the door still sticks once the hinges have been fixed, a pro would probably dress the edges with a belt sander or hand plane. For a homeowner there's no point in using a hand plane unless you know how to sharpen it. Even right out of the box, the plane may not be sharp enough. You don't have to worry about sharpening a belt sander, but you do have to worry about the speed with which it can wreck your door. A belt sander will sand ⅛ inch of wood away in no time, leaving you with an edge that isn't straight and a door that is too small once you straighten it. You're better off sanding by hand.

2

INSERT WOODEN GOLF TEES OR DOWELS

Coat tees or pieces of wooden dowel with epoxy and drive them into the holes widened by the loose screws. Let the epoxy dry completely and then cut off the excess wood.

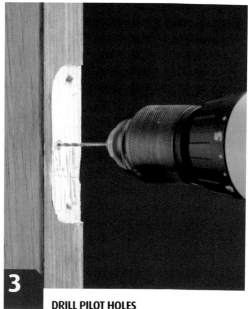

3

DRILL PILOT HOLES

Drill holes in the new wood slightly smaller than the original screws. Reinstall the hinge with the new wood as a base for the screws and rehang the door.

Installing a door lock

When you move into a new home, the locks are usually already in place. Deadbolts may not be installed; however, they're worth adding. Not only will you sleep better at night, you usually get a break on your homeowner's insurance. As new owners of the house, you should consider changing all the exterior door locks and deadbolts.

The biggest choice to make when buying a deadbolt is how you want to open the door. Single-cylinder locks can be opened from the inside with a thumb latch. Double-cylinder locks require a key from either side.

In most applications a single cylinder is fine. A key opens it from the outside; a twist of the thumb screw opens it from the inside. But if you have a door with a window, a double cylinder provides more security. Someone breaking the window will still need a key to get in. However someone needing to get out—in the case of a fire, for example—will also need a key.

All door locks have a setback—the distance from the edge of the door to the center of the knob or cylinder. The two standard setbacks are 2¾ and 2⅜ inches. Neither has an advantage over the other; however if you're replacing a lock and the hole is already there, measure the setback and get a lock that matches. If you arrive at the store only to discover you forgot the measurements, don't panic—both locks and deadbolts are available with an adjustable setback.

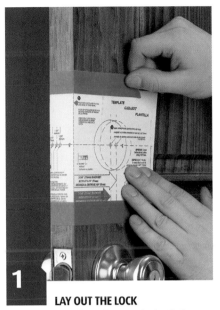

1 **LAY OUT THE LOCK**

Tape the cardboard template, supplied with the lockset, onto the door. Use a nail or awl to mark the center of the cylinder on the face of the door and the center of the latch bolt on the edge of the door.

2 **BORE A HOLE FOR THE CYLINDER**

Drill a hole the recommended size using a drill and hole saw. To avoid splintering the door, drill through one side until the drill bit just starts to come out the other side. Remove the hole saw and then complete the hole by drilling from the opposite side of the door.

3 **BORE THE LATCH BOLT HOLE**

Put a spade bit in your drill and bore a hole for the latch bolt from the edge of the door into the cylinder hole. Keep the drill perpendicular to the door edge while drilling.

4 **LAY OUT A RECESS FOR THE BOLT**

The plate on the bolt mechanism sits in a shallow pocket so that it's flush with the edge of the door. Lay out the recess by putting the bolt in its hole. Line up the plate parallel with the edges of the door and screw it into the door. Trace around the plate with a utility knife. Remove the plate from the door.

Installing a door lock *(continued)*

WORK SMARTER

BUT I'M JUST REPLACING AN OLD LOCK

If you're just replacing a lock and not drilling holes for a new one, the job is much simpler. Find the setback by measuring from the edge of the door to the center of the cylinder—it will be either 2⅜ or 2¾ inches. Remove the screws holding the thumb latch (or interior cylinder) and pull it and the exterior cylinder off the door. Unscrew the bolt from the edge of the door and remove it too. Buy a lock with the same setback as the old one. Reverse the process to install the new lock.

5

DEEPEN THE LAYOUT LINES

Cut the outline of the recess by holding a chisel with the bevel side facing the inside of the recess. Tap the butt end lightly with a hammer until the cut is as deep as the plate is thick. To help gauge the depth, measure back from the cutting edge of the chisel by the thickness of the plate and draw a line on the chisel.

6

BREAK UP THE WASTE

Make a series of parallel cuts about ¼ inch apart across the face of the recess. Strike the chisel with a hammer to make the cuts. Try to make them no deeper than the layout lines.

7

CUT OUT THE WASTE

Hold the chisel at a low angle with the bevel side toward the recess. Push the chisel by hand to make the cut. Striking the chisel with a hammer will drive the chisel too deep.

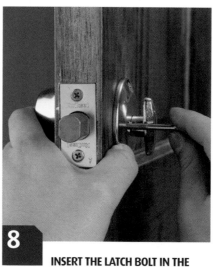

8

INSERT THE LATCH BOLT IN THE EDGE HOLE

Put the latch bolt back in the door and screw it in place. Insert the lock tailpiece—the long thin finger on the cylinder that goes through the latch bolt—and see how everything fits. If the tailpiece is too long, snap it at the indentations by bending it with one set of pliers while holding it with a second set.

9

INSTALL THE STRIKE PLATE

Close the door and turn the lock. Mark where the bolt touches the jamb. Center the strike plate on the lines and trace around the hole. Drill a matching hole in the jamb it may take two smaller holes side by side. Temporarily screw the strike plate in place. Trace around it and cut a recess for it in the same way you did for the bolt. Attach the plate.

Repairing windows

Repairing broken windows is messy but not hard. Sooner or later you'll probably have to repair one.

Before you cut or buy a replacement pane, put on a pair of heavy leather gloves, remove the broken pane, and measure the opening for a new one. The replacement should be 1/16 inch to 1/8 inch smaller than the opening.

Codes require that you use shatter-resistant panes in applications such as doors and sidelights. Let the salesperson know what the glass is for so you purchase the right type. Paint the putty channel before you install the glass and apply the glaze. Unfinished wood is dry and will pull the moisture out of the putty so it won't stick.

Glazing—putting in the glazing compound that holds the window in place—is the messy part. Traditional glazing compound is a puttylike substance. A modern variation comes in a tube, like caulk. If you're adept with caulk, this is the route to go. Rest the nozzle (which is square) on the window frame and on the glass, and caulk away. By pulling the trigger gently and taking your time, you'll get a flat bead that slopes from the muntin to the window at the perfect angle. If your timing is a little off, you'll get some extra caulk here and there, which can be difficult to clean up.

Traditional putty (shown on pages 160–161) has more body and takes direction better. Bed it firmly in the channel and then create the slope by pulling a putty knife or glazing tool along it.

CLOSER LOOK

REPLACING GLASS IN NEWER WINDOWS

If you're replacing glass in a factory-built window, you may not be able to do so by following the directions here—especially if the glass is double- or triple-paned. The major manufacturers recommend you call your distributor to get the parts you'll need for repairs. In some cases you can replace the pane; in others you'll need to replace the entire sash.

Cutting glass

1
PUT THE GLASS ON A FLAT, PROTECTED SURFACE

Although it's easiest to have the store cut the glass to size, you can do it yourself. Cover your work surface with several layers of newspaper or a drop cloth. Make sure you have at least 1/2 inch or so between the edge of the glass and your cut. Smaller cuts are extremely difficult.

2
LAY OUT THE CUT

Draw a line with a marker or a grease pencil, indicating where you want to cut for the replacement pane. A framing square will help ensure a square cut.

3
MAKE A SINGLE FIRM PASS ALONG THE LAYOUT LINE

Firmly guide a glass cutter along a straightedge. The cutter will score the glass rather than cut through it. Put the scored line atop the edge of the framing square and then tap along the scored line with the butt end of a glass cutter to snap it free.

4

PREPARING YOUR NEW HOME

Repairing a broken windowpane

1 REMOVE THE GLASS

Most windows can be repaired while they are still in the frame, but if you're removing the window for other repairs, it's a bit easier to work on a table or workbench. Start by putting on heavy leather work gloves and removing the loose pieces of broken glass.

2 REMOVE THE OLD PUTTY

To soften the old putty, use a heat gun, being careful not to scorch the wood. Scrape away the soft putty with a putty knife and remove the remaining glass. Small pieces of metal that hold the glass in place—called glazing points—probably remain in the frame. Pry them out with a putty knife or pull them out with pliers. Wire-brush the channel to completely remove the old putty and sand the grooves to clean them.

3 PAINT THE BARE WOOD WITH AN OIL-BASE PAINT

Using oil-base paint or linseed oil, coat the bare wood so the new putty will stick. (Bare wood pulls the moisture out of putty, making it too dry to adhere.)

4 SET THE PANE IN PLACE

Put a thin bead of glazing compound in the channel that holds the glass. Gently press the replacement pane into the compound. Press in new glazing points every 10 inches with the tip of a putty knife or glazing tool. Avoid pushing the glazing points toward the glass; the pressure may break the pane.

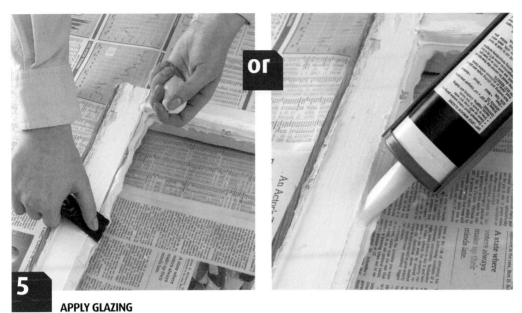

5
APPLY GLAZING
If using a puttylike glazing compound, roll a ball of it between your hands to make a long thick noodle. Press the noodle against the glass and the side of the channel. Set it firmly with the tip of a putty knife or glazing tool.

If using a caulklike glazing compound, put it in a caulking gun and poke a hole in the seal. (The nozzle is already shaped and need not be cut.) Move the tip along the glass, applying even pressure to the trigger.

6
SMOOTH THE GLAZING COMPOUND
Slide a putty knife along the glass and muntin. If using a glazing tool, like the one shown here, position the notch on the muntin and the edge on the glass; pull the tool from corner to corner. This takes some practice, so be patient. Learn to hold the putty knife at the correct angle while pulling it smoothly along with just the right pressure.

Let the glazing compound dry, as directed by the manufacturer, before priming and painting the window.

GOOD IDEA

TRY A LITTLE LINSEED OIL
If you have trouble smoothing the putty, try adding a light coat of linseed oil. It should lubricate the putty just enough to let the knife blade move along without catching on the putty.

Preparing for moving day

Being prepared is the key to success when moving. You probably take a shopping list when you go to the grocery store, make a to-do list at work, and have a list of things to fix around the house. This planning helps in everyday events.

But moving is anything but an everyday event. While 16 percent of the population moves each year, another 15 percent has lived in the same house for at least 20 years. Whether you moved last year or last century, making a plan is an important part of making your move.

The first part of preparing for moving day is knowing what to do and how to do it. How do you get everything ready in time? What do you do with your pets? What do you tell movers when they ask where to put a piece of furniture?

One homeowner recounts diligently asking the electric company to close her account the evening of moving day. Unfortunately the utility switched off the power 24 hours early, plunging the house into darkness while the family was frantically packing. So just knowing what to do isn't

Chapter 5 highlights

enough. You have to know when to do it too. This chapter opens with a countdown to moving day, covering everything from when to choose a mover to when to defrost the refrigerator. It helps you organize the things you'll need once you arrive and helps you anticipate the things that shouldn't happen, but will.

The following pages also answer some questions you might have about utilities, school records, forwarding mail, and the countless other details you'll have to deal with. You'll find advice, too, about minimizing the impact of the move on your children and pets. Above all, this chapter emphasizes that there is nothing about moving that should be underestimated. Planning will make all the difference, especially when it comes to that crunch time when the packing is done and it's time to really get moving.

Countdown to moving day

When you're moving time is the great enemy. Even with a well-planned move, almost everything will take longer than you expect. Things may begin smoothly, but they will inevitably end up rushed. If they begin badly they will only get worse.

So plan ahead. Moving companies and real estate agents say that you should begin working on the move at least two months beforehand. Anyone who has moved recently, however, will tell you it's never too early to pack away the items you don't need daily, like holiday decorations, books, or the good china.

Whether you start two months, three months, or a year in advance, begin with a calendar. Get one that lets you see an entire month at a glance. Write in the moving date and then start planning around it. Assuming a two-month schedule your life will look something like what follows.

Eight weeks before the move
■ Packing aside, the first thing to do is line up the movers. Begin by getting estimates from moving companies (see page 28) or if this will be a do-it-yourself move, check into prices from truck rental companies (see pages 92–93).

■ Make an inventory of everything you have. Decide what gets packed in the truck, what gets packed in the car, and what gets put out for trash.
■ Start planning where you want to place the furniture in the new house (see page 112). The movers already know the couch goes in the living room, but ifyou already know which wall it should go against, the move will be smoother.

Six weeks before the move
■ Clean out your closets (see pages 16–17). Be ruthless.
■ Have your first yard sale (see pages 18–19). Moving companies charge by weight. If you're renting a truck, larger rental trucks are more expensive than smaller trucks. Get rid of as much as you can.
■ Transfer your children's school records to their new school and get vaccination records from the pediatrician.

Four weeks before the move
■ Reserve a truck or trailer for a DIY move. If a moving company is handling the move, you should have selected one by now. If they're doing the packing too, arrange to have them do so two days before the move.

5

PREPARING FOR MOVING DAY

■ If you're doing the packing, get boxes and packing tape (see pages 62–64). Start packing out-of-season clothes and other items you don't need immediately.

■ Start taking care of paperwork. Fill out change of address cards available at the post office. Tell everyone from your charge card company to your great aunt what your new address will be. Don't forget the bank and your insurance agent. Send change of address messages directly to any magazines you subscribe to. The post office will only forward magazines for 60 days.

■ Make copies of all important papers like birth certificates, passports, and medical and dental records. Put them in a safe place (see page 54).

Three weeks before the move
■ Arrange to have utilities cut off. Schedule the cutoff for a couple of days after the move to allow for mishaps or a last-minute change in the schedule. Also arrange to have service established at your new residence.
■ Start working your way through the house, packing up one room at a time.
■ Find someone to help take care of the kids on the day of the move (see pages 168–169).
■ If you're moving into or out of a building with several floors, reserve the freight elevator for moving day.

Two weeks before the move
■ Arrange to move plants (see pages 78–79) and pets (pages 170–171).
■ Get rid of items you're not allowed to move, such as gasoline or propane. (For a complete list, see page 55.)
■ Keep packing.
■ If you're renting a truck, line up helpers.
■ If you are moving appliances and aren't comfortable disconnecting them yourself, make arrangements with a plumber and/or an electrician.

One week before the move
■ If making a long distance move, open your new bank accounts. Cancel the paper. If you have a safe deposit box, decide whether to close it now or wait until after the move.
■ If you take medication make sure you have enough to last through the move. Have your doctor write new prescriptions that you can have filled once you move.
■ Defrost the refrigerator two days before the move. Disconnect any appliance you'll be moving (see pages 88–89).
■ Make arrangements to pay the mover, who will probably require a certified check or cash.
■ Drain gas and oil from the lawn mower and other power equipment you'll be moving.
■ Finish packing.

Day of the move
■ Be there to oversee the move.
■ Have beds stripped and ready to go.
■ If it's a professional move, accompany the driver as he or she takes an inventory of everything that will go on the truck (see page 37).

■ Let the moving crew disassemble things, like beds, that need it.
■ Fill out the bill of lading (see page 36), which includes the inventory and the price of the move. Read it carefully and sign it. Hang on to it until everything is delivered and any claims are settled.
■ Be sure to give your mover directions to your new home.

Details, details

1 t's the little things that get away from you when you're moving and it's the little things that can turn a move into a disaster. Doubtful? Try getting into the new house when you've forgotten to pick up the keys from your real estate agent—and the movers are already there waiting to unload.

Keep paperwork close at hand
One of the easiest and worst things to lose during a move is the voluminous paperwork. Set up a portable organizer (see page 54) for all the paperwork relating to the move and take it with you in the car. The organizer can be anything from an old briefcase to a fancy file box you pick up at an office supply store. Put everything in its own folder, including all the paperwork from the moving or truck rental company. Include health certificates, if necessary, for any pets.

Make sure you've also got estimates for any repairs you're having done at either house, along with the business card of whomever is doing the work. Put the name and number of your insurance agent in the organizer, as well as a copy of your homeowner's insurance and auto policy. Have your real estate agent give you the name of a good electrician and a good plumber in your new neighborhood and file them away too.

Precious documents
You'll have other important papers that you won't need during the move, but which you'll need later—birth certificates, marriage licenses, wills, passports, school records, and so on. Make photocopies of everything and put them wherever you usually keep the originals. Put the originals in a portable fireproof box, lock it, and keep it in the car trunk until you've arrived at the new home. Once there, put it someplace obvious, like the cupboard that holds the dinner plates, until you have time to file everything away properly.

Last call
Make it someone's job to double-check closets, built-ins, and kitchen drawers to make sure everything is empty. Whether it is something as insignificant as a broom, or a pair of beloved downhill skis left at the back of the closet, check for overlooked items. Leave your old home as cleared out and clean as you expect to find your new one.

Check the signals
Check in with the truck driver before you hit the road. Make sure the driver has the address of the new house, directions, and a number to call if lost. But who will he call if you're on the road? Cell phones are a great way to keep in touch, but there are plenty of spots where there's no reception. What if your new employer wants you to start a week early? What if your sister has twins? Ask your real estate agent to take messages or accept faxes for you while you're on the road. Check for messages once a day using a landline if there's no cell phone reception.

WORK SMARTER

CONFIRM ARRANGEMENTS
Check with everyone a few days before the move to make sure everything is ready. If you're using pros, call and double-check arrival dates and times. If you're renting a truck, check in with the rental company and remind your friends too. If you've lined up babysitters, check with them as well.

Settling in

Even before you move consider subscribing to the local paper in your new town. You'll learn a lot about your community—what the local issues are, whether and where there are crime problems, what the school board is up to—even how the high school football team is doing. Not only will you find out the latest news, you'll see what the local stores are and perhaps who has the best prices.

You'll want to have the utilities connected before you arrive. If you're moving during cold weather, you want the house to be warm before you spend your first night in it. Come nightfall, lights and a working shower are going to feel pretty good too. There's often a delay between your call and connecting the account, so call two if not three weeks before the move.

The utility companies may ask for a deposit as part of setting up a new account. They'll usually waive the fee if you've had an account elsewhere. The phone company usually won't ask for a deposit, unless you're ordering your first phone. Have the names and numbers of the old accounts handy when setting up new service. If you'll be using the same utility, you can avoid deposits by asking to transfer service rather than set up new service.

Once you arrive, do one of the most important things a homeowner ever does: Change the batteries in the smoke detectors (see page 184).

Use those local contacts

Your real estate agent (or the former owner's real estate agent) can be a great help when you're settling in. They've likely lived in the community for a long time and their job brings them in contact with people you need to know. They've worked with banks to make sure the mortgages go through. They've worked with the lawyers at closing. They've worked with contractors to make sure the house is up to code. They know who can fix a roof fast, who's slow but good, and who to avoid.

Don't lose track of your real estate agent as you settle in and don't think you're imposing. There's a nice check in the real estate agent's account as a result of your move. He or she should be happy to help, in hopes that you'll refer friends. Ask your real estate agent to recommend local plumbers, electricians, builders, and even car mechanics. Talk to your real estate agent about good local attorneys.

If you've financed the mortgage locally, your banker is another good resource for recommendations and advice.

Pick up your trash

You don't want to have to go back to the old house to put out the trash—especially if you've moved across the country. If you have a private trash hauler, you may be able to have them make a pickup the day after the move. Call and ask. If they'll do it, put everything in trash bags instead of cans, so that you don't have to go back for the cans. If you rented a dumpster as part of your housecleaning, schedule the pickup for the day after you move and put any last-minute trash in it. If neither of these is an option, ask a neighbor for one last favor on trash day.

Moving with kids

For an adult a move is generally a positive thing; there is a new job and a new home to look forward to, perhaps a change of geography and exciting cultural life as well. The move itself may be stressful, but the hundreds of tasks to be completed are a more-than-adequate distraction.

For kids the process is more disruptive. They're leaving familiar surroundings and close friends. They'll likely adapt quickly to their new situation, but the move itself can be stressful.

It will help to get your children involved on whatever level you can. For a young child it may be putting his blanket and favorite toy in a box that will be unloaded and unpacked first. For older kids it might be checking to make sure each room has been emptied or giving the rug a final vacuuming.

Toddlers and young children

Younger children should be told as soon as possible about the move, so that they can adjust to the idea. Tell them why you're moving. Stress the benefits. ("There's a playground in the backyard," or "You'll have a bigger room.")

The youngest children won't really understand what it means to move, but need to know that changes are coming and that they won't necessarily be bad. Make sure they know the family and all their special things—bed, toys, security blankets, etc.—will all be together in the new home. Reassure them that they won't get left behind.

Make moving an adventure for them. Let them draw pictures and stick labels on the boxes. Younger children tend to think that things that have been packed have disappeared, so wait until the move is close at hand before packing their

rooms. Encourage them to pack their own things, but remind them to leave a few favorite toys unpacked so they can play with them now and put them into a box that will be first off the truck later.

Have photos of the new house and the new community and share them with your child. If your child is old enough to understand maps, show them where the new home is and help them understand the scale by relating it to known distances: "It's a bit further than Grandma's house," or "It's as far as we went on vacation this summer."

As moving day approaches help them understand what it means. Keep it simple, but complete: "On Saturday after breakfast, a big truck will pull up into the driveway. We'll take the driver and his helpers all through the house and show them what to take to our new home. And when the truck gets to our new home, we'll show them where everything goes and you can tell them where everything goes in your new room."

On moving day line up someone who can keep an eye on younger children, be it a relative or a favorite babysitter. Let the child "supervise" the move in his or her room, but have a safe place for the children somewhere else in the house or yard. Check on them regularly so they'll know you haven't left and have the babysitter bring them to you whenever they ask.

Preteens and teens

Involve older children as soon as you've decided to move. If possible take them house-hunting with you. Let them keep sales brochures or take photos of houses they like. Don't expect their likes and dislikes to be completely reasonable— a cute neighbor or a nearby skateboard park isn't a good reason to buy a house you hate. But looking at houses together will give you and your children common ground and a way to talk about what the family needs.

Once you've chosen a house, have your children start sketching out where they want furniture to go. If you'll be painting or wallpapering, let them pick out their own paint or paper. Let them pick out the curtains too. Make them feel their new space is their own.

Help them keep in touch with their friends both before and after the move. Get them each an address book. Let each child throw a pizza party prior to the move and have everyone who comes put their name, address, phone number, and e-mail address in the book. Give your child a prepaid phone card that he or she can use to keep in touch.

Put your moving calendar (see page 164) somewhere everyone can see it and let the kids enter important dates— both those related to the move and those related to their social life, so that they don't miss big events in their lives.

What to do on moving day

■ Younger children will need a relative, neighbor, or babysitter to keep an eye on them. Set aside a place where they can play and be out of the way. Have a new game, puzzle, or toy that they can unwrap and play with. Begin the day by having them pack their "special box" that holds a few toys and special items, and that goes on the truck last and comes off first.

■ Older children can watch, help, or play on their own. Let them invite a friend over to keep them company while you're busy.

■ Give younger and older children jobs that involve them in the move. Younger children can be "Nook and Cranny Inspectors," who make sure nothing gets left behind. Older children can carry things if it's a DIY move or sweep up dust bunnies once a room gets emptied.

■ Put a child in charge of making or passing out refreshments to the movers. If they can mix powdered soft drinks, they're old enough.

■ Teenagers may be the only ones in the house who have any idea how the computer, television, and stereo are connected. Let them disconnect and reconnect them. If you've kept the original boxes, let them help you pack things away. (If you don't have the original boxes, see page 77.)

Getting pets from here to there

As if the move weren't hard enough, you can't put your pets on the moving van. It's best for all concerned—huge temperature swings and the lack of food and sanitation in the moving van would make life extremely hard on your pet. But it does mean you have one more thing to plan for, the sort of thing that lives and breathes and depends on you.

On the other hand, if you're driving solo cross-country (or across town), your pet might make pretty good company. Get a pet carrier, if you don't already have one and put it in the backseat where it's safest. Take your pet for a few short rides to get it used to the car. If the animal gets carsick on short drives and continues to do so, talk with your veterinarian about medication that may help.

Smaller animals such as rabbits, gerbils, hamsters, and birds can travel in their regular cages. Make sure they have food and water and the cage door closes securely. Cover the cage with a cloth to help keep them calm.

Fish are harder to move. What you need to do will depend on the type of fish. Check at the pet store to see if you'll need special containers or battery-powered aerators.

Feed your pet five or six hours before leaving, but not any closer to the time of departure. Make plenty of rest stops when traveling and protect the upholstery by covering it with a plastic tablecloth. Get a collar for your pet that bears its name, your name, your new address, and a phone number where you can be reached. (Use the real estate agent's phone number if you don't have a phone yet.) When you take your pet out of its carrier for any reason, put it on a leash.

Pets—especially those that get carsick—need plenty of air. Run the car's air-conditioning or leave the windows open an inch or two. Smaller animals such as gerbils, rabbits and hamsters are sensitive to temperature extremes. Keep the car at a temperature you find comfortable, and they'll be comfortable too. Don't leave any pet unattended in the car for any length of time. The summer's heat or winter's cold

 **CLOSER LOOK**

PET TRAVEL KIT

When you travel with a pet, you'll need to keep it both safe and comfortable. Vets recommend the following:

- A kennel, cage, or appropriate container that you keep the pet in while traveling
- Food, a dish, and a can opener, if necessary
- Drinking water brought from your old home
- Bedding
- A favorite toy
- A pooper-scooper and plastic bags
- A collar with license, rabies tag, pet's name, your name, and contact information attached
- A leash where appropriate

can be fatal. If you have to leave the animal in the car for a short period during warm weather, open the windows partway to keep them from overheating.

If you'll be on the road for more than a day, check to make sure the hotel or motel you're staying at allows pets in the room. Pack a jug or two of tap water from your old home, and water and feed your pet once daily. Strange water can mean upset stomachs.

Check state and local pet regulations before you leave home. Regulations for cats are usually as simple as getting the animal a health certificate, rabies shots, and a local license. But if Floppy is a dog, chicken, horse, llama, or something more exotic than your average turtle, there will be stricter requirements that you need to know about and meet before making the move.

 GOOD IDEA

KEEP CATS CALM

Cats, as all cat owners know, upset easily. The noise and commotion of having strangers cart furniture out of the house can frighten even the calmest cat, and a frightened cat is liable to run away. On moving day, find an out-of-the-way room for your cat. Give it some favorite toys, some food, and a litter box, and close the door. When moving, transport your cat in a cat carrier. Don't assume your cat has calmed down once you reach the new home. Put it in its own room again, with litter box, food, and toys. Open the carrier door, but let the cat venture out at its own speed. Keep the room door closed. When the cat starts roaming around the room and poking its head out the door when you open it, it's ready to see the rest of the house. Let it explore, but don't let it outside for several more days. When you do take it outside, keep it on a leash for the first few trips.

 REAL WORLD

FLYING YOUR PETS TO THEIR NEW HOME

If you're flying to your new home—or even if you wish you were—it might make sense to fly your animals. Regulations vary from airline to airline, but most will allow you to take small dogs, cats, and birds into the cabin with you, as long as they are in a kennel that fits under the seat.

You can check larger animals with your luggage. They'll be kept in temperature-controlled holds, although the airlines generally won't transport animals if the temperature outside the plane is expected to be exceptionally hot or cold.

There are regulations regarding health certificates and when the animal should be fed prior to departure. Check with the airline for specifics and notify them well in advance of your plans. You'll be charged extra if you surprise the carrier on the day of the flight.

Finding a home for your furniture

Putting your furniture in a new home is part science and part art. On the one hand the question is "Will it fit?" On the other hand the question is "How do I make this house look like my house?"

Approach the problem the way a general moves toy soldiers across a scale-model battlefield. Get a floor plan. Move scaled drawings of your furniture around in each room until you like what you see. In new construction getting a floor plan is easy—it's usually part of the literature they give you when you tour the model house. In older houses rely on the real estate agent, who measured the rooms as part of establishing a sales price for the home. Or once you're about to make a bid, ask to make one more visit and take a tape measure so you can draw your own floor plan.

Once you have measurements there are several ways to make a floor plan. You can draw one on graph paper with each square equaling a foot. You can use a computer program—either online or out of the box—and key in the dimensions. Or you can buy a kit that comes with scale drawings of furniture that you place on a floor plan you create yourself.

If you're comfortable with computers, it's fairly easy to use one of the computer programs. You key in the room dimensions and then select furniture from a menu. Drag it where you want it and go on to the next piece of furniture. You can reposition anything and everything at any time.

If you want to create a low-tech floor plan, draw the room on a piece of graph paper with a ¼-inch grid. A three-sided ruler called an architect's triscale measures distances in different ratios, such as ¼ inch equals a foot, one inch equals a foot, and so on. They're available at office supply stores and are a good way to measure without having to count squares on the graph paper. Measure your furniture, cut out scale top views of each piece, and move them around until you find a layout you like.

Equally low-tech, but slightly more sophisticated, are kits that come with punch-out furniture that you move around on a scale floor plan you draw on a board, mat, or tablet that comes with the kit. At least one kit is plastic peel-and-stick (see opposite page); others have paper punch-outs.

Be your own interior decorator

Once you've created your floor plan, the trick is making your existing furniture fit in the new house. Nobody can tell you how to arrange your furniture to your satisfaction. It's your home, your taste, and your furniture. But there are some commonly held principles. Some are obvious: Don't put your stove in the living room. Others are common sense: Don't block the traffic flow. Still others are the guidelines that designers and architects use when they lay out a room. Guidelines are flexible, but here are some of the principles professionals use when laying out furniture.

Create a focal point. Every room tells a story. In the dining room the plot revolves around the table. In the living room the main character may be the fireplace (opposite page), the entertainment center, or an armoire. Wherever you are and whatever it is, it's a focal point. Identify it and then group furniture around it.

Step away from the walls. Lining everything against the wall gives the room a boxy look. In a big room it creates a void in the middle. Group seating in comfortable clusters around the focal point. Fill in along the walls with accents, plants, or smaller pieces of furniture. If the space outside a cluster is big enough, treat it as a separate room or small nook by filling it with its own cluster.

Create a skyline. While laying your furniture out on graph paper is about the only way you can plan where your furniture will go, there is a drawback. A room can look great in two dimensions, but will look flat in reality if all the furniture is the same height. The problem usually solves itself in bedrooms because dressers, beds, chairs, and TV stands are all different heights. But in a living room or family room, the chairs, sofa, and tables are all about the same height.

Add a dividing screen, some bookcases, an entertainment center, plants, or tall floor lights to break up the landscape.

Light the space. Rooms need two types of light to function, and a third type of light to be interesting. Ambient light is the light that helps you see the room and navigate through it. It can come from an overhead fixture or several freestanding lights. Task lighting is the light you need to read your book or prepare dinner. It can come from a floor or table lamp, overhead lighting, or track lighting. Accent lights give the room drama—they might do nothing more than wash across a brick or stone wall, or they might light a painting or work of art. Include ambient and task lighting in your floor plan. Accent lighting might take the form of track lighting or a light in a china cabinet. It won't show up on your floor plan, but keep it in mind once you're actually settling in.

Direct traffic. Rooms with a stairway or more than one door do duty both as a room and as a passageway. Group furniture to separate the two. Put a long table or the back of a sofa along one edge of the passageway, for example. If that doesn't work, try breaking the room into clusters that fall on either side of the passage and bridge them with a rug.

Work out. Start laying out furniture from the center of the room (or at the focal point if it's built into the room) and work out toward the walls. This will position pieces of furniture in relation to each other and the way they'll be used instead of in relation to the walls.

Scale it. A large table in a small room can make it impossible to arrange furniture comfortably. Put it elsewhere. If the table is too small for the room on the other hand, make the table larger by adding a leaf or two. In large rooms mix large and small pieces to achieve a comfortable balance.

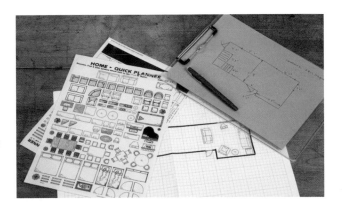

Expect the unexpected

t wouldn't be a move if something didn't go wrong. With luck it will be minor, and with a little preparation even the largest problem will be manageable.

Be prepared. There's no knowing if the problems that pop up are going to be big or small, or what you'll need to solve them. Keep the essentials handy. Among them you'll want a cell phone, a toolbox, a first aid kit, and a flashlight. Have about $100 extra in cash on hand too. You may spend it having pizza delivered for dinner. You may spend it buying extra moving blankets, or you may spend it on duct tape and plastic to cover a broken window, but you will spend it.

Immediate use boxes

In addition to the general household open-me-first box (see page 56), pack an immediate use box for every member of the family. Put them on the truck last and take them off first. Contents will vary. Yours will have the toolbox, the vacuum, the flashlight, a good supply of rags, some towels, and the coffee. (Pack the first aid kit in the car, so you can get to it quickly.) Younger children may want to pack a favorite toy or their blanket in their boxes. Slightly older children may want to pack video games. Let the kids pack what they want and then you can pack what they need—pajamas, toothbrush, comb, towel, and a change of clothes for starters. Pack the same for yourself and be sure that anyone who wears contacts has packed the appropriate paraphernalia.

On the road

If you're driving a rental truck, it's no less likely to break down than any other truck. Because even

CLOSER LOOK

RUNAWAY PETS
Relocating is stressful on pets as well as people. A stressed dog or cat is likely to run away from the source of the stress—which is anything to do with the move—and end up lost. To prevent runaways keep your pets in a pet carrier when moving and on a leash when you take them out. Put collars on your pets that bear the pet's name, your name, phone number, and new address. Moving is especially tough on cats, who need to be acclimated to their new home for a few days before you can even let them roam indoors. For more on moving cats and other pets, see pages 170–171.

New homeowner basic tool kit

At the very least, you will probably need to hang a curtain rod. You may also need to tighten the nut on a drainpipe, attach a speaker wire to the stereo, or connect an old-fashioned antenna to the TV. You can get the tools listed below at a home center. Get a good toolbox too. This is the beginning of a set of tools you're going to use again and again.

Hammer	Assorted nails and screws
Nail set	Assorted picture hangers
Tape measure	Spare curtain hanger
Pencil	Putty knife
Slot-head screwdriver	Utility knife
Phillips screwdriver	Spackle
Large adjustable wrench	Drill
Small adjustable wrench	Drill bits
Allen wrenches	Screwdriver bit
Water pump pliers	Duct tape
Wrench set	Yellow glue

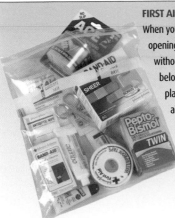

FIRST AID KIT

When you move, people are lifting heavy things, walking down ramps, and opening unfamiliar windows and doors. It's a rare move that comes off without at least a cut finger. The ingredients for a good first aid kit are listed below. Once you've gathered your kit, put everything in a large resealable plastic storage bag, a cloth bag, or an old (but clean) tackle box. You can also buy ready-made kits at drugstores, home centers, and backpacking shops. Once you're done with the move, put the first aid kit in your car so you'll have it on trips or during your kid's soccer games.

Ibuprofen or acetaminophen

Adhesive bandages in
   several sizes

Butterfly adhesive bandages

Antiseptic wipes

Triple-antibacterial first aid
   ointment

Soap

Sterile gauze

Adhesive tape

Elastic bandage

Tweezers

Scissors

Sunscreen

Lip balm

Antacid

Antidiarrhea medicine

FROZEN PIPES

It's seldom that someone moves into a house with frozen pipes, but winters get colder the farther north you move and it does happen. If water won't flow from the faucets when you move in, turn up the heat and check with the city to make sure the water is turned on. Once you're sure water is getting into the house, be ready to call a plumber. A frozen pipe may start to leak once it has warmed up, and you want a pro there to patch it. If some faucets work and others don't, letting a trickle of water run out of the unfrozen taps will help keep the pipes that feed them from freezing. Don't try to thaw the pipes with a blowtorch. It won't work, it may start a fire, and operating a blowtorch in an enclosed space can create a lethal dose of carbon monoxide.

---

small rental trucks are pretty big, fixing a simple thing like a flat tire isn't very simple. Because of the danger involved, fixing a flat yourself is out of the question. Most rental companies have an 800 number that you can call for roadside assistance seven days a week, 24 hours a day. Make sure the company you're renting from has roadside assistance and that you have the number when you leave the rental lot. Pack a cell phone and call the number for anything from a flat to a blown engine. Then be prepared to wait. At best it will take time for the mechanic to leave the shop and find you. At worst it's the mechanic's day off and three other people have already called in for help. Pack a book along with your cell phone.

A few tools

As anyone who has ever moved will tell you, the most essential skill any homeowner can have is the ability to take a door off its hinges. It may be the couch or it may be the fridge, but without doubt at

some point the doorway will be too small and something will be too big. You can make a doorway as much as a couple inches wider by removing the door from its hinges (see page 67).

Hinges or no hinges, you may end up with a piece of broken furniture. If you're using professional movers, fixing it is their responsibility. Let the driver know what the problem is, and he or she should have a company repairman come out to fix it. If you're moving yourself, you're probably the driver and you're certainly the repairman. When things break they usually don't shatter completely— a leg falls off instead or maybe a drawer falls apart.

Make the repair with glue and a band clamp, which is a long nylon belt that you loop around the furniture at the break. Put glue on the joint, wipe off the excess, and tighten the ratchet that's built into the clamp. If you're working on a drawer, measure the diagonals, and push on the long one until the diagonals are equal. This keeps the sides parallel and the corners at 90 degrees so that the drawer will slide easily. If the fix doesn't work—and sometimes it doesn't—look in the yellow pages under furniture repair. Refinishers often do repair work too. Have them do the repair, which can

usually be done without a refinishing job (no matter what they say).

Rain ready

If it's raining when you move, try to keep wood furniture dry. A bit of moisture shouldn't hurt upholstered furniture, but water can turn the lacquer on wood furniture white. Cover the furniture with a tarp as it travels from house to truck and wipe the furniture down with a towel as soon as you get it on the truck. Reverse the process when you unload and tape one or two moving blankets to the floor by the entrance to pick up water and mud that gets tracked in.

Settling in

The moving truck is empty. If you've used professional
movers, you've reviewed and signed off on your
inventory. If you've moved yourself, you're folding the
moving pads and preparing to take the truck back to the rental agency.
You've put one set of stressful experiences behind you and now you face
a new set of challenges—or adventures. You've got to create a new home.

Settling in can be unsettling at first. Maybe your new house has been
sitting empty for awhile and smells funny. Perhaps the previous owners

didn't leave it broom clean, though they did take with them bathroom
mirrors you thought were part of the deal. You've finished a huge job,
are tired, and maybe more than a bit discouraged. And although you are
in the new house, you still aren't really home.

You've still got strenuous physical work ahead of you as you face the
clusters of unpacked boxes and unassembled furniture. You've got to
make decisions about where to put lamps, how to set up your closet,
and where to store the good china. You need to learn how appliances
work and what you'll need to replace. And you'll also have some

Chapter 6 highlights

emotional strain, as you and your family go about creating a new set of routines, support systems, and friends.

After the stress of moving day, it's often a relief to have all of your possessions under one roof—even if they're scattered in many places under that roof. Putting your house in order and returning to a predictable routine can help relieve some of that stress, but accomplishing that can sometimes seem a little overwhelming. Where do you begin?

Unpacking

At this point in the move, you've probably spent so much time worrying about how things need to be packed that unpacking seems as though it should be a snap—just start opening boxes. But do yourself a favor and set priorities about how and when you'll unpack your household.

The necessities

What will you absolutely need first? Think about the basics: You need to eat. You need to sleep. You'll need a bathroom. You'll need to clean. If you've packed an open-me-first box for each family member, put them in an easy-to-reach location (either in individual bedrooms or a central—and less busy—spot).

Be sure to plan for food for the first few days. Besides needing to keep up your physical and emotional strength, mealtime, however short, can provide a welcome respite from unpacking. Fast food and delivered pizza are always handy, but keep a supply of other foods and beverages on hand as well—fruit, nuts, milk and juice, bread and cereal. You may opt for paper plates and cups or you may pull out a few dishes for family use. Unpack or connect any kitchen equipment that you'll need for quick meals as well: coffeemaker, microwave, saucepan, utensils. If you've moved any major appliances—refrigerator, stove, dishwasher, washer, or dryer—connect those and make sure they're working.

Unpack any tools you'll need for assembling furniture, opening boxes, or other moving-in chores. These might include a screwdriver, hammer, scissors, utility knife, and pliers. Have cleaning supplies on hand as well—sponges and rags, a bucket or two, cleanser, and a broom, mop, or vacuum.

After you've assembled the beds, unpack bedding and go ahead and make them. There's a lot to be said for sinking into a comfy, familiar bed at the end of moving day.

Set up a bathroom, including towels for everyone, soap, some toiletries, and basic medicine-chest items—especially aspirin, adhesive bandages, and antibiotic ointment.

What's next?

After the basics, your own priorities should dictate the order of unpacking. You'll need to start unpacking clothes and kitchen items such as dishes, pots and pans, and utensils. Designate a place for files and important papers so that they're safe and easy to get to. If you have a home office, you may need to get that set up and running in order to ensure that your work isn't disrupted. Unpack, set up, and connect other electronics as well: CD player, television, DVD player, or VCR. Kids can begin to unpack toys and items for their rooms.

Unpack larger bulky boxes to help free up space: packed lampshades (which will also help you to set up and place lamps), pillows, and cushions. Items that have a definite destination—books on bookshelves, linens in the linen closet—can come out too.

Make a trip to the grocery for staples: seasonings, canned goods, condiments, and special dietary items, as well as food for the next few days.

If it's in season you may schedule an unpacking session in the garage to unpack and organize some basic outdoor tools and equipment, such as the garden hose, the lawn mower, some clippers, and a shovel or trowel. Or maybe the snowblower and snow shovels.

What can wait

You're not going to need the winter coats in June nor your college diaries anytime soon. If you already know where you're going to be storing seasonal clothes, decorations, and personal archives, take those boxes to that location. Check for breakage or damage, but there's no need to unpack them now.

You might also want to leave more fragile items, such as china, decorative items, or artwork, safely boxed up until some of the moving disorder subsides. Do check for breakage or damage though.

You will also find, as you unpack, that you've moved items that don't fit your new house or that you just don't want any more. Start a box for these, but do not seal the box and do not put it in a storage area. Give them or throw them away as soon as you can. You don't want to move them again.

Empty boxes

While emptying boxes can give you a feeling of accomplishment, you're also faced with a more immediate problem: what to do with that stack of broken-down boxes? You could throw them away or recycle them, although that seems like a waste of good, sturdy moving boxes. You could try placing a notice on an online board such as craigslist.com or freecycle.org, to see if others who are relocating could use your discards.

If you have the room, you may also save some, particularly if you anticipate moving again in the next five years or so, or if you have friends who move a lot. One group of Midwestern coworkers passed around a sturdy set of boxes through four or five moves, as they each bought houses. By the time the last person used them, the boxes were pretty marked up with successive scratched-out lists of contents on each, but they'd held up remarkably well.

It's an adjustment

Once the initial excitement—and exhaustion—of moving wears off, some cold reality of your moving experience may set in.

Your first shock may be seeing your new home as a cavernous series of empty rooms instead of the cozy, clean, please-buy-me abode that the real estate agent showed you. How could you not have noticed the stain on the floor near the door or that unusual shade of green in the downstairs powder room? Add to that the certain amount of wear and tear caused by the previous occupants' move: smudged walls, some scratches on the floors, maybe an unswept hallway. The windows and floors are bare; the heat may not be switched on.

Some of this may be very real; not every homeowner or renter is conscientious about cleaning when they move out. Others may be exaggerations that are the byproduct of a long and tiring move. So take a step back. You can see lots of flaws in an empty house. Some of them you'll be able to live with; some of them you'll be able to fix.

You may also start to entertain thoughts of ambitious home improvement projects: a larger kitchen, a better bathroom. Some of these may be realistic and necessary; but for some of them, you may be wise just to live in the house a while and see what really works for you and what doesn't.

Where's the microwave that was here?

One of the best ways to avoid unpleasant surprises in an empty house, according to real estate agents, is to do a thorough walk-through the day before closing. A good real estate contract should specifically state what stays in the house (anything that's screwed in or nailed to the walls or floors) and should note any exceptions, like an heirloom chandelier that the sellers want to take, or window treatments that match a bedroom set. The contract can also specify if there are things that must be moved, like piles of paint cans, old appliances, or firewood.

When you do the walk-through, be observant—don't just treat it as one more opportunity to plan where furniture can go. You may spot missing or downgraded light fixtures, a leaky water heater, or other elements that weren't present when you signed the contract. By doing the walk-through before closing, you have a negotiating position when it does come time to close. If the missing items are substantial, some agents recommend you come prepared with estimates on replacement costs to help in your negotiations.

This is home?

Even as you start to unpack and the house begins to look more like a home, you and your family are in for a period of

adjustment. Part of it is simply the unfamiliarity of a new home that has a different physical layout, a different set of noises, a different feel.

While you may be able to talk yourself into getting used to these changes, other members of your family are going to need your help.

Helping children adjust

Give kids some control over their personal space in the new house. Set them to work unpacking their bedrooms; it will be helpful to see familiar toys and books. Let them help decide furniture placement in their rooms and help them hang favorite artwork on the walls.

Teach your children their new address and phone number. Take them out to explore the neighborhood as soon as you can, and if the children aren't starting school immediately, at least plan a trip within the first few days to see the new school.

If you have toddlers or crawling babies, you'll need at least one clean room for them to move around in and you'll have to be vigilant about childproofing, even in the chaos of the move. Watch for exposed plugs, ungated stairs, and unguarded cleaning products.

Helping pets adjust

Familiarity also helps pets settle in after a move. Pet experts recommend that in a new home, cats be kept inside, confined to one room during the moving-in process. Give your cat its litter box as well as familiar toys and bedding, but keep the cat contained; it'll begin to get used

to the new house and, more importantly, won't wander off to hide or get lost (see also pages 170–171).

You can give dogs a little more leeway, but if your dog is a wanderer, you may need to make provisions to keep it contained if there's a lot of opening and shutting of doors—and always keep it on a leash when you take it outdoors. As with cats, give it familiar items such as its bed, water and food bowls, and toys. Check your new yard to make sure there are no hazards or escape routes.

For all pets, make sure they have ID tags with your new address and phone number. Find out if your town has any pet regulations, such as leash laws or licenses.

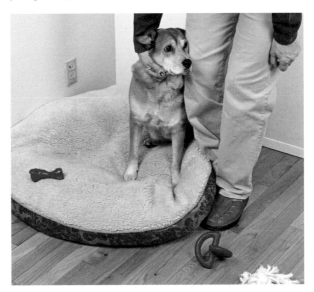

Getting organized

Y ou've figured out where those two extra end tables are going to go and you've decided which kitchen cabinet is going to hold the spices and which will hold the dinner plates. Now that you've covered the basics, you've got to start organizing your new household.

What do you need?

Even if it feels like you've just moved more household items than you ever imagined you owned, you'll still probably need to buy some new things. Take a notebook and a tape measure and make a room-by-room list. Some things may be big—a piece of furniture, a room-sized rug, window treatments; others may be minor, such as a new dish drainer or a box of 60-watt lightbulbs. Measure for sizes and note colors.

Once you've made the list, go through it and prioritize: What do you need right away? What can wait until next week—or next year? You probably don't want to live too long in a house without window coverings or overhead lights, but a new entertainment center could go on the longer-term list.

Once you've winnowed down your immediate-needs list, you can make up a focused shopping list and cut down on those innumerable back-and-forth trips that seem to crop up after a move.

Tuneups and service

You'll also need to turn your attention to things you already have. You may have household goods that need adjusting, servicing, or cleaning after a move. You'll probably want to change the locks on the house. You may have put off cleaning upholstered furniture until after the move; if so, call and schedule an appointment to have the living room set cleaned. If you have a piano, you may need to have it tuned. You may need to have the gutters cleaned or the cable television connected. Check the maintenance schedule of your new home's heating or air-conditioning system; if they need service schedule that as well.

Your maintenance file

If the former residents of your home haven't done it already, you should gather and organize the owner's manuals and instructions for major appliances in your new home. As you do so, read through them and note recommended maintenance schedules and suggestions.

There are plenty of ways to organize these papers; some people swear by three-ring binders; other use sturdy file boxes. You can group the manuals by location (all basement appliances, for example) or by function (heating and cooling, cleaning, etc.). The key is to settle on a system that's easy and convenient for you to use.

This piece of organization is particularly important if you've moved from being a renter to being a homeowner. Things that you didn't have to think about before—heating systems, yard maintenance, plumbing—are now your responsibility, and learning their maintenance schedules and procedures will help keep them in good operating order.

6

SETTLING IN

Maintaining your new home

Get off to the right start in your new home by doing a little bit of work on it every month. If you catch little problems before they become big ones, fixing them is both easier and more affordable. On the other hand, if you wait until the pipes freeze (and burst) before you drain the outdoor water spigot, you'll end up paying for a plumber and any water damage.

Many of these jobs can be done any time of year, so use this schedule as a guide. If you live in an area that gets very cold early in the season, get the furnace cleaned before you're knee-deep in snow. If it's warm where you live, you won't winterize the lawn mower, but don't forget to change the oil and plugs. Most of these jobs are low tech; a ladder is probably the most elaborate tool you'll need.

January
- Start the year by pushing the test buttons on the smoke and carbon monoxide detectors to make sure they are working. Repeat monthly.
- In the garage put your hand over the sensor that's near the bottom of the garage door opening to make sure the electric door's safety cutoff switch is working.
- Push the test button on special receptacles (called GFCIs) near the sinks in the kitchen and bath to make sure the receptacle will cut off power in the event of a shock.
- Make sure the safety valve on your water heater is working by testing it now and again in June.

February
- If you have a sump pump, make sure it works now, before the rainy season starts.

March
- Inspect the roof from the ground to see if shingles are worn or loose. Check flat roofs from a ladder for bubbles or loose granules. Check for wet spots in the attic after a rainstorm. Make any necessary repairs.
- Clean the gutters, patch any holes, and repair loose joints.
- If you have a bypass humidifier, clean the drum and tray to keep it working efficiently.

April
- Put fresh batteries in your smoke and carbon monoxide detectors with the beginning of daylight saving time. Continue testing them monthly.
- Sharpen your lawn mower and garden tools.
- If you have a septic tank, check the level of the sludge and have the tank pumped out, if necessary, to avoid sewage backups.

May
- Keep the sunlight pouring in by cleaning windows now and again in the fall.
- Clear debris and obstructions from attic fans and vents to let out summer heat.

June
- Remove debris from window wells and around doors to avoid insect damage.
- Repair any decayed wood by scraping away the damage, patching, and applying a new finish.
- Inspect the siding and other painted surfaces for mildew or paint failure. Wash off mildew; scrap away damaged paint and repaint.
- Make your second check of the hot water heater safety valve.

GOOD IDEA

ADD COLOR TO YOUR LIFE
If you're moving into a newly built home, chances are good that the walls are off-white, off-white, or off-white. Painting them yourself is one of the least expensive ways to dress up a home. You can paint an entire room in less than a day. You can also pick an accent wall, paint it a color you like, and leave the rest of the room alone.

July
- Extend the life of your driveway, walks, and patio by repairing cracks and removing weeds.
- Patch loose or cracked mortar in brick or concrete block walls to avoid more extensive repairs later.
- Check the chimney for loose bricks or damaged joints and make repairs to eliminate fire hazards.

August
- Check the foundation inside and out for signs of termite infestation.
- Inspect the siding and trim for damage and make repairs. Check cable TV and phone line entry points and caulk any unsealed openings.
- Caulk around windows and doors.
- To prevent rain and ice damage, check flashing around chimneys and vents.
- If you have a crawlspace, clean vents and louvers to prevent moisture buildup that can damage the framing.
- Have your furnace serviced now and avoid the rush when the weather turns cold.

September
- Prepare for winter by checking that storm windows are in good repair. If you have old-style storms, install them. If you have sliding track storms, put in place before the first frost.
- Clear the weep holes at the base of metal storm windows so that water condensation can drain.

- Wash the windows so you can enjoy the winter light.
- If you have a fireplace, inspect the chimney yearly for creosote buildup and clean it every two or three years.
- Clean and inspect chimneys connected to woodstoves yearly.
- Make your second roof inspection of the year. Inspect the attic again for signs of roof leaks.

October
- Change the batteries in your smoke and carbon monoxide detectors with the end of daylight saving time. Continue to test the detectors every month.
- Clean the gutters again, patching any holes and repairing loose joints.
- To maximize baseboard heater efficiency, vacuum the fins that distribute the heat.
- If you have window air-conditioners, seal the units with insulated covers during the off-season.
- If you have a whole-house attic fan, insulate the opening to eliminate heat loss.
- Drain the supply lines to outdoor water spigots so that they don't freeze.
- To avoid damage to paint and siding, trim trees and shrubs so they don't rub against the house.
- To lower heating costs clean or replace your forced-air system filter monthly during the heating season.

November
- Patch dings and dents in walls, and paint the repaired areas.
- To keep a bypass humidifier working efficiently, clean the drum and tray.
- Wrap cold-sensitive shrubs with burlap to keep the cold from damaging them.
- Winterize your lawn mower and power garden equipment. Drain the gas and change the oil and spark plugs.

December
- Drain two gallons of water from your water heater to remove sediment that collects on the bottom and shortens its life.
- Check the caulking around ceramic tiles and all sinks and countertops. Recaulk as necessary to avoid water damage.
- Inspect ceramic tile and regrout as needed.
- Make sure the fire extinguisher in the kitchen is fully charged.

CLOSER LOOK

LANDSCAPING

The landscaping at a newly built home generally consists of grass and not much else. If you're on a limited budget and would like to dress up the yard, flowers look great. Keep it simple until you're settled in. Seeds are cheaper than starter plants. Impatiens grow in the shade, but need to be planted every year. Poppies grow in the sun and replant themselves. Periwinkle and pachysandra are good for covering bare spots on slopes or around trees. Periwinkle prefer shade but will grow in the sun. Pachysandra need full to partial shade. Periwinkle and pachysandra are widely available as plants. Seeds may be hard to find.

Establishing yourself

At your old house the mail came to the door and your kids went to school. You had electricity, water, and heat. You were in the phone book. You voted. You were somebody.

At your new house you're nobody until you get all those records and utilities transferred to the new address. You can begin the process from the old address: Talk to the post office about forwarding your mail. Arrange with all your utilities to end service at one address and begin it at another. Work with the old and new schools to make the transition smooth for your children. Other things will have to wait until you've made the move, but the time to prepare for them is now.

If there's anything you need immediately after a move, it's your mail. The post office recommends that you notify everyone from banks to relatives at least 30 days before the move. You should also notify the post office of your new address, either by filling out a form at the post office or online. (If some family members are staying at the old address, you'll have to fill out a separate form for everyone moving.)

The post office will forward first-class mail, priority mail, and express mail for 12 months at no charge. Newspapers, magazines, and periodicals will be forwarded for 60 days at no charge. After that it gets expensive, so notify the publisher of your new address as soon as possible.

Getting a driver's license

A driver's license is probably the single most important document you have. You'll need one to get on an airplane, cash a check, open a bank account, get a library card, and of course to drive. The federal Real ID Act of 2005 standardized the requirements for getting a driver's license and increased the documentation you'll need to do so.

Under the terms of the act, anyone applying for a driver's license must have either photo ID or a birth certificate; proof of birth date; proof of residency; and proof of having gotten a social security card. This usually requires showing the actual card, so find it or replace it before all your records are packed in boxes. You can usually prove residency with one or two of the following: tax records, lease, mortgage, W-2 form, or current utility bills.

Starting a new school

If you're moving your school-age children to a new school district, contact the school before you make the move to find out exactly what you'll need. It will be easier to find or replace missing records at your old address than it will be at your new address. It will also be easier to work with your current pediatrician to get any immunizations that may be needed.

Once you've gathered the records you need, make an appointment with whoever handles registration of new students. The paperwork you'll need is pretty standard, though it varies from district to district. Generally schools ask for a birth certificate or passport. Copies and hospital-issued proof of birth are generally not acceptable. They'll want complete immunization records, and your child may need to get some additional shots. You'll need proof that you live in the district—a driver's license, bank statement, pay stub, vehicle registration, utility receipt, or voter registration card with your new address is usually sufficient. And finally they'll want to see a report card or current transcript of grades. Special needs or gifted students may need additional documentation.

Stopping and starting utilities

As part of your move, you'll have to contact two sets of utilities. At the old house notify each

of the utilities that you're moving out. At the new address notify the new utilities that you're moving in.

There are a lot of services involved: cable or satellite television, Internet, phone (often with different long distance and local providers), cell phone, gas and/or heating oil, water, and electricity. Most utilities say you should contact them at least two weeks before the move. Given the number of calls you have to make, you may want to start earlier.

If you're moving to a cold climate in winter, contact the appropriate utilities so you can turn the heat on as soon as possible. Have the rest of the utilities turned on the day before you arrive. Having phone, lights, and water makes the first night at the new address seem like home instead of a campout.

Build a little time into the schedule at the old house. Have the utilities disconnected a day or two after the move. Scheduling the power cutoff for moving day risks having the lights go out as you and your friends are carrying the big-screen TV down the steps. You'll appreciate having a phone and heat or air-conditioning during the move too.

Utilities often require a deposit when opening up new accounts. Make sure you get any deposits back from your old utilities and ask for a letter that says you were a customer in good standing. A letter from your old utility often gets you out of having to pay a deposit to the new utility.

Give your old utilities your new address. Have them take a final read of the meters and mail you a statement. It will come in handy if there's a dispute with the new owners about when utilities became their responsibility.

Utilize the web

Depending on your lifestyle and your heating system, you may have to call nine utilities at your old home and at your new one. Instead of making 18 calls (and who knows how many follow-ups), make all your arrangements on the web. There are several sites that, once you've typed in your address, take you to sign-up pages for all the appropriate utilities. Each page lists the services offered, lets you choose which services you want, and lets you open an account online. Depending on the site you can often transfer an account from one address to another. If you want to close an account, however, you will probably have to call the utility.

Register to vote

Registering to vote is almost as simple as getting a library card. Federal law allows you to register when you get your driver's license or by mailing in a postcard available at the post office. There are also several sites that let you register online. As long as you register 30 days before an election (or mail the card by that date), the law says you are registered to vote in that election.

Your new community

Finding the services, stores, and activities that are important to you will help you settle into your new community.

Ask your real estate agent for recommendations. Some real estate firms have information packets. The chamber of commerce may have a newcomer service with local directories and coupons or small gifts from merchants. Get a current telephone directory, and subscribe to the local newspaper.

State and civic services

Go to city hall for information about trash and recycling pickup, parking regulations, and so forth. Some towns host new-resident meetings to review laws and procedures. Learn and post your town's emergency fire and police numbers.

Contact your state department of motor vehicles to change the address on your vehicle registration or driver's license. If you've moved to a new state, get a new license and registration.

Register to vote. You may do this at city hall or you may have to visit the county courthouse. Or watch for voter registration drives, particularly during election season.

Medical services

Your search for a new doctor or dentist may be limited by your health insurance; consult the insurance company's list of participating doctors in your area.

You can ask your current provider for recommendations. The American Medical Association's online DoctorFinder at http://webapps.ama-assn.org/doctorfinder lets you look up doctors by geographic location and specialty.

The bank and the post office

Scout out the location of your local post office; you'll be visiting it often in the next few months to pick up forwarded mail. Set up local bank accounts soon after arrival. You're the best judge of what you require from a bank, and you may choose one based on a variety of services or convenience .

Day-to-day services

One of the most disorienting things about moving is setting up your new support network: a good hair stylist, the best pizza place, a reliable plumber, and so forth. Ask your new neighbors, coworkers, and even similar service providers (the plumber probably knows a heating contractor) for advice.

What's going on?

The library is a good place to start connecting to the community. Sign up for a library card and ask about activities at the library and elsewhere in the community.

Take the time to explore your new neighborhood and town. Try some of these ways to connect too: Volunteer for a group that interests you, join a professional organization, get involved in a church, tutor at your child's school, join a gym, or take an adult-ed course.

6

SETTLING IN

Index

Many thanks to the employees
of The Home Depot® whose
"wisdom of the aisles"
has made *Moving 1-2-3*® the
most useful book of its kind.

Connie Bryant
Atlanta, GA

Leslie A. Camp
Atlanta, GA

Chris Kruger
Atlanta, GA

Julia Thomas
Atlanta, GA

Tom Sattler
Atlanta, GA

Toolbox essentials: nuts-and-bolts books for do-it-yourself success.

Save money, get great results, and take the guesswork out of home improvement projects with a growing library of step-by-step books from the experts at The Home Depot®.

Packed with lots of projects and practical tips, these books help you design, remodel, decorate, and repair your home or garden. Easy-to-follow, step-by-step instructions and colorful photographs ensure success. Projects even estimate time, skills, materials needed, and tools required.

**You can do it.
We can help.**